# Yoga As An Intervention Strategy For Learning Disability

D1722308

**By:**
**Shubratha K. P.**

## CONTENTS

# LIST OF TABLES

# LIST OF CHARTS

# LIST OF GRAPHS

*Chapter- I*

**INTRODUCTION**

## 1.1 Learning Disability

We live in a literate society. In today's knowledge based world, literacy is the foundation for all learning.Socioeconomic development of a country depends directly on the literacy rate of that country. Such is the importance of literacy today. UNESCO defines literacy as the ability to read, write and use arithmetic. It is the ability to use the dominant symbol systems of a culture to understand, communicate and gain knowledge. This high socio-cultural need has impelledculturally constructed handicap. Learning Disability is such a handicap for acquiring literacy.

### 1.1.1 Definition

Learning Disability (LD) is defied as a group of neurodevelopmental disorders manifested as persistent difficulties in learning to efficiently read, write or perform mathematical calculations despite normal intelligence, conventional schooling, intact hearing and vision, adequate motivation and socio-cultural opportunity (Lagae, 2008; Karande et al, 2011).

### 1.1.2 Terminological clarification

LD is characterized by specific deficits in scholastic skills, and hence the term specific learning disability (SLD) is also used. LD is broadly classified into different types such as reading disability/dyslexia, spelling disability and arithmetic disability. Different terminologies are also used in different places. But LD in general refers to heterogeneous group of disorders manifested by significant difficulties in the acquisition of reading, writing, reasoning or mathematical abilities. Hence the term LD is used throughout the thesis.

1

### 1.1.3 Characteristics

The characteristic features of LD are that the scholastic backwardness in children stem from developmental neurological disturbances and that the difficulties continue to exist, despite appropriate instruction and intervention. A number of cognitive, neuropsychological and imaging researches over the past four decades have confirmed cognitive and neurological deficiencies in children with LD. LD is also known as a hidden disability because of its subtle manifestations, heterogeneous expressions and difficulties in identification. The disability manifests mainly in academic related activities where affected children display adequate reasoning and intelligence baffling the teachers and parents as to their inability to acquire simple academic skills. Its heterogeneity expresses differently in different children in the form of poor attention and concentration, poor recall, poor planning ability, inability to read or slow and incorrect reading, making persistent spelling mistakes, illegible hand-writing, reversing letters, poor sequencing, lacking number concept, inability to perform simple arithmetic calculations, etc.

### 1.1.4 Learning Disability in India

LD is a culture specific disorder even though the underlying cause is neurodevelopmental. Its expression is affected by the nature of orthographic system andteachingmethods. Educational system, school and government policies invariably influence identification and management of the disorder

### 1.1.4.1 Problems in identification

Identification of the disability is complicated and has gone trough several modifications in the west from IQ-achievement discrepancy method, grade level achievement discrepancy method, and neuropsychological assessments to the present

2

reaction to intervention method. To emulate the western methods of identification is impractical in India due to several factors like the lack of uniformity in quality of education where quality greatly varies from public to private schools and rural to urban schools, lack of uniformity in curriculum, where schools follow different curriculums like state syllabus, Central Board of Secondary Education (CBSC), Indian Certificate of Secondary Education (ICSC), International Baccalaureate (IB), International General Certificate of Secondary Education (IGCSE) syllabus that greatly differ from each other in their grade level difficulties, multilingualism where the medium of instruction in schools may not be the same as children's mother tongue. All these factors make it difficult to follow a uniform diagnostic method throughout the country.

The definition of LD clarifies that any scholastic backwardness due to low intelligence, poor or no schooling, inadequate hearing and vision, poor motivation and lack of socio-cultural opportunities are not due to LD. Hence, a proper diagnosis ideally requires a multidisciplinary team comprising of pediatrician, clinical psychologist and special educator to rule out the above possibilities for scholastic backwardness (Karande et al, 2011). Another complication associated with diagnosis is that a conclusive diagnosis of LD is difficult to make until the child is in the fourth grade, or about 7-8 years old because of the developmental variances among children. This late diagnosis leaves them unattended until they develop huge grade level discrepancies and show obvious signs of LD and prevent them from availing early interventions. Remedial education started early in life has better benefits on account of the neural plasticity in developing children. To overcome this difficulty, Reaction to Intervention (RTI) method is adopted in the US since the 2004 reauthorization of the Individuals with Disabilities Education Act to identify LD. The primary intention of this model is to support the "at risk" children at the earliest. The program identifies children at some level of risk for not meeting academic expectations at earlier grades and is given intense instructions through tier 1 and tier 2 programs. These instructions are intense classroom teaching carried out in small groups and are planned by the teachers with less regard to individual strengths and weaknesses or cognitive deficits. These instructions are to provide special attention to at risk children and more opportunities to practice skills. Children who do not possess cognitive deficits may reach successful level of competence by these instructions and may not want any further special attention. But children who do not respond to these special instructions may qualify for LD and may require special education service. This method requires immense support from the class teacher and school authorities. Class teacher is the first to observe child's academic performance and play important role in early identification and thus needs to be sensitive to notice such signs as delayed language development, inability to attend to the sounds of words, trouble playing rhyming games, or confusing words, etc. The school authorities must also be supportive in providing resources, time and space for the at risk children. Such a supportive environment is available in handful of schools in India, today. Presently exclusion criteria, IQ assessment, scores below 2 standard deviations in grade level assessments, and other neuropsychological assessments are being practiced to identify children with LD, in India.

### 1.1.4.2 Limited recognition and policies

Every disability needs recognition from the government to safeguard rights, ensure equal opportunities and full participation of the disabled. In this regard, LD has got minimal recognition from the government of India. The enactment of three legislations for the rehabilitation and welfare of people with disabilities viz, The

4

Persons with Disabilities Act, 1995; The Rehabilitation Council of India Act, 1992; and The National Trust Act, 1999 have been important milestones in India. They deal with all aspects pertaining to rehabilitation, from prevention, training, employment, long-term settlement, human resource development and research, and documentation. However, LD is not included in any of these acts. As of now, the only facilities that can be availed by these children are concessions in examinations conducted by the various examination boards. There is no uniformity in these provisions among states and examination boards. The Indian Certificate of Secondary Education (ICSE) board provides extra time 15 minute/per hour or 25% of total time, exemption from second language, use of calculator in some cases for mathematics, use of a writer and question paper can be read out to the student if required. The Central Board of Secondary Education (CBSE) board provides use of a writer, additional 1 hour for each paper and one compulsory language as against 2 in addition to any 4 of the following subjects: mathematics, science, social science, another language, music, painting and home science. Maharashtra Board of Secondary & Higher Secondary Education provides extra time of 30 minutes for SSC and 1 hour for HSC students, exemption from third language (Hindi/Marathi) for SSC students. HSC students may take a vocational subject instead of the second language, exemption from paper II in Mathematics (Algebra and Geometry) for SSC students, students may take a vocational subject of 75 marks in lieu of Mathematics Paper II and a writer may be provided as per the rules of the board. For students of standard I to IX, the school may apply to the Deputy Director of Education through the Divisional Inspector for similar provisions. Maharashtra remains the only state where children with LD are trained to take examinations, incorporating the provisions, from primary classes onwards. Recently the Higher and Technical Education Board extended these provisions to

5

technical Institutions, nonagricultural and agricultural universities, effectively covering students in undergraduate and postgraduate courses. Tamil Nadu provides extra time to answer examination paper, use of calculator, using Clarke's table, appointment of scribe to read the question paper or answer the paper. (Karande et al 2011) The other provision that children with LD in other states can avail is to take admission in the NIOS which allow a choice of subjects. However, NIOS is not available at all schools. The above provisions and concessions are accessible on producing disability certificate in the prescribed form issued by the recognized institution. In Karnataka, candidates with LD need to be certified either from the National Institute of Mental Health and Neuro Sciences (NIMHANS), Bangalore, St John's Hospital, Bangalore, All India Institute of Speech and Hearing (AIISH), Mysore, any psychiatrist working in a government hospital, any clinical psychologist with an M.Phil qualification and attested by a government doctor,not below the rank of a district surgeon (Karande et al, 2011). As to the participation of schools, no law in any state of India mandates schools to provide remedial education within its premises or government funding for remedial education services. The help and support children with LD in India today are getting from a handful of NGOs, and special schools and hence only a small number of children are receiving the benefits.

**1.1.4.3 Limited intervention facilities**

Interventions for children with LD are individualized with special consideration to their deficits, strengths and weaknesses. Phonologically based and neuropsychologically based interventions like are common. Remediation first target their cognitive deficiencies through tasks and practices to either enhance deficient cognitive skills or use compensatory cognitive mechanisms and then transfer the training to academically specific tasks. Remediation is not carried out in schools but isavailable in private or government special remedial centers. Since the process is time, cost and resource demanding only a few children are getting the attention.

### 1.1.4.4 Limited public awareness

LD awareness in India is also in its nascent stage. In the west, the disability has attracted considerable attention, owing to the long efforts of the parents, teachers and researchers, which has enabled children with LD avail the much needed support from the educational institutions and the government. In a country like India where at most importance is placed to academic achievements, such awareness in the public, parents, and teachers is highly required to reduce the negative attitude and prejudices that are attached to children with LD and to provide them adequate educational, psychological and legal support. The high prevalence of the disability also warrants considerable attention. It has been estimated that of the 416 million children in India, about 5-15% have LD. It is also reported that at least five students in an average classroom are affected with this disability (Kamala, 2014). However, children with LD have been bluntly condemned as dull, lazy, and this neglect has been resulting in chronic scholastic backwardness, detention in class and even dropping out of schools in rural areas. The problems are not restricted to academics but extend to child's quality of life, peer and family relationships, social interactions and self-image. Studies up till 2010 on teacher's awareness of the disability indicate a general lack of awareness and understanding of the disorder in the school teachers (Saravanabhavan&Saravanabhavan, 2010). Lately there has been an optimistic rise in the awareness among the professionals including educationalists, psychologists and pediatricians but a wave of awareness has yet to traverse beyond the professionals and reach the general public.

7

At present, the country's socio-cultural structure, educational system, lack of government recognition, lack of public awareness, highly demanding remediation methods all seem to be unfavorable and stressful to the parents and the children with LD.

## 1.2 Contemporary Yoga

Yoga is a traditional system of lifestyle which has its roots in Indian philosophy and had goals of spiritual attainment. Today it is practiced for physical and mental well-being. In this context, yoga is mostly associated with physical postures, breath control and meditation. Of the eight limbs of the age-old art of right living; Yama, Niyama, Asanas, Pranayama, Pratyahara, Dharana, Dhyana, and Samadhi, the three; Asana, Pranayama and Dhyana are the emblem of modern yoga. The teachings and research in yoga are predominantly centered on these three fold practice of yoga.

Modern yoga has undergone variations suiting the temperament and physical needs of the practitioners. There are 43 identified variations or schools of Yoga. Some of them are HathaYoga, Iyengar Yoga, Integrated Yoga Approach, Sudarshan Kriya Yoga, Nidra Yogasana, Viniyoga Yoga, Sahaja Yoga, Ashtanga Yoga, Yoga-based lifestyle modification, Silver Yoga, Kundalini Yoga, Yoga of Awareness, Vinyasa Yoga, Restorative Yoga, Kripalu Yoga, Dru Yoga, Chair Yoga, Bikram Yoga. As a result of expanding off shoots of classic yoga, borders between yoga and other similar practices are blurred. For example Transcendental meditation is usually seen as distinct from yoga, but is actually based on yoga principles. In the same way, mindfulness-based stress reduction uses yoga postures, but is not commonly seen as a yoga intervention (Cramer et al, 2014). Hence, modern yoga is an umbrella term used for the several variations each having its own distinct emphasis regarding the relative

8

content of physical postures and exercises (asanas), breathing techniques (pranayama), deep relaxation, and meditation practices.

### 1.2.1 Yoga as Complementary and Alternative Medicine

Though the therapeutic aspect of yoga is not described in any of the traditional systems of healing, except in the yoga sutras of Patanjali where the word vyadhi meaning disease is used in the list of disturbing factors of mind that are obstacles to spiritual liberation Gharote (1987), the modern yoga has found its way in the complementary and alternative medicine. The ministry of AYUSH in India, National Center for Complementary and Integrative Health (NCCIH), in the United States, National Health Service in the United Kingdom have been recognizing yoga as a safe and effective approach, in health and illness, for people of all ages. The therapeutic application of yoga started with the beginning of laboratory experiments done on the yoga practitioners in the early 90s. The first systematic medical application of yoga started in India in 1918 at the Yoga Institute at Versova near Mumbai, and the Yoga Institute at Santa Cruz. This was soon followed by the clinical work at the Kaivalyadhama Yoga Institute in Lonavala under Swami Kuvalyananda in the 1920s. The early researches on the psychophysiological effects of yoga practice were published in the first scientific journal devoted to scientific investigation into yoga called Yoga Mimamsa. Subsequently, yoga therapy has proliferated in India with the establishment of yogic hospitals and clinics, notably the Swami Vivekananda Yoga Research Institute near Bangalore (SVYASA). (Khalsa, 2004).

### 1.2.2 Increasing interest in Yoga research

A 2014 review article stated that the number of Yoga research articles published has been constantly rising since the 1970s and a large rise is seen post millennia (Cramer et al, 2014). The total number of studies published in 2014 was three times as high as in 2010. 86.9% of the articles available were published after the year 2000 and the maximum of them were published between 2010 and 2012. Randomized Control Trials on yoga were published from 23 countries some of which include India, USA, United Kingdom, Australia, Iran, Germany, Canada, Brazil, Japan, Taiwan, China, and Korea.

Research on the effectiveness of yoga has been done on various population including general, student, employee and patients with specified medical conditions. Yoga as intervention has been tested on various conditions like Breast cancer, Asthma, Depression, Type 2 diabetes mellitus, Chronic low back pain, Hypertension, Pregnancy, Schizophrenia, Menopausal symptoms, Multiple sclerosis, Metabolic syndrome, Stress, Coronary artery disease, COPD, All cancer types, Chronic neck pain, Eating disorder, Fibromyalgia, Heart failure, Menstrual irregularities, Osteoarthritis, Overweight/obesity, Smoking, Substance abuse and Others. Of the 312 studies reviewed 46.4% of studies were reported from India and 26.8% were reported from the US. 84.6% studies included adults (18-64 years), 33.7% involved older adults (≥65 years) and 9.9% were with children (<18 years). (Cramer et al, 2014).

**1.2.3 Increasing acceptance by general public**

A study conducted by Yoga Journal and Yoga Alliance in 2016 estimated that more than 36 million people practice yoga in the US and 80 million people are likely to try yoga in the near future. (http://www.yogajournal.com/yogainamericastudy/). Apparently, the reason for this rise in popularity of yoga and yoga as therapy among general public and the researchers is the increasing incidence of chronic lifestyle diseases, which the mainstream health care systems are failing to adequately address and yoga being a mind-body system promises to serve as a preventive intervention.

10

The popularity and global acceptance of yoga is marked by the declaration of the International day of Yoga by The United Nations. The United Nations stated its aim is "to raise awareness worldwide of the many benefits of practicing yoga" (www.un.org/en/events/yogaday/).

### 1.2.4 Yoga for LD

Yoga's relaxing effects on the body and mind, effects on the cardiovascular, pulmonary, musculoskeletal, autonomic nervous system in promoting general wellbeing is well acknowledged.Its effects on specific clinical conditions are the popular research interest today. Previous studies conducted on children with mental retardation & attention deficit hyperactivity disorder using yogic practices have yielded positive results.But there were no published studies where yoga was tried as an intervention on children with LD when this research was commenced. Nor such studies have been reported till date, to the best of my literature search in Google Scholar, PubMed, ERIC, Shodha Ganga, & Mysore University e- library, etc. Hencein the preset study, an attempt is made to evaluate the effects of yoga on the cognitive and behavioral variables of children with LD.

*Chapter -II*

**REVIEW OF RELATED LITERATURE**

## 2.1 Introduction: Processing deficits in LD

LD is a central nervous system dysfunction. Owing to the heterogeneous nature of LD, several neuropsychological theories like; double deficit theory, magnocellular deficit theory, temporal processing deficit theory, cerebellar theory, etc have been proposed to explain the causes of LD. Different theory explains different cognitive, functional and structural deficits exhibited in LD. In the present study, Planning, Attention, Simultaneous & Successive processing (PASS), and Phonological Processing are seen as the underlying cognitive functions involved in the acquisition of literary skills in children. Hence the following literature review revolves around the relationship between these cognitive processes in children with LD.

### 2.1.1 Planning, Attention, Simultaneous & Successive processing in LD

One of the perspectives for understanding LD is the PASS theory of cognitive processing. The PASS theory holds the view that the PASS cognitive functions, particularly successive and simultaneous processes, have a bearing on the reading, spelling and writing tasks while planning process is related to problem solving capacities in children. A below average functioning ability in all or some of these four cognitive processes are known to be the reason for the poor processing skills in children with LD. The validity studies for the PASS theory with children with LD have shown that successive process is associated with word attack skills in children and planning is associated with mathematical computation (Naglieri & Gottling, 1997).

PASS theory of intelligence is an information processing theory based on the ingenious work of A.R Luria (Luria, 1973). Luria's theory of functional units proposed that, all cognitive functions fall within the framework of three separate but related brain systems or functional units. The first unit provides regulation of cortical arousal and attention, the second, receives codes and stores information and the third provides strategy development, self monitoring and cognitive control. Luria proposed that attention is a mental process that is closely related to orienting response which allows the organism to direct focused selective attention toward a stimulus over time and resist loss of attention to other stimuli. This according to Luria forms the first unit of the brain, the attention-arousal system, and is located in the brain stem, the diencephalon, and the medial regions of the cortex. This unit is responsible for the appropriate level of arousal or cortical tone, and for selective attention. The second unit is the simultaneous and successive processing unit. The simultaneous processing is essential for organization of information into groups or a coherent whole while successive processing is involved when the stimuli are processed in a specific serial order. This includes for example serial organization of sounds and movements in order and therefore it is integral to working with sounds in sequence and early reading. This second functional unit is associated with the secondary and tertiary zones of occipital, parietal and temporal lobes posterior to the central sulcus of the brain. This unit is responsible for receiving, processing, and retaining information a person obtains from the external world. The third functional unit is planning. Planning helps in achieving selection and development of plans or strategies needed to complete tasks for which a solution is needed and is critical to all activities where one has to determine how to solve a problem. This includes generation, evaluation, and execution of plan as well as self-monitoring and impulse control. This functional unit associated with the prefrontal areas of the frontal lobes of the brain.

Luria expressed that every conscious activity is always a complex functional system and takes place through the combined working of all three brain units, each of which makes its own contribution (Luria, 1973). The relationship between the third and first functional units is particularly strong. The first functional unit works in cooperation with, and is regulated by, higher systems of the cerebral cortex, which receive and process information from the external world and determine individual's dynamic activity. The unit has a reciprocal relationship with the cortex. It influences the tone of cortex and is influenced by the regulatory effects of the cortex. This is possible through the ascending and descending systems of the reticular formation, which transmits impulses from the lower parts of the brain to the cortex and vice versa.

This theory of functional units by A.R.Luria formed the basis of a subsequent theory of Intelligence; Planning, Attention, Simultaneous and Successive theory of intelligence (Das, Naglieri & Kirby, 1994). According to its proponents, Das, Kirby & Jarman (1975), intelligence is the sum total of all cognitive processes and that it entails planning, coding of information and attention as well as arousal. The model proposes that information in the cognitive system are processed by the four main units namely Planning, Attention, Simultaneous and Successive processes which are broadly associated with the frontal lobe, brain stem and lower part of cerebral cortex, occipital and parietal lobes and frontal- temporal lobes respectively. When the information arrives at the senses, these four cognitive processes are activated to analyze its meaning within the context of individual's knowledge base. Planning processes involves making some decisions about how to solve a problem, setting goals, anticipating consequences, using feedback and carryout an activity. Attention-Arousal involves the ability to selectively attend to stimuli while ignoring other

14

distracters. It is a simple process to keep one awake and alert. Simultaneous process involves the ability to integrate separate stimuli into a cohesive, interrelated whole. Successive process involves the ability to integrate stimuli into a sequential order.

The PASS theory suggests that successive processing is the underlying cognitive process that is responsible for phonological skill and word reading. PASS theory is operationalized using the tool Cognitive Assessment System which can be regarded as neuropsychological assessment tool useful in the assessment of LD.

Naglieri and Gottling (1997) expressed their view that the PASS theory, operationalized by the tool CAS, is helpful in identifying specific cognitive weakness in children and is appropriate for successful aptitude by treatment interaction if the specific and relevant aptitude is identified and a particular treatment pertaining to that specific aptitude is applied. In a study they grouped 12 students with LD from schools that specialized in the treatment of students with significant learning problems, into two groups as low and high planning groups on the basis of cognitive assessment system. They theorized planning to be important for mathematical computations. Students with LD in math lack effective use of problem solving strategies and hence the interventions particularly addressed their inefficient planning strategies. Following the intervention the students with low planning scores showed significantly better performance than those with high planning scores. The researchers concluded that to design an appropriate academic instruction that meets the students cognitive needs, professionals require a complete and accurate picture of a person's level of cognitive processing in specific areas and that PASS model helps meet this needs.

Das, Mishra, and Pool (1995) proposed that, word decoding which is a basic reading skill is linked primarily with successive process than with any other cognitive process. They conducted a study with 51 children aged between 8 years 9 months and

15

11 years 11 months who demonstrated word decoding problems. The subjects were assessed in successive and planning processes using cognitive assessment system. Their word decoding ability was also tested using two subtests from WRMT-R. Following the intervention which addressed their cognitive deficit, a significant improvement in the successive processing as well as in the word decoding test was observed.

A study conducted by Van Luit, Kroesbergen, and Naglieri (2005) examined the utility of the planning, attention, simultaneous, successive ( PASS) theory of intelligence as measured by the cognitive Assessment system (CAS) for evaluation of children with attention deficit hyperactivity disorder ( ADHD). The CAS scores of 51 Dutch children without ADHD were compared to the scores of a group of 20 Dutch children with ADHD. The scores of the Dutch children were also compared to American standardization samples of children with and without ADHD. The findings showed that children with ADHD in both the countries demonstrated relatively low scores on the planning and attention scales of the CAS, but average scores on the simultaneous and successive scales. They concluded that the findings are similar to previously published research suggesting that the PASS theory, as operationalised by the CAS, has sensitivity to the cognitive processing difficulties found in children with ADHD.

Hayward, Das and Janzen (2007) conducted experiment in order to find the effectiveness of two cognitive enhancement programs (COGONT and PREP developed particularly to enhance PASS processes) on variables such as phonological awareness, rapid naming speed, word reading ability, listening comprehension and also on the four cognitive processes planning, Attention, successive and simultaneous processes, which are thought to be the underlying factors contributing effective

16

reading skills. Forty five grade 3 children from a reservation school in Western Canada were selected for the study. They were divided into two remedial groups and a non-risk control group. The group means across the four scales did reveal differential improvements following intervention but there were no significant group differences.

### 2.1.2 Phonological Processing in LD

LD is predominantly a language related problem. Research states that most reading difficulties stem from deficits in phonological processing. (Bradley &. Bryant, 1978; Bryant, Bradley MacLean & Crossland, 1990; Bryant & Goswami, 1986; wagner& Trogesen 1987. Phonological processing is generally defined as the conscious use of phonological or speech sound knowledge in processing written and oral language (Wagner & Torgesen, 1987). Children as young as 2-3 years of age, start picking up sound units in spoken language which progress during their preschool and early years in school. Studies have shown that the phonological skills possessed at an early age is significantly predictive of later phonemic ability and hence reading ability (Muter, 2000; Muter & Snowling, 1998; Wagner, Torgesen &. Rashotte, 1994).

According to the phonological deficit hypothesis, phonological awareness (PA) is the key to learn to read languages that have alphabetic spelling systems. Phonological awareness is related to accurate identification of words and to applying letter/sound knowledge to decode unfamiliar words. Failure to discover the underlying sound structure of written language is a major cause of problems in LD. Correlation studies show that phonological processing and its relationship to reading are concomitant. Intervention studies have shown that children with low phonological awareness demonstrate improved reading performance after phonological awareness

17

intervention (Sodoro et al, 2002). PA facilitates the development of reading skills in early readers and the development of reading skills reciprocally facilitate the development of phonological awareness in later years of reading. There is a general sequence in the development of phonological awareness. Children become increasingly sensitive to smaller and smaller parts of words as they grow older. They first learn to detect or manipulate syllables and then become sensitive to onsets and rimes, and finally can attend to individual phonemes within intra-syllabic word units. Children are able to blend phonological information before they are able to segment phonological information (Anthony & Francis, 2005).

Phonological awareness of a child is assessed using tasks that require accessing and manipulating sounds in words. Phonological awareness is thus operationally defined as unified ability that manifests itself in different skills such as one's ability to recognize, discriminate, and manipulate the sounds in one's language (Anthony, & Francis, 2005). It has been measured by using many different tasks that range from recognition of rhyme and sound-to-word matching to isolating single sounds from words, blending, deleting phonemes, and other even more complex manipulations, such as children's secret languages. According to Adams, 1990 the tasks used to measure phonological awareness fall into five levels of difficulty. The first level consists of having an ear for the sounds of words, which is revealed by the ability to remember familiar rhymes. A second level consists of the ability to recognize and sort patterns of rhyme and alliteration in words, which requires more focused attention to sound components; this ability is revealed in oddity tasks. A third level requires familiarity both with the idea that syllables can be divided into phonemes and with the sounds of isolated phonemes; this level is indicated by blending tasks and by syllable-splitting tasks, for example, isolating initial phonemes.

A fourth level of difficulty is encountered in tasks that require full segmentation of component phonemes, e.g., tapping tests. Most difficult of all are tasks that require children to add, delete, or otherwise move phonemes and to regenerate the resultant word or pseudoword.

Functional neuroimaging studies involving various PA tasks have indicated activation of regions in the prefrontal and temporal cortex of the brain. With proficiency in reading and PA, activation in left temporo-parietal and temporo-occipital regions are reported. Studies using visually presented PA tasks in typically developing children have indicated involvement of left inferior frontal gyrus, superior temporal gyrus, middle temporal gyrus, and fusiform gyrus (Temple et al. 2001; Booth et al. 2004; Bitan et al. 2009). In older and proficient readers increased activations in left posterior temporal and parietal regions are reported (Hoeft et al. 2006; Shaywitz et al. 2007), and reduced activation in these areas are reported in children with dyslexia relative to age- or ability-matched typical readers (Temple et al. 2001; Cao et al. 2006). With remediation for dyslexia increased activation in left posterior temporal and parietal regions are reported (Simos et al. 2002; Meyler et al. 2008). Kovelman et al (2011) reported that typically developing children, but not children with LD, recruited left dorsolateral prefrontal cortex (DLPFC) when making explicit phonological judgments. In their study LD children who exhibited weakness in phonological awareness as assessed by standardized test of phonological awareness (CTOPP) showed reduced activation in left DLPFC. They concluded that left DLPFC may play a critical role in the development of phonological awareness for spoken language critical for reading and in the etiology of dyslexia. Katzir et al. 2005, suggested that phonological awareness without print engages the frontal lobe, whereas the engagement of left posterior regions may reflect the integration of printed and

19

auditory information during reading (Pugh et al. 2000; Booth et al. 2004; Shaywitz et al. 2007). Many studies have reported that left middle frontal gyrus (MFG) may support both verbal and nonverbal auditory processes important for reading acquisition (Gaab et al. 2007; Poldrack et al. 2001). Some studies have implicated different networks in posterior left-hemisphere regions, including posterior temporal and parietal regions as being important for reading due to their engagement for tasks involving phonological analysis of print. (Pugh et al. 2000; Temple et al. 2001; Cao et al. 2006; Hoeft et al. 2006; Shaywitz et al. 2007). Activations in posterior left hemisphere regions, including posterior temporal, temporoparietal, and temporooccipital regions are reported with increased phonological awareness competence (Temple et al. 2003; Frost et al. 2009).

### 2.1.3 Phonological processing in Kannada

It is now found that the scripts or orthographies of a language also influence the ability to learn to read them. Orthographies or scripts differ from one another in terms cognitive challenges they place in representing and decoding them. In India, children learn two to three languages; one or two Indian languages and English. English is an alphabetic script where as Indian languages are alphasyllabary scripts. Studies in phonemically represented scripts or alphabetic scripts like that of English for example, report phonological awareness as a very important predictor of reading ability in children, i.e, in such scripts phonological awareness precedes and determines the reading acquisition in children. In contrast, studies in alphasyllabic scripts suggest that phonological awareness does not precede or predict reading acquisition but is in fact the product of practice and successful reading skill (Nag, 2007).

20

Kannada is an alphasyllabic script. It is both phonemically as well as syllabically represented in the script and is called as an alpha syllabary script or abugida. This characteristic enables mapping or representation both at the phonemic as well as at the syllabic levels. This in other words means both smaller as well as larger units are available for mapping. For example letters can be recognized by the phoneme markers present in it or can be recognized as a whole letter. The primary mapping happens at syllable level but each syllable is constructed by stacking many phoneme markers (Nag, 2007).

The characteristic nature of Kannada orthography is that it is a transparent script i.e., it has consistent grapheme to phoneme correspondence unlike the English script. It has extensive set of symbols or phoneme markers to master and recall them. There are primary and secondary vowels and consonants which cluster around a base consonant. It is syllabically represented but each syllabic representation is clustered by phoneme markers (Nag et al,2011). This nature of the script makes it a dense unit for the extraction of visual information. In terms of visuo-spatial organization, it is non-linear. Kannada script is nonlinear and require mapping from left to right, right to left as well as up and down. Phonemically represented scripts rely on phonological processing skills while visually complex scripts must rely on visual analysis for decoding (Yeh et al, 2003). Therefore, Kannada script with extensive symbol set and dense visual information, necessitate visual analysis for effective reading acquisition.

## 2.1.4 Emotional and Behavioral Problems in LD

Children with LD develop emotional and behavioral problems due to the incompetence in academic and cognitive abilities they face more than their non LD peers. This leads to lack of motivation, poor self-efficacy, internalization and externalization problems. They generally exhibit poor self efficacy ad lackbeliefs in one's capabilities to organize and execute the courses of action required to produce given attainments. The self-efficacy is the vital element in influencing the line of thinking and executing the one's responsibilities. (Bandura,1997). One's belief about their self-efficacy has a direct impact on one's performance. Many researchers noted that the children with LD make poor judgment when it comes to their self-knowledge, the motivation and the knowledge towards their task (Butler, 1998; Meltzer et al., 1998).The students with fully developed Meta cognitive skills possess the ability to evaluate and understand their strength, weakness, and cognitive abilities which are much necessary to become successful in the academic setting. This becomes difficult for the children with LD because they exhibit deficiencies in analyzing their own skills and monitoring their tasks (Flavell, 1976).

The children with LD exhibit different behavior problems in social as well as academic settings. They generally show deficits in social competence when comparing to their peers without LD. The LD students exhibit low level of peer acceptance than the non LD students. Gresham (1986) in their comparative study between LD and non LD children reported that the LD children were .75 standard deviations below the non LD children in peer acceptance. Many researches suggest that the children with learning disability express the negative social behaviors like problems in inter personal relationships with their peers, which leads to the reduced level of acceptance. Studies reveal that the socio-metric status of students with LD is one half to a full standard deviation below of the non LD students (Bryan, 1982;La Greca & Mesibov, 1981). In class room and home setting children with LD are known to demonstrate poor social skills towards their peers, teacher and parents. The social skill deficit is consistent in both school and home settings and also its same irrespective of the teachers, and peers. The parent and teachers recognize that they exhibit poor social skills such as greeting others, conversing, listening to others, smiling and laughing, and complimenting others. Gresham reported that children with LD are two standard deviations below the non LD students in the behavioral area.

## 2.2 Introduction: Yoga as intervention

When viewed from psychotherapeutic interest, yoga is nothing but techniques to develop attention, concentration, introspection, volition and metacognition. Yoga intrinsically has qualities of biofeedback therapy with techniques for greater awareness to body and mental states with the goal of being able to manipulate them at will.

Regardless of the schools, there are some core components that provide psychotherapeutic values to yoga. As explained by (Schmalzl et al. 2015) movement and the execution of specific physical postures or movement sequence in yoga, fine-tune interoceptive and proprioceptive awareness, and provide a context for training attention. These slow, controlled and rhythmic movements synchronized with breath, train one to balance, coordinate, and constantly track ones of the body positions in space, postural alignment, fluidity and fine tune the movement. The postures are characterized by a hypertonic (e.g., arm balances that require a high level of muscle tension) or hypotonic (e.g., a supine relaxation pose) states provide balanced muscle tone. The overall aim of the practice is to create a state of well-balanced muscle

23

tension which allows the movement to feel stable, well rooted, light and effortless. These practices provide submaximal levels of load on the joints which are said to be beneficial for bone remodeling and osteogenesis. The intensity employed in these movements increase parasympathetic tone as opposed to sympathetic nervous activation as in other forms of exercises and consequently promote down-regulation of stress levels. The postures are taught using precise alignment cues. The postures are designed to expand range of motion, strength and flexibility of the body. The belief is that physical and emotional stress over time manifests as stiffness and blockages in our muscles, joints and connective tissue. Therefore the aim of posture practice is to release this tension by directing attention to the physical limitation, while directly moving towards and breathing into it. There are practices of interior muscle activations which are called "bandhas". These are static and soft contraction of interior muscle groups at pelvic floor, the lower abdomen and the throat. The contraction of these muscle groups aid breathing practices and facilitates the maintenance of strong core musculature while moving through the postures.

Breathe awareness is a very important component in yoga. Breath is precisely coordinated with movements so that specific movements help enhance the breath and *vice versa*. The breath are used as a tool to direct attention to specific body parts while holding a posture or performing a movement, and to consequently increase interoceptive and proprioceptive awareness. There is the practice of consciously altering breathing patterns which have a number of different effects depending on their characteristics. Slow and rhythmic breathing is said to promote a shift to parasympathetic dominance via vagal afferent stimulation and consequently reduces stress, whereas more forceful breathing practices promote sympathetic activation. In some practices the focus is on cultivating an even rhythm of inhalations and exhalations, with no specific emphasis on linking movement with breath. There is a relationship between breathing and emotional states. Emotional states are expressed in breathing patterns, and subsequently that voluntary change of the breathing patterns can alter emotional states. A typical autonomic reaction to stressful situations is rapid thoracic breathing, which in turn leads to hyperventilation, altered tidal volume and hypocapnia. These symptoms are frequently observed as chronic manifestations in individuals with anxiety and depressive disorders and may be alleviated by the types of breathing techniques. The breath also serves merely as an object of attention in many meditation practices. A fundamental aspect of yoga is paying attention to interoceptive, proprioceptive, kinesthetic and spatial sensations, and using that information to adjust and fine-tune one's movements. These lead to body awareness. Interoceptive awareness refers to the awareness of internal bodily states and sensations, including heart rate, respiration, as well as several autonomic nervous system responses related to emotional states. The processing of bodily sensations is also a key for our sense of bodily self, which originates through the integration of interoceptive, proprioceptive, kinesthetic, tactile and spatial information. Meditation practices are often classified as engaging focused attention (FA) or open monitoring (OM) techniques. FA techniques involve directing and sustaining attention on a single selected object, whereas OM techniques emphasize non-reactive metacognitive monitoring of perceived sensory, emotional or cognitive events that may arise from moment to moment during one's practice. The beginners tend to primarily engage in FA, where as advanced practitioners gravitate more toward an OM approach. Individuals engaging in yoga gradually transition from a FA to a more OM attentional orientation. Novice practitioners may only be able to provide their attention to one single element of the practice at the time, but as their practice advances they are likely to become increasingly skilled at simultaneously monitoring movement, breath, and any concomitant interoceptive and exteroceptive sensations that may arise. Hence, in more advanced practitioners, primarily engage an OM type of attention. Another component is gaze.

Gaze, like breath are used as a tool for training attention and inducing a calm state of mind. Some use eye exercises including gazing techniques in which the eyes are held in a particular position (e.g., upward, inward or downward). These exercises are recommended to aid powers of concentration and prevent one's attention from being distracted.

Finally, metacognition is the conscious and mostly intentional monitoring of our own mental processes and behaviors. It is the action of "stepping back" to observe ones own inner sensations and thoughts. This aspect differentiates yoga from many common forms of exercise, which are often practiced without a primary goal of paying attention to bodily or mental states. Mindfulness-based practices represent interplay between metacognition and mind-wandering (MW), which refers to spontaneous and undirected thought processes that mostly occur without our volition. In FA, metacognition has the "suppressive" function of noticing drifts of attention from a selected object, and subsequently redirecting attention towards it. In OM, metacognition has the more "integrated" function of monitoring one's stream of thought, while attempting to maintain detachment and refrain from any cognitive elaboration or judgment.

### 2.2.1 Allostatic regulation and Polyvagal theory for Yoga

Yoga has a place in complementary and alternative medicine. It is an evidence based practice. The exact mechanisms of how it brings about clinically significant changes are not clearly known yet. But it has been recommended and practiced based on clinically relevant research, experiences of patients and expert practitioners. The popular theories proposed to account for the wellbeing promoted by yoga are the allostatic regulation and polyvagal perspective. It is believed that yoga has intrinsic properties to promote vegal tone and facilitate decrease of allostatic load. Allostatic load is the ability of an organism to maintain homeostasis by actively adapting to both predictable and unpredictable event in the environment. This adaptation is mediated by the hormones in the hypothalamo-pitutary-adrenal (HPA) axis. An imbalance in these mediators results in allostatic state and cumulative effect of sustained state over time result in allostatic load. The regulation of allostatic load is done by the vegal nerve, the 10th cranial nerve. Its axons emerge from and converge into brain stem nuclei and it regulates several visceral organs as well as muscles of face, head and neck. The parasympathetic activation brought about by yogic slow and rhythmic breathing, postures that enhance the depth of breath and postures that emphasize abdominal tone through activation of interior muscles are know to stimulate vagal nerve and regulate the vegal tone. This theory is accounted for the hormonal balance, positive cardio pulmonary functioning and body-mind integration brought about by yoga.

The positive effects of yoga are reported on endocrine system, nervous system, physical health, metabolism, circulatory system, cognition and behavior are reported following the practice of yoga. Decreased salivary cortisol levels, enhanced serotonin, melotonin, and oxytocin (Vera et al, 2009; Brotto, 2009; Oswal et al, 2011; Kinser et al , 2012) production are reported following yoga. These changes in hormones are believed to be responsible for the observed decrease in stress and anxiety, improved immunity and sleep in practitioners. On the nervous system, yoga is known to influence sympathetic and parasympathetic activity of the ANS. Respiratory effects of breathing exercises, visualization and calming techniques in meditation as well as physical movements are known to produce sympathetic activation, increased levels of gamma aminobutyric acid (GABA) (Streeter et al, 2012), regulated hypothalamic-pituitaryadrenal (HPA) axis (Kiecolt-Glaser et al, 2010) to produce improved outcomes in mood disorders, stress, well-being and provide an anxiolytic effect. Lowered resting heart rate, oxygen consumption rate, decreased basal metabolic rate (BMR) and decreased body mass index (BMI) (Bera et al, 1993; Innes et al, 2005) and fat mass are reported which indicate preventative effects for cardiovascular disease, diabetes and obesity and promote physical health. Improved glucose tolerance and insulin sensitivity following yoga are reported which suggests that regular practice may replace drug therapies in type 2 diabetics (Innes et al, 2005). Clinically significant improvements after yoga intervention are noted in fasting plasma glucose (FPG) and postprandial plasma glucose (PPPG) (Sahay, 2007). Increased hepatic lipase and lipoprotein lipase at the cellular level and subsequent increase in uptake of triglycerides by adipose tissues (Balaji et al, 2012) suggest positive effects of yoga on metabolism. In the circulatory system health-related outcomes included lowered blood pressure and improved arterial function, enhanced cardiovagal function and slowed atherosclerosis to prevent cardiovascular disease, increased blood flow and restored baroreceptor sensitivity (Innes et al, 2005). Numerous findings provide evidence for increased levels of total antioxidant status (TAS) and other naturally occurring antioxidants in human cells such as glutathione (GSH) and plasma vitamin E (Dun et al, 2008) following yoga intervention.

## 2.2.2 Yoga for children

Of the 312 studies reviewed in 2014 only 9.9% of the studies were done with children (Cramer et al, 2014). A review of literature of randomized controlled trials of yoga on children suggests that yoga has positive impact on the general health and physical fitness of children. Increased muscular fitness (Moorthy, 1982), improved tweezer dexterity (Telles et.al, 1993), grip strength (Raghuraj, 1997; Madanmohan, 2003), motor speed (Dash & Telles, 1999) were reported. Physical fitness in terms of body composition (Seo, 2012), muscular strength, cardiopulmonary functions (Udupa et al, 2003, Chen et al, 2009), abdominal strength (Komathi et al, 2011), vital capacity (D'Souza & Avadhany 2014) had improved. Decreased heart rate, improved cardiac function, improved lipid profile and insulin resistance, increasing parasympathetic activity and decreasing sympathetic activity (D'Souza & Avadhany 2014; Seo, 2012) were also observed following the practice of yoga in children. On psychological wellbeing, children showed reduced levels of fear and anxiety (Rauhala, 1990; Berger & Owen, 1999), improvements in self image (Clance, 1990), behavioral adjustments (Telles, 1997), and increased emotional balance in terms of healthy stress management (Stueck & Gloeckner, 2005) following yoga intervention.

## 2.2.3 Yoga and cognitive functions

Studies on the effect of yoga on cognition have reported improvement in some cognitive functions. A study by Naveen KV,et al (1997) involving 108 school children aged 10 to 17 years who practiced four types of yoga breathing; right nostril breathing, left nostril breathing, alternate nostril breathing, and breath awareness without manipulation of nostrils, in four independent groups for 10 days. Verbal and spatial memory was assessed. All 4 trained groups showed a significant increase in spatial memory test scores at retest, but the control group did not show change. They

29

concluded that yoga breathing improves spatial memory in children. Similar results were showed by Manunath&Telles (2004). Manjunath&Telles (1999) studied the effect of yoga on the visual perceptual sensitivity in children. The experiment included 14 children, aged between 12 to 17 years, who were given training in Yogasanas, Pranayama, and Kriyas which included eye-cleansing techniques, meditation and Bhajans, 8 hours per day for a period of 10 days. The children were assessed on for visual perceptual sensitivity through an apparatus called Critical Flicker Fusion Frequency which recorded the binocular responses of the children. The degree of optical illusion was also measured using Muller-Lyer apparatus. At the end of $10^{th}$ day, the subjects were assessed. The results revealed significant increase in the CFF and significant reduction in the degree of perceived optical illusion in the experiment group. They concluded that training through yoga to focus and defocus might influence cognitive judgmental factors of subjects to significantly reduce the degree of illusion perceived. The effect of yoga on maze learning task was studied by Telles, Ramaprabhu& Reddy (1999). They reported that Following 30 days of Yoga training in asanas, Pranayama, Kriya, Meditation, devotional sessions, guided relaxation and lectures on the theory and philosophy of yoga for approximately 6 hrs a day, the experiment group showed significant decrease in the time taken to trace the maze and also reduction in the number of errors they made. They concluded that yoga helps in improvement of higher levels of mental functioning, including the process of choosing, trying and rejecting or adopting alternative courses of conduct or thought. Manjunath and Telles, 2001 reported improvements in problem solving ability in a group of female school children after 7 days of yoga practice, who were compared to a group of children performing the same amount of regular physical exercise. Children in the yoga group showed significant reduction in planning time, execution time and in the number of moves in both simple and complex tasks in Tower Of London. Children participating in the yoga classes were reported to have come up with more efficient solutions (planning time, execution time and number of moves) on the Tower of London Task. Decreased visual and auditory reaction time in 22 healthy schoolboys following practice of yoga was reported by Bhavanani et al 2003. They reported that yoga has the potentiality to improve sensory-motor performance and enhance processing ability of the central nervous system. Jensen P, Kenny D (2004), Peck HL, (2005), Harrison ,Manocha&Rubia (2004) reported improved attention in children with Attention Deficit Hyperactivity Disorder. Subramanya and Telles (2009) showed the effect of cyclic mediation on improved performance in memory scores. Narayana, 2009 found that yoga group compared to non yoga group performed faster in a visual color discrimination task. He attributed it to increased alertness and visuospatial attention due to the practice of yoga. Gothe and colleagues (Gothe et al., 2013) found greater improvements in working memory in novice practitioners after a single session of yoga compared to a single session of general aerobic exercise. Verma (2014) studied the effect of yoga practices on cognitive development variables in 82, 11-15 years adolescents in rural residential school children. Cognition Function tests, an Indian adaptation battery based on Guilford's Structure of Intellect Model was administered at the baseline and at the end of 12 weeks of yoga training in both groups. Results showed significant improvement in measures of mental ability and memory in experimental group. No statistically significant changes were observed in measures of mental ability and memory tests in control group. They concluded that yoga training has effect on primary cognitive processes such as attention, perception and observation and that yoga, being a simple and inexpensive health regimen, can be

31

incorporated as an effective adjuvant therapy to governmental child health initiatives in school curriculum.

### 2.3.4 Yoga curriculum in schools

Since 2010, some studies have shown interest in using yoga or yoga based intervention within the school settings and exploring its effects on school children. Some authors have speculated the use of having a yoga based curriculum in the school. In the following section some of the studies on yoga that were conducted in the school settings are reviewed. Of the many published articles only a few followed the recommended experimental procedures. In all these studies Yoga or yoga based interventions were given to school age children within the school setting and the effects on psychological well-being or cognitive functions were analyzed. Telles et al. 2013 observed the effects of yoga and physical exercise on physical fitness, cognitive performance, selfesteem, and teacher-rated behavior and performance. 98 children between the ages of 8 and 13 were selected from a primary school in Haridwar. Participants were assessed for physical fitness, performance in the Stroop task (the Stroop color-word naming task), self-esteem, and analog scales (attention, punctuality, behavior with friends, and behavior with teachers) rated by the teachers. Post assessment was done at the end of twelve weeks. Yoga practice involved yoga breathing techniques, loosening exercises, postures, chanting, and yoga relaxation techniques 45 minutes per day, during school hours which lasted three months with a frequency of five times a week. Physical exercise had the same time and frequency and consisted of jogging in place as well as bending and spinal twists. Results indicated significantly higher social self-esteem in physical exercise group. Both groups showed an increased BMI, and number of sit-ups. Balance worsened in the physical exercise group, while plate tapping improved in the yoga group. In the

Stroop task both groups showed improved color, word- and color-word naming, while the physical exercise group showed higher interference scores. Total, general and parental self-esteem improved in the yoga group. Authors concluded that both Yoga and physical exercise are useful additions to the school routine, with physical exercise improving social self-esteem. Noggle et al. (2015) evaluated the effects of a yoga program on psychological well-being, psychological attitudes, and self-regulatory skills in 11$^{th}$ and 12$^{th}$ grade adolescents at a public high school in Massachusetts. They compared a Kripalu based yoga program conducted within the school curriculum for adolescents and compared them to the regular physical education classes. Both the interventions were done two to three times a week for 30 minutes. Yoga practice consisted of 5 minutes of centering and breathing exercises, 5 minutes of warm-up, 15 minutes of yoga postures, and 5 minutes of closing relaxation. After 10 weeks of program, students attending physical education classes showed decreases in primary outcomes like in profile of mood states while Yoga students were maintained or improved. Total mood disturbance improved in yoga students but worsened in controls. Positive affect remained unchanged in both, negative affect significantly worsened in controls, but improved in yoga students. Secondary outcomes, such as the scores in resilience scale, and the child acceptance mindfulness measure were not significant. The authors concluded that Kripalu yoga program at school can have preventive benefits in psychosocial well-being. A study by Butzer 2015 explored the effects of a 12-week school-based yoga intervention on changes in grade point average (GPA) in 9th and 10th grade students. Participants included 95 high school students who had registered for physical education (PE). The class was group randomized to receive either a yoga intervention or a PE control condition. The yoga intervention took place during the entire third quarter and half of the fourth quarter of

33

the school year, and quarterly GPA was collected via school records at the end of the school year. Results revealed that GPA differed between the yoga and control groups over time. While both groups exhibited a general decline in GPA over the school year, the control group exhibited a significantly greater decline in GPA from quarter 1 to quarter 3 than the yoga group. Both groups showed equivalent declines in GPA in quarter 4 after the yoga intervention had ended. The results suggest that yoga may have a protective effect on academic performance by preventing declines in GPA however these preventive effects did not persist once yoga practice was discontinued. Schonert-Reichl(2015) designed a mindfulness social and emotional learning (SEL) program for elementary school students involving mindfulness and caring for others. 4th and 5th graders (N = 99) were randomly assigned to receive the SEL with mindfulness program versus a regular social responsibility program. Measures assessed executive functions, stress physiology via salivary cortisol, well-being (self-reports), prosociality and peer acceptance (peer reports), and math grades.would enhance cognitive control, reduce stress, promote well-being and prosociality, and produce positive school outcomes. Relative to children in the social responsibility program, children who received the SEL program with mindfulness (a) improved more in their cognitive control and stress physiology; (b) reported greater empathy, perspective-taking, emotional control, optimism, school self-concept, and mindfulness, (c) showed greater decreases in self-reported symptoms of depression and peer-rated aggression, (d) were rated by peers as more prosocial, and (e) increased in peer acceptance (or sociometric popularity). The researchers suggested that mindfulness SEL intervention strategies are good to ameliorate children's problems and to cultivate their well-being and thriving. Daly LA, 2016 evaluated the impact of mindful awareness, self-compassion and body awareness through yoga

34

effect the emotion regulation of high school students as compared to physical education. The study involved thirty-eight high school students, in good general health from school in Brooklyn New York. Yoga intervention had 42 sessions of 40 minutes yoga classes, approximately three times a week- for 16 weeks. Each class included postures, breathing, relaxation and guided meditation techniques. And Control group had common games, such as football and baseball, as well as walking and running, relays and other socially focused activities. Pre-post data analyses revealed that emotion regulation increased significantly in the yoga group as compared to the PE group. Authors concluded that preliminary results suggest that yoga increases emotion regulation capacities of middle adolescents and provides benefits beyond that of PE alone. Folleto, J.C. et al. (2016) investigated the effects of yoga program in physical education classes on the motor abilities and social behavior parameters of 6–8-year-old children in a public elementary school in the South of Brazil. 16 children from grade 1 of were selected. The children participated in a 12-week intervention, twice weekly, with 45 min each session. The Bruininks-Oseretsky Test of Motor Proficiency, the flexibility test, the Pictorial Scale of Perceived Competence and Social Acceptance for Young Children and semi-structured interviews with children, parents, and classroom' teacher were used. Results showed that the yoga program was well accepted by children and children demonstrated significant and positive changes in overall motor abilities scores (balance, strength, and flexibility). In addition, the interviews reported changing in social behavior and the use of the knowledge learnt in the program in contexts outside of school.

## 2.3 Rationale for the study

The prevailing interventions for children with LD are individualized, time and cost effective. The review of yoga literature suggests that yoga brings about biochemical changes, neural activation, improved metabolism and can be regarded as a holistic medicine which operate both on the body as well as on the mind. Its effects on the cognitive system have been demonstrated in many studies. Studies have shown structural and functional changes in the brains of yoga practitioners. Hence it can be hypothesized that the neural activation created by the practice of yoga may result in synaptic proliferation as well as in the resumption of functioning of certain malformed nerve cells and reactivate the circuits that may have pertinence to the acquisition, processing and storage of knowledge. Since it is difficult to pay individual attention to children with LDin the current educational system, the challenges faced by are going unnoticed. In order to overcome, a remedial method which can be given to a group of children is necessary. Hence, the present study was carried out to examine the effectiveness of yoga as an intervention method for the children with LD.

*Chapter -III*

# METHODOLOGY

## 3.1  Title

"Yoga as an Intervention Strategy for Learning Disability"

## 3.2  Aims and Objectives

The aim of the study was to evaluate the effectiveness of yoga on the cognitive functions involved in reading and arithmetic problem solving in children with Learning Disabilities. Hence the specific objectives of the study included analysis of the effects of yoga practice on the following cognitive and behavioral processes.

1. Attention

2. Planning

3. Simultaneous processing

4. Successive processing

5. Phonological processing

6. Reading efficiency

7. Arithmetic problem solving skills

8. Behavioral adjustments in school

## 3.3  Variables

### 3.3.1  Dependent Variables

In the study, the following variables are taken as the dependent variables

1.  Cognitive process of Attention

2.  Cognitive process of Planning

3.  Cognitive Simultaneous process

4.  Cognitive Successive process

5.  Phonological process

6.  Word reading efficiency

7. Arithmetic ability

8. Behavioral adjustments

### 3.3.2 Independent Variables

1. The first independent variable in the study is an intervention that combined yoga techniques and academic activities. (Y&AA)The yoga practice included yogic eye exercises, pranayama techniques, standing, sitting, prone and supine asanas, and quick relaxation and guided imagery techniques. The academic skill training included paper-pencil activities related to word reading in English and Kannada and basic arithmetic calculations.

2. The second independent variable is also an intervention that combined neuropsychological methods and academic activities. (N&AA). The Neuropsychological techniques included tasks that are designed to improve cognitive processes like attention, planning, simultaneous, successive processes and phonological skills, combined with the same academic activities for English, Kannada word reading and basic arithmetic calculations.

3. The third independent variable is an intervention that included only academic activities (AA) for English, Kannada word reading and basic arithmetic calculations.

4. The fourth Independent variable is a control condition where no intervention was given.

### 3.4 Operational Definitions

#### 3.4.1 Learning Disability

Learning disability is determined by the criteria of persistent failure in the acquisition of reading and arithmetic skills, and at least two grade levels below performance that which cannot be attributed to inadequate intelligence, physical (vision and/or hearing) handicap, psychological disturbances, and inadequate educational and socio cultural opportunities. In this study, sample consisted of children who were identified as learning disabled in The All India Institute of Speech and Hearing, Mysore according to the above mentioned criteria.

#### 3.4.2 Planning

Planning is a higher cognitive function which involves programming regulation and verification of behavior before and during the action. The planning is assessed by the subtests in Cognitive Assessment System (Das, Naglieri & Kirby, 1994)that require children to create a plan of action, apply the plan, verify that an action taken conforms to the original goal, and modify the plan as needed.

#### 3.4.3 Attention

Attention is the focusing of perceptive awareness on a particular stimulus (or set of stimuli) which results in the relative exclusion of other stimuli and is often accompanied by an increase in the readiness to receive and to respond to the stimulus (or set of stimuli involved). The attention is assessed by the subtests in the Cognitive Assessment System (Das, Naglieri & Kirby, 1994)that requires the focus of cognitive activity, detection of a particular stimulus, and inhibition of responses to irrelevant competing stimuli.

### 3.4.4 Simultaneous processing

Simultaneous processing is a cognitive process by which individual integrates several different stimuli into a whole. It involves integration of stimuli into interrelated stimulus arrays (Naglieri,& Das, 1997)

### 3.4.5 Successive processing

Successive processing is a process in which the individual integrates stimuli in a specific order. Successive processing is necessary when a person has to store, retrieve and analyze information that follows a strict, defined order, especially serial and syntactical information. The Successive process is assessed by the subtests in Cognitive Assessment System (Das, Naglieri & Kirby, 1994)that require preservation and comprehension of a serial organization of events.

### 3.4.6 Phonological processing

It is an ability to process the units of sound in a given language. The process is assessed by the ability to identify and manipulate these sound units of different size and complexity by deleting, segmenting, integrating, reversing them in a target word(Wagner, Torgesen & Rashotte, 1999).

### 3.4.7 Word reading

It is a process of reading a word with different Consonant and Vowel combinations and syllable lengths from the print either by phonetically decoding them or by identifying and recalling them by their sight(Torgeson, Wagner, & Rashotte, 1999).

### 3.4.8 Arithmetic problem solving

Basic arithmetic involves understanding numbers as quantities, counting, knowing smaller and greater numbers, increasing and doubling quantity by addition and multiplication, decreasing or halving quantity by subtraction and division, knowing the concept of whole and fraction numbers, etc., upon which higher and mental calculations rely. (Kapur, Rozario, Oommen, 1991).

### 3.4.9 Behavioral adjustments

Behavioral adjustment refers to adjustment of children to the school environment and the absence of maladaptive behavior in the school.

### 3.4.10 Yoga

Yoga refers to traditional yogic postures, breathing methods and meditation. It includes sitting, standing, prone and supine postures, different types of conscious breathing, and concentration, relaxation and imagery meditations. In the present study Hatha yoga is practiced.

### 3.4.11 Academic Activities

In the study academic activities refer to training children in word reading skills and basic arithmetic problem solving skills.

### 3.4.12 Neuropsychological Intervention

Neuropsychological intervention refers to those tasks that have been traditionally used in the clinics targeting the cognitive abilities whose repeated presentation over time is believed to enhance person's cognitive functions, due to learning and adaptation that would not happen as quickly or at all on its own due to injury in the brain or developmental disorders (Stuss& Benson, 1986).

41

## 3.5 Research Questions and Hypotheses

### 3.5.1 Research Questions

The broad purpose of the study is to know whether yoga exercises can be utilized as an intervention for improving cognitive deficits in children with learning disability which in turn should improve their receptiveness for academic targeted interventions. Therefore the research questions are:

1. What are the effects of yoga practice on the cognitive functions of attention, planning, simultaneous processes, successive processes and phonological processes in children with learning disability?

2. What are the effects of yoga on the target specific interventions for word reading efficiency and arithmetic problem solving skills?

3. What is the effect of yoga on the behavioral adjustments in the school for the children having learning disabilities?

### 3.5.2 Hypotheses

Hypothesis 1: Practice of yoga will improve the planning process in Children with LD

Hypothesis 2: Practice of yoga will improve the attention process in Children with LD

Hypothesis 3: Practice of yoga will improve simultaneous process in Children with LD

Hypothesis 4: Practice of yoga will improve successive process in Children with LD

Hypothesis 5: Practice of yoga will improve phonological process in Children with LD

Hypothesis 6: Practice of yoga will improve word reading efficiency in Children with LD

Hypothesis 7: Practice of yoga will improve arithmetic efficiency in Children with LD

Hypothesis 8: Practice of yoga will improve behavioral adjustment in Children with LD

### 3.6    Design of the study

The study is a repeated measure design which involved pre, post and follow up intervention assessments of four independent groups of children; (a) those who were exposed to yoga practice and academic specific activities (Y & AA Group ), (b) those who were exposed to cognitive intervention and academic specific activities (N & AA Group ), (c) those that are exposed only to academic specific activities (AA Group) and (d) those that are not exposed to any kind of intervention (C Group). The four groups are compared with respect to the enhancement of performance on PASS, Phonological process, word reading, arithmetic problem solving and behavioral adjustment.

Initially Academic Activities was not planed in the study. But when data collection was started, increasing demands from the parents and their unwillingness to send children to interventions that did not have any academic related activities, led to the introduction of AA in yoga and neuropsychological interventions. Hence as control a separate only AA group was also introduced.

### 3.7 Participants

### 3.7.1    Participant Selection

All the participants for the study were drawn from The All India Institute of Speech and Hearing, Mysore. It is one of the national institutions in Karnataka which undertakes diagnosis and certification of children with learning disabilities. Children showing difficulty in acquiring academic skills in the schools are directed to the institution by the school head master/ mistress or physicians or clinical psychologists for diagnosis.

With official consent, the records in the institution were accessed. A list of children diagnosed with LD, falling in the age range of 8 to 13 years was made. The individual profiles of these children were again accessed and all children falling at around $2^{nd}$ grade performance level in reading, spelling and arithmetic were short listed. The parents of these children were contacted either through phone calls or in person and some parents were approached soon after the diagnosis in the institution and were informed about the program. Those children whose parents were willing to send their children for intervention program were selected for the study. Thus participation in the study was voluntary.

The method of randomization in sample selection could not be followed due to certain constraints. The selection of samples depended heavily on the availability of children performing at around $2^{nd}$ grade level, parental consent and their commutability to the place where interventions were carried out. And hence a convenient sampling was followed.

### 3.7.2  Sample Description

#### 3.7.2.1  Sample size

The study included a total of 57 participants, 14 of them were girls and 43 of them were boys. Yoga and academic skill training group (Y & AA group), Neuropsychological and academic activitiesgroup (N & AA group) and no-intervention groups (C group) consisted of 15 children respectively and the Academic Activities group (AA group) comprised of 12 children.

#### 3.7.2.2  Age

The chronological age of the children ranged from 9 to 13 years. The average age of the participants was $M=11.49$; $SD=1.16$

| Table 3.1: Description of the participants | | | | |
|---|---|---|---|---|
| Groups | Size | Age | Boys | Girls |
| Y&AA | 15 | $M$=10.75; $SD$=1.01 | 13 | 2 |
| N&AA | 15 | $M$=10.81; $SD$=1.15 | 10 | 5 |
| AA | 12 | $M$=10.78; $SD$=.93 | 9 | 3 |
| C | 15 | $M$=10.68; $SD$=1.21 | 10 | 5 |
| Total | 57 | $M$=11.49; $SD$=1.16 | 42 | 15 |

### 3.7.2.3 Inclusion criteria

Children (a) who were diagnosed with LD, (b) who were aged from 9 to 13 years and (c) who performed at around $2^{nd}$ grade level in reading and arithmetic as assessed by the institution were included for the study.

### 3.7.2.4 Exclusion criteria

Children with (a) attention deficit disorders, (b) below average mental ability and (c) any of the pervasive developmental disorders were not included in the study.

Children who had previous exposure to any kind of intervention for LD were also not included.

### 3.8 Tools and Measures

Children with LD possess inherent cognitive deficits which manifest as inability to perform academic specific tasks. And hence, in the present study the assessments were done both at the cognitive as well as at the manifestation levels. Assessment at the manifestation level included assessment of reading and arithmetic skills and assessment at the cognitive level included assessment of processes involved in these academic specific skills such as attention, planning, simultaneous processing, successive processing and phonological processing.

The tools used for assessments were:

1. Cognitive Assessment System (CAS)

2. Comprehensive test of phonological processing (CTOPP)

3. Kannada Phonological Processing Tests

4. Test of word reading efficiency (TOWRE)

5. Test of Kannada Word Reading Efficiency

6. NIMHANS Specific Learning Disability Index

7. Rutter's proforma B

1. **Cognitive Assessment System (Das, Naglieri & Kirby, 1994):** It is an individually administered test for children and adolescents from 5 to 17 years of age. It consists of four scales; Planning, Attention, Simultaneous, and Successive processes (PASS). The PASS scales standard scores are set at a mean of 100 and 80 and SD of 15. The CAS has high internal reliability, ranging from 0.95 to 0.97 for the different age groups. The average reliability coefficients for the scales are .88 (P) .88 (Attention). 13 (Simultaneous) .93 (Successive processes (Van Luit, 2005).

2. **Comprehensive Tests of Phonological Processing (Wagner, Torgesen& Rashotte, 1999):**CTOPP is individually administered test to assessee the phonological awareness in individuals aged through 5.0 to 24.11 years. The subtests provide a measure of an individual's ability to access the sound structure constituting the English language. Five subtests; Elision, Blending words, Blending non-words, Segmenting non-words, and Phoneme reversal are used in the study. The reliability coefficients for the scales are .79 (Elision), .72 (Blending words), .77 (Blending non-words), .86 (Segmenting

46

non-words), .79 (Phoneme reversal). The scoring for the subtests is done by giving 1 point for the correct response and 0 for the incorrect response.

3. **Kannada Phonological Processing Tests**: is individually administered test to assesses an individual's ability to access and manipulate the sound structure constituting the Kannada language The test is developed in Learning Disabilities Unit, Department of Psychology, in the University of Mysore. It consists of four sub-tests; Phoneme oddity, Phoneme deletion, Phoneme reversal and spoonerism. The reliability coefficients for the scales are .64 (Phoneme oddity), .95 (Phoneme Deletion), .88 (Phoneme reversal) and .95 (Spoonerism). The scoring for the subtests is done by giving 1 point for the correct response and 0 for the incorrect response.

4. **Test of Word Reading Efficiency (Torgeson, Wagner, & Rashotte, 1999)**: is individually administered, speed testfor children/adults aged between 6.0 to 24.11 years to assesses an individual's ability toindividual's word reading skills in terms of (a) capability to convert graphemes to phonemes and (b) quick recognition of a word by the word's structural form sight-word reading. The reliability coefficients for the scales are .91 (Sight words) and .91 (Phonemic decoding). Scoring is done by taking number of correct words read in 45 seconds.

5. **Test of Kannada Word Reading Efficiency**: The test is developed at Learning Disabilities Unit, Department of Psychology, in the University of Mysore and is Kannada adaptation of TOWRE. It is individually administered, speed test. It consists of two sub-tests Sight word reading efficiency and phonemic decoding efficiency. The reliability coefficients for the scales are

.98 (Sight words) and .95 (Phonemic decoding). Scoring is done by taking number of correct words read in 45 seconds.

6. **NIMHANS Specific Learning Disability Index Arithmetic subtests (Kapur, Rozario, Oommen, 1991):**Only arithmetic subtests from the complete index were used in the present study. Arithmetic subtest consists of addition, subtraction, multiplication, division and fraction tests.The tool has a test-retest reliability of 0.53 and criterion validity ranging between 0.75 and 0.61.(Anuja, Panicker, Uma, Subbakrishna, 2006).Scoring is done by giving 1 mark to the correct answers and 0 for incorrect ones.

7. **Rutter's Proforma B (Rutter, 1967):** is a teacher rating scale that measure emotional and behavioral difficulties in children. It consists of 26 statements and each statement is given a score of 1, 2 or 0. Scores obtained on all the items are totaled to obtain a total score. A total score of nine and above indicates clinically diagnosable emotional/behavioral difficulty. The scale has reliability and validity of 0.69.

All of the above tests have been used in the Indian context and are found to be reliable and valid.

**3.9   Description of the intervention**

The present study was designed to compare two types of interventions i.e., a Yoga intervention combined with Academic activities (Y&AA) and a Neuropsychological intervention combined with Academic activities (N&AA). Both these interventions incorporate a common component that is Academic activities (AA). Academic skills refer to those skills that are acquired only through schooling. They include ability to read, write, understand arithmetic concepts and do mental calculations. These skills are also called secondary skills. Unlike primary skills, which are learnt simply by the interaction with the environment like that of language acquisition, secondary skills can only be acquired through explicit training. Skills like reading, writing are acquired only through exclusive teaching and practice and not simply by living in a literate environment.

Therefore, the present study assumed that acquisition or improvement in skills like reading and arithmetic problem solving are possible only by explicit target specific training. Any other intervention that explicitly target only the cognitive functions of children with LD can act as a supplementary cognitive specific intervention, which can boost the acquisition of these specific skills.

The study also assumed that when a child with LD, whose cognitive deficits are corrected or near-corrected should be able to acquire or improve in the academic specific tasks, when trained in the same.

When both the interventions carry a common component of AA, any significant difference in the post-test performance should be attributed to the supplementary cognitive specific intervention introduced in the program.

The study also included two control groups, one group that gets only AA, and the other group that do not get any intervention. The AA group is introduced in order to know the extent of improvement that can be expected from only AA and the no-intervention group is introduced to control the maturation factor.

All the interventions given to children in the study followed a pre-decided schedule and activity plan. The interventions were planned for a period of 120 days excluding Sundays and holidays and were carried out in a regular place.

### 3.9.1 Yoga combined with Academic Activities

In this intervention, the children with LD were introduced to academic skill training along with the practice of selected yoga techniques. The interest of the study was to assess the cognitive functions and specific skill acquisition following the intervention. Yoga and AA were introduced simultaneously, practicing yoga techniques four days in a week and AA twice a week for a period of 120 days. The 120 days period constituted 90 days of yoga practices and 30 days of AA

### 3.9.1.1 Selection of Yoga Techniques

As a preliminary step, a set of asanas and pranayama appropriate for children, which are said to have positive influence on the mind (memory functions) and body (hormones regulations) were listed out from the books published by Bihar School of Yoga which pioneered the spreading of yoga practices among lay people for specific problems and has extensive expertise in teaching yoga for children.

In the second step, a set of open-ended questions were prepared for the expert yoga teachers in order to obtain their opinion and suggestions of asana, pranayama and dhyana techniques which can be safely taught and performed by children and has a positive effect on, as in their own words, memory and learning capacity of children.

In the third step, the common techniques suggested by all the yoga teachers and The Bihar School of Yoga as well as techniques from a pilot program to test the feasibility of some asanas and pranayama were selected for the study.

The contentious opinion of all the yoga teachers were that the effects of yoga practice can only be noticed following a regular practice of yoga for a period of three months. Hence, the yoga intervention was decided for 90 days.

The yoga intervention was given by the researcher as she has completed yoga instructor's course from Swami Vivekananda Yoga Anusandhana Samstana, Bangalore.

### 3.9.1.2 Focus of the Yoga Intervention

In teaching yoga besides emphasizing on learning the postures and breathing correctly, psychological aspects of yoga was also included. It was ensured that these focuses were imparted and reminded to children in each and every intervention session.

1. To sensitize children to listen and follow instructions.

2. To teach children the verbal meaning of attention and concentration and then gradually make them experience and have a meta-cognitive awareness of it.

3. To teach children the act of inhibiting impulsive actions by making them perform controlled muscle movements and breathing and gradually introducing the concept to class room situations.

4. To teach children tolerance to physical and mental stress and the importance of volition in learning by slowly encouraging them to achieve perfect postures.

5. To introduce them to feel the silence and thereby let them experience an agitation-free mind.

6. To teach them to form (visual) mental imagery as they receive continuous auditory stimuli.

7. To introduce them to the experience of physical relaxation especially in the head and neck regions.

### 3.9.1.3  Description of the Yoga Techniques

| Table 3.2: Yoga techniques practiced | |
|---|---|
| Beginning Exercises | 1. warming exercises, |
| | 2. A six step eye exercise, (alternative days) |
| Breathing Exercises | 1. Kapalabhati 60 strokes, |
| | 2. One nostril breathing, (both left and right) |
| | 3. Nadishudhi pranayama 9 rounds |
| Asanas | 1. Suryanamaskara 6 rounds (alternative days) |
| Standing Asanas | 1. Tadasana |
| | 2. Ekapadanamaskarasana |
| | 3. Garudasana |
| | 4. Padahastasana |
| | 5. Ardhachakrasana |
| Sitting Asanas | 1. Vajrasana |
| | 2. Pashchimotasana |
| | 3. Suptavajrasana |
| | 4. Hamsasana |
| Prone Asanas | 1. Bhujangasana |
| | 2. Shalabhasana |
| Supine Asanas | 1. Sarvangasana |
| | 2. Halasana |
| | 3. Chakrasana |
| | 4. Ardhashirasasana |
| Relaxation and Meditation | 1. Instant relaxation technique (alternative days) |
| | 2. Yoga Nidra (alternative days) |

### 3.9.1.4 Yoga Techniques Teaching Strategies

Within the first 30 days all the techniques were introduced to the children. In the following 60 days, they practiced the same techniques. However, they were constantly encouraged to better their skills by verbal reinforcements. A step wise method was used to teach the asanas and breathing techniques to the children.

| Table 3.3: Step-wise method to teach Asana and Pranayama | |
|---|---|
| Teaching Asana | |
| Step 1 | The name of the asana was told to the children and let each child pronounce it |
| Step 2 | The Picture of the final position of the asana was showed and informed them that there are some steps to reach the final posture |
| Step 3 | Demonstrated the asana with counts |
| Step 4 | Children repeated the procedure with counts |
| Step 5 | Demonstrated the asana with counts and breathing |
| Step 6 | Children performed it. Corrections were made and wrong postures were explained and demonstrated |
| Step 7 | Children performed it in pairs and corrected each other |
| Step 8 | Discussed about their physical and subjective experience and information about the benefits of the asana was given |
| Teaching Pranayama | |
| Step 1 | The name of the breathing technique was told to the children and let each child pronounce it |
| Step 2 | Demonstrated the technique |
| Step 3 | Explained the technique by rough drawings in a paper |
| Step 4 | Children performed the technique and corrections were made |
| Step 5 | Incorrect methods were explained and demonstrated |
| Step 6 | Children performed in pairs and correct each other |
| Step 7 | Discussed about the subjective experience and informing the usefulness of the technique was told |

### 3.9.2 Neuropsychological methods combined with Academic Activities

In this intervention, another group of children with LD were introduced to selected neuropsychological activities along with academic activities. Children practiced Neuropsychological intervention activities and AA simultaneously for six days a week for a period of 120 days.

### 3.9.2.1 Selection of Neuropsychological Techniques

The neuropsychological techniques were selected form PREP (PASS Reading Enhancement Program) and COGENT (Cognitive Enhancement Training) programs. These are two remedial programs developed based on PASS theory, incorporating the principles of Luria and Vygotsky, by Das and colleagues in 2004. The activities in COGENT are designed for pre-school children as well as for older children. Fourteen activities from the PREP and COGENT were selected for neuropsychological training program. The intervention did not involve direct academic related activities but consisted of activities to improve PASS as well as Phonological processes.

### 3.9.2.2 Description of the Neuropsychological Techniques

| Table 3.4: Description of Neuropsychological intervention in N&AA Group (Appendix-VII) | |
| --- | --- |
| Activity 1 (Joining shape-global) | The task aims at improving successive processing in general. The task enhances scanning, rehearsal, verbalization and short-term sequential memory for instruction. |
| Activity 2 (Joining shape-bridging) | The task enhances successive processing in general. It also enhances scanning, rehearsal, sound blending and short term memory for letters. |
| Activity 3&4 (Connecting letters) | The task enhances successive processing in general. It fosters scanning, using rehearsal as a memory technique, sounding out words and predicting words. |
| Activity 5 (Sound Memory) | The task aims at developing sound discrimination and working memory capacity in children. |
| Activity 6 (Syllable discrimination) | The task improves phonological processing. It increases sound discrimination. |
| Activity 7 (Onset & Rime) | The task improves phonological processing. It increases children's attention to onset and rimes in words. |
| Activity 8 (Onset & Rime) | The task improves phonological processing. It increases children's attention to onset and rimes in words. |
| Activity 9 (Deletion) | The task improves phonological processing in children. |
| Activity 10 (Window sequencing-global) | The task enhances successive processing. The task improves children's discrimination of colors and shapes and attention to patterns in color and shape, verbalizing and rehearsal |
| Activity 11 (Window sequencing-bridging) | The task enhances successive processing in general. The task improves sounding, blending, predicting and rehearsal. |
| Activity 12 (Shape design-global) | The task improves simultaneous processing in general. It promotes associative strategies, proximity and spatial relationships. |
| Activity 13 (Shape design-bridging) | The task develops simultaneous processing in general. It promotes sentence comprehension, proximity and spatial relationships. |
| Activity 14 (Shapes and objects-bridging) | The task enhances simultaneous processing in general. It fosters recognition and understanding the key concepts in sentences and categorization and classification of the key concepts. |

### 3.9.3  Academic Activities

Academic Activities consisted of activities to practice decoding skills and perform arithmetic calculations. The activities were designed for 30 days.

#### 3.9.3.1  Selection of Academic Activities

Academic skills focused in the present study includedbasic abilities such as decoding scripts, understandingnumber concepts and performing basic arithmetic calculations. Academic skill training program was drafted based on the level of performances showed by typical 2<sup>nd</sup> grade children. Children with LD show partially acquired skills which need to be improvised, corrected andreinforced. Therefore, the training program aimed at these factors and not at introducing a novel task.The activities were not tailor made for individual children but were mere syllabus followed and introduced to all children.

#### 3.9.3.2  Description of the Academic Activities

Children performed 19 English word decoding activities, 13 Kannada word decoding activities and 12 arithmetic activities

| Table 3.5: Description of the intervention in Academic Activities (AA) Group English Word Decoding Activities(Appendix-VIII) | |
|---|---|
| Activity 1 | Children practiced English alphabets. They wrote capital and small letters and also practiced the sounds of consonants and vowels. |
| Activity 2 | Children identified the alphabets randomly presented to them and also to say the sounds of consonants and vowels randomly presented to them. |
| Activity 3&4 | Children practiced to blend a vowel and a consonant said to them orally by the teacher and then they blended the vowel and consonant presented to them in print. |
| Activity 5&6 | Children practiced to blend onset and rimes presented to them orally by the teacher and then they read three letter words presented to them in print. |
| Activity 7&8 | Children practiced to blend three sounds presented to them orally by the teacher and then they blended three letters presented to them in print. |
| Activity 9&10 | Children practiced to blend more sets of onsets and rimes said to them by the teacher and then they read four letter words presented to them in print. |
| Activity 11&12 | Children practiced to blend four sounds presented to them by the teacher and then they blended four letters presented to them in print. |
| Activity 13&14 | Children practiced more complex consonant-consonant blending and they read four to five letter blend words |
| Activity 15&16 | Children practiced to blend double vowels and they read words containing double vowels presented to them in print. |
| Activity 17 | Children practiced long vowels and they read words containing long vowels |
| Activity 18 | Children practiced novel sounds and they practice to read having novel sounds |
| Activity 19 | Children read randomly presented words. |

| Table 3.5 (continued): Description of the intervention in Academic Activities (AA) Group Kannada Word Decoding Activities(Appendix-VIII) | |
| --- | --- |
| Activity 1&2 | Children practiced swaras and identified randomly presented swaras. |
| Activity 3&4 | Children practiced vyanjanas and identified randomly presented vyanjanas. |
| Activity 5 | Children read simple words formed by swaras and vyanjanas. |
| Activity 6 | Children practiced kagunitaaksharas using kagunitha symbols and identified randomly presented kagunithas. |
| Activity 7 | Children practiced to write words read out to them in kagunitha symbols |
| Activity 8 | Children read short and long words made up of kagunithaksharas |
| Activity 9 | Children practiced to read long and short words containing anunasikaaksharas |
| Activity 10 | Children practiced to identify vottakshara symbols presented randomly |
| Activity 11 | Children practiced to read long and short words containing sajatiyavotakharas |
| Activity 12 | Children practiced to read long and short words containing vijatiyavottaksharas |
| Activity 13 | Children practiced to read long and short words containing arkavottu |

| Table 3.5 (continued): Description of the intervention in Academic Activities (AA) GroupNumber concept and basic arithmetic calculations(Appendix-VIII) | |
|---|---|
| Activity 1 | Children practiced rote number counting from 1 to 10,000 |
| Activity 2&3 | Children practiced concept of place values |
| Activity 4, 5 & 6 | Number concept by writing preceding and following numbers, identifying greater and smaller numbers, writing numbers in ascending and descending order, memorized multiplication tables from 2 to 12 |
| Activity 7&8 | Activities to impart money concept |
| Activity 9 to 12 | Children practiced simple addition and addition requiring borrowing involving four digit numbers, simple subtraction to subtraction with four digit numbers and requiring borrowing, simple multiplication to complex multiplication involving three and three digits and simple to division complex division involving three digit divider and dividend |

## 3.10 Data Collection Procedure

The data collection was done in All India Institute of Speech and Hearing, Mysore.

### 3.10.1 Pre-intervention assessment

The pretest assessment was done a week before the start of intervention. The assessment was done individually to children that took about two hours. Hence assessment was done in two sessions.

### 3.10.2 Post-intervention assessment

Post test assessment was done at the end of 120 days of intervention for Y&AA, N&AA and C groups. For AA group intervention lasted for 30 days, hence post intervention assessment was done at the end of 30 days.

### 3.10.3 Follow up assessment

Follow up assessment was done at a time common to all the groups. After the end of interventions to all the groups, it was decided to do a follow up assessment, hence there was 2.6 to 2 years of time gap between pretest and follow up for Y&AA group, 1.8 to 1.7 years of time gap between pretest and follow up for AA group and 1.6 to 1 year time gap between pretest and follow up for N&AA group. Follow up assessment was not done to control group.

### 3.11 Intervention Procedure

Intervention was carried out for 6 days a week in two places. On the week days' intervention was done in All India Institute of Speech and Hearing (AIISH) and on Saturdays intervention was carried out in the department of psychology, Mysore University. For Y&AA and N&AA groups, yoga or neuropsychological interventions were carried out from Monday to Thursday, and Academic Activities was done on Fridays and Saturdays.

Yoga asanas were performed on soft blankets spread on the carpet floor of the room in AIISH. The AA on Fridays was carried out in the same room. Children sat in semi-circle around the instructor, spreading instruction materials on the floor during academic activities. The Saturday sessions of AA were carried out in department of psychology where children sat around a table and instruction materials were spread on the table. The intervention for 15 children was completed in two seasons. In the first season (Y&AA1) a group of 8 children and in the second season (Y& AA2) a group of 7 children were introduced to the intervention. Both the seasons had a gap of 5 months between them. Hence subgroups Y&AA1 and Y&AA2 were formed. The problems due to conducting interventions in two seasons were addressed in the analysis section.

60

The N&AA interventions were carried out on the carpet flour of the room in AIISH, all children sitting in semi circle around the instructor and the instruction materials spread on the floor. The intervention for 15 children was completed in two seasons. Hence subgroups N&AA1 and N&AA2 were formed. In the first season (N&AA1) a group of 7 children were introduced to the intervention and in the second season (N&AA2) 8 children were introduced to the intervention. Both the seasons had a gap of 5 months between them.

The academic activities for only AA group was carried also out on the same room in AIISH, children sitting in semi-circle around the instructor, spreading instruction materials on the floor. Intervention for 12 children was carried out in two sessions, hence subgroups AA1 and AA2 were formed. In the first (AA1) session 7 children and in the second (AA2) session 5 children were introduced to intervention. Both the seasons had a gap of 1 month between them.

## 3.11 Data Analysis

Prior to data analysis, a homogeneity test was done between Y&AA1 and Y&AA2, N&AA1 and N&AA2, AA1 and AA2 subgroups. If there was no statistical difference between the seasons in their pretest scores, they were merged together as single group in all further analysis. If there was significant difference between the subgroups groups that got same interventions in different seasons, the groups were retained separately for all further statistical analysis.

The data was analyzed using non parametric statistics. Within group and between group analyses were made to assess the effects of intervention.

*Chapter -IV*

# ANALYSIS AND RESULTS

**4.1 Introduction to analysis of data**

The statistical techniques used to analyze the data are depicted in the flow chart (fig.4.1).The data was tested for homogeneity (Kruskal-Wallis). Since the data was small and not distributed normally nonparametric techniques were employed. Significance is assessed at the 5% level of significance. Wilcoxon Signed Rank test (two-tailed, dependent) was used to make within group analysisfor the Yoga and Academic Activities intervention group (Y&AA), Neuropsychological and Academic Activities intervention group(N&AA), Academic Activities intervention group (AA) and no-intervention group (C). To make between group comparisons Kruskal-Wallis test (two-tailed, independent) and to make post hoc comparisons Mann-Whitney U test was employed (two-tailed, independent). Effect sizes were computed to assess the effects of interventions on the four groups and to assess the extent to which the groups differed from each other. SPSS 16.0 software is used to analyze the data.

The obtained results are presented with reference to eight hypotheses that were proposed related to different cognitive processes.

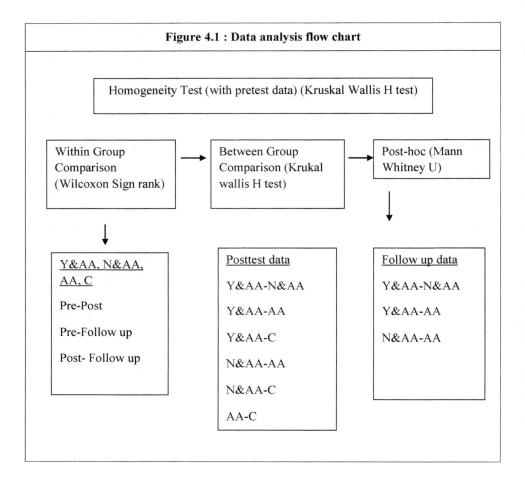

**Figure 4.1 : Data analysis flow chart**

Homogeneity Test (with pretest data) (Kruskal Wallis H test)

Within Group Comparison (Wilcoxon Sign rank) → Between Group Comparison (Krukal wallis H test) → Post-hoc (Mann Whitney U)

Y&AA, N&AA, AA, C

Pre-Post

Pre-Follow up

Post- Follow up

Posttest data

Y&AA-N&AA

Y&AA-AA

Y&AA-C

N&AA-AA

N&AA-C

AA-C

Follow up data

Y&AA-N&AA

Y&AA-AA

N&AA-AA

## 4.2 Testing Hypothesis 1: Practice of yoga will improve the planning process in children with LD

### 4.2.1 Homogeneity test for intervention subgroups for planning

**Table 4.1 : Homogeneity test for intervention subgroups pretest data planning**

| Groups | $n$ | Mean ranks | $Chi\ sq$ | $df$ | $p$ |
|--------|-----|------------|-----------|------|-----|
| Y&AA1 | 8 | 16.00 | | | |
| Y&AA2 | 7 | 24.86 | | | |
| N&AA1 | 7 | 17.07 | | | |
| N&AA2 | 8 | 23.38 | 5.40 | 5 | .369 |
| AA1 | 7 | 21.00 | | | |
| AA2 | 5 | 29.50 | | | |

There was no statistically significant difference ($p$=0.37) between the experimental sub groups carried out in two sessions in planning subtest scores before the commencement of the intervention. Hence the groups Y&AA1 & Y&AA2, N&AA1& N&AA2, AA1 & AA2 are merged respectively in further analysis

### 4.2.2 Homogeneity test for Planning pretest data

**Table 4.2: Homogeneity test for Planning pretest data**

| Groups | $N$ | Mean ranks | $Chi\ sq$ | $df$ | $p$ |
|--------|-----|------------|-----------|------|-----|
| Y&AA | 15 | 27.50 | | | |
| N&AA | 15 | 28.10 | 1.29 | 3 | .73 |
| C | 15 | 27.37 | | | |
| AA | 12 | 33.79 | | | |

There was no statistically significant difference ($p$=0.73) between the experimental and control groups in planning subtest scores before the commencement of the intervention.

64

### 4.2.3 Within group analysis for planning

#### 4.2.3.1 Within group analysis for planning Y&AA group

**Table 4.3 : Descriptive statistics for Planning subtest data (Y&AA group)**

| Data | $n$ | Median | $M$ | $SD$ | Min | Max |
|------|-----|--------|-----|------|-----|-----|
| Pretest data | 15 | 89.00 | 91.00 | 10.86 | 79.00 | 119.00 |
| Posttest | 15 | 100.00 | 101.73 | 9.97 | 87.00 | 124.00 |
| Follow up | 15 | 100.00 | 101.93 | 7.20 | 92.00 | 123.00 |

**Table 4.3 A: Pre, Post & Follow up intervention comparisons within (Y&AA) group**

| | $z$ | $p$ | Effect size |
|---|-----|-----|-------------|
| Pretest-Posttest | -3.41 | .001* | -0.88 |
| Pretest-Follow up | -3.41 | .001* | -0.88 |
| Posttest-Follow up | -.67 | .50 | -0.17 |

*significant at 0.05 level

There was a significant increase from pretest (median= 89.00) to posttest (median= 100.00), $z$=-3.41, $p<0.001$, r= -0.88, pretest (median=89.00) to follow up (median=100.00) $z$=-3.41, $p<0.001$, r=-0.88 in planning scores and the decrease was large. There is no significant difference in posttest (median=100.00) to follow up (median=100.00) $z$=-.67, $p$=0.50 scores. This indicates that the group has significantly improved from Y&AA intervention in their Planning ability.

#### 4.2.3.2 Within group analysis for planning N&AA group

**Table 4.4: Descriptive statistics for Planning subtest data (N&AA group)**

| Data | $n$ | Median | $M$ | $SD$ | Min | Max |
|------|-----|--------|-----|------|-----|-----|
| Pretest | 15 | 89.00 | 90.80 | 10.92 | 75.00 | 110.00 |
| Posttest | 15 | 94.00 | 97.53 | 11.20 | 81.00 | 115.00 |
| Follow up | 15 | 98.00 | 100.27 | 8.96 | 85.00 | 115.00 |

**Table 4.4 A: Pre, Post & Follow up intervention comparisons within (N&AA) group**

|  | z | p | Effect size |
|---|---|---|---|
| Pretest-Posttest | -2.74 | .006* | -0.708 |
| Pretest-Follow up | -3.42 | .001* | -0.883 |
| Posttest-Follow up | -2.79 | .007* | -0.720 |

*significant at 0.05 level

There was a significant increase from pretest (median= 89.00) to posttest (median= 94.00), z=-2.74, p<0.001, r= -0.71, pretest (median=94.00) to follow up (median=98.00)z=-3.42, p<0.001, r=-0.88 and posttest (median=94.00) to follow up (median=98.00) z=-2.79, p<0.001 r= -0.72 in planning scores, and the increase was large. This indicates that the group has significantly improved from N&AA intervention in their planning ability and the improvement continued over a period of time till the follow up assessment was made.

### 4.2.3.3 Within group analysis for planning AA group

**Table 4.5 : Descriptive statistics for Planning subtest data (AA group)**

| Data | n | Median | M | SD | Min | Max |
|---|---|---|---|---|---|---|
| Pretest | 12 | 98.00 | 93.50 | 9.49 | 77.00 | 104.00 |
| Posttest | 12 | 97.00 | 94.77 | 8.26 | 83.00 | 102.00 |
| Follow up | 12 | 102.00 | 98.75 | 6.65 | 85.00 | 104.00 |

**Table 4.5 A: Pre, Post & Follow up intervention comparisons within (AA) group**

|  | z | p | Effect size |
|---|---|---|---|
| Pretest-Posttest | -1.47 | .14 | -0.424 |
| Pretest-Follow up | -2.81 | .005* | -0.812 |
| Posttest-Follow up | -2.96 | .003* | -0.855 |

*significant at 0.05 level

There was no significant increase from pretest (median= 98.00) to posttest (median= 97.00), z=-1.47, p=0.14, but there was significant increase in pretest (median=98.00) to follow up (median=102.00)z=-2.81, p<0.001, r=-0.81 and posttest

66

(median=97.00) to follow up (median=102.00) z=-2.96, p<0.001 r= -0.85 in planning scores, and the increase was large. This indicates that the group has significantly improved from AA intervention in their planning ability.

### 4.2.3.4 Within group analysis for planning C group

**Table 4.6 : Descriptive statistics for Planning subtest data (C group)**

| Data | $n$ | Median | $M$ | $SD$ | Min | Max |
|------|-----|--------|-----|------|-----|-----|
| Pretest | 15 | 89.00 | 90.00 | 9.24 | 75.00 | 108.00 |
| Posttest | 15 | 92.00 | 93.73 | 8.34 | 81.00 | 108.00 |
| Follow up | - | | - | - | - | - |

**Table 4.6 A: Pre, Post & Follow up intervention comparisons within (C) group**

| | $z$ | $p$ | Effect size |
|---|-----|-----|-------------|
| Pretest-Posttest | -2.94 | .003* | -0.759 |
| Pretest-Follow up | - | - | - |
| Posttest-Follow up | - | - | - |

*significant at 0.05 level

There was a significant increase from pretest (median= 89.00) to posttest (median= 92.00), z=-2.94, p<0.001, r= -0.76 in planning scores, and the increase was moderate. This indicates that the group has significantly improved in planning ability in control group.

### 4.2.4 Between group analysis for planning post intervention data

**Table 4.7: Planning subtest data between groups analyses (Post-test data)**

| Groups | $n$ | Mean ranks | Chi sq | df | $p$ |
|--------|-----|-----------|--------|-----|-----|
| Y&AA | 15 | 36.23 | | | |
| N&AA | 15 | 29.17 | 4.73 | 3 | .19 |
| C | 15 | 23.63 | | | |
| AA | 12 | 26.46 | | | |

There was no statistically significant difference between the groups in planning ability in the posttest data ($x^2(2) = 4.73$, $p= .19$) with a mean rank of 36.23

(Median= 100.00) for Y&AA group, 29.17 (Median= 94.00) for N&AA group, 23.63 (Median= 92.00) for C group and 26.46 (Median= 97.00) for AA group. Hence no further analysis was done.

**4.2.5 Between group analysis for planning follow up data**

**Table 4.8: Planning subtest data between groups analyses (Follow up data)**

| Groups | $n$ | Mean ranks | *Chi sq* | *df* | *p* |
|--------|-----|------------|----------|------|-----|
| Y&AA | 15 | 23.47 | | | |
| N&AA | 15 | 20.27 | .61 | 2 | .74 |
| C | 15 | - | | | |
| AA | 12 | 20.58 | | | |

There was no statistically significant difference between the groups in planning ability in the follow up data ($x^2(2)$ = .61, $p$= .74) with a mean rank of 23.47 (Median= 100.00) for Y&AA group, 20.27 (Median= 98.00) for N&AA group, and 20.58 (Median= 102.00) for AA group. Hence no further analysis was done.

Graph 1

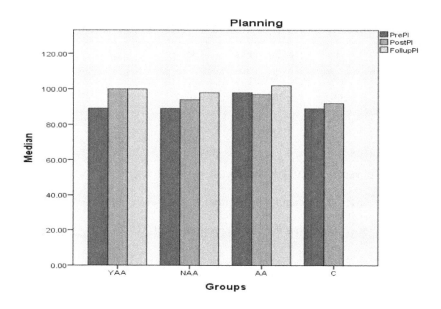

68

## 4.3 Testing Hypothesis 2: Practice of yoga will improve the attention process in children with LD

### 4.3.1 Homogeneity test for intervention subgroups for attention

**Table 4.9: Homogeneity test for intervention subgroups preintervention data Attention**

| Groups | n | Mean ranks | Chi sq | df | p |
|--------|---|-----------|--------|----|----|
| Y&AA1 | 8 | 22.13 | | | |
| Y&AA2 | 7 | 17.00 | | | |
| N&AA1 | 7 | 28.57 | 4.74 | | |
| N&AA2 | 8 | 24.06 | | 5 | .448 |
| AA1 | 7 | 18.36 | | | |
| AA2 | 5 | 17.20 | | | |

There was no statistically significant difference ($p=0.45$) between the experimental sub groups carried out in two sessions in attention subtest scores before the commencement of the intervention. Hence the groups Y&AA1 & Y&AA2, N&AA1 & N&AA2, AA1 & AA2 are merged respectively in further analysis

### 4.3.2 Homogeneity test for attention pretest data

**Table 4.10: Homogeneity test for Attention pre-intervention data**

| Groups | n | Mean ranks | Chi sq | df | p |
|--------|---|-----------|--------|----|----|
| Y&AA | 15 | 30.40 | | | |
| N&AA | 15 | 38.37 | 10.37 | 3 | .016* |
| C | 15 | 19.17 | | | |
| AA | 12 | 27.83 | | | |

*significant at 0.05 level

Since p value ($p=0.01$) is significant the three intervention group and the control group differ significantly on attention ability before the commencement of intervention. N&AA Group has the highest mean score of 38.37.

### 4.3.3 Within group analysis for attention

### 4.3.3.1 Within group analysis for attention Y&AA group

**Table 4.11: Descriptive statistics for Attention subtest data (Y&AA group)**

| Data | $n$ | Median | $M$ | $SD$ | Min | Max |
|------|-----|--------|-----|------|-----|-----|
| Pretest | 15 | 84.00 | 83.20 | 7.32 | 71.00 | 94.00 |
| Posttest | 15 | 108.00 | 104.60 | 7.05 | 90.00 | 115.00 |
| Follow up | 15 | 102.00 | 101.20 | 6.32 | 90.00 | 112.00 |

**Table 4.11.A: Pre, Post & Follow up intervention comparisons within (Y&AA) group**

| | $z$ | $p$ | Effect size |
|---|-----|-----|-------------|
| Pretest-Posttest | -3.41 | .001* | -0.881 |
| Pretest-Follow up | -3.41 | .001* | -0.881 |
| Posttest-Follow up | -1.86 | .06 | -0.480 |

*significant at 0.05 level

There was a significant increase from pretest (median= 84.00) to posttest (median= 108.00), z=-3.41, p<0.001, r= -0.88, pretest (median=84.00) to follow up (median=102.00)z=-3.41, p<0.001, r=-0.88 and posttest (median=108.00) to follow up (median=102.00) z=-1.86, p=0.06 in the scores of attention, and the increase was large. This indicates that the group has significantly improved from Y&AA intervention in their attention.

### 4.3.3.2 Within group analysis for attention N&AA group

**Table 4.12: Descriptive statistics for Attention subtest data (N&AA group)**

| Data | $n$ | Median | $M$ | $SD$ | Min | Max |
|------|-----|--------|-----|------|-----|-----|
| Pretest | 15 | 88.00 | 88.93 | 10.13 | 75.00 | 108.00 |
| Posttest | 15 | 94.00 | 94.53 | 10.43 | 80.00 | 112.00 |
| Follow up | 15 | 100.00 | 99.86 | 6.06 | 90.00 | 112.00 |

**Table 4.12.A: Pre, Post & Follow up intervention comparisons within (N&AA) group**

|                   | z     | p     | Effect size |
|-------------------|-------|-------|-------------|
| Pretest-Posttest  | -3.43 | .001* | -0.886      |
| Pretest-Follow up | -3.41 | .001* | -0.881      |
| Posttest-Follow up| -2.67 | .007* | -0.689      |

*significant at 0.05 level

There was a significant increase from pretest (median= 88.00) to posttest (median= 94.00), z=-3.43, p<0.001, r= -0.88, pretest (median=88.00) to follow up (median=100.00)z=-3.41, p<0.001, r=-0.88 and posttest (median=94.00) to follow up (median=100.00) z=-2.67, p<0.001 r= -0.69 in the scores of attention, and the increase was large. This indicates that the group has significantly improved from N&AA intervention in their attention and the improvement continued over a period of time till the follow up assessment was made.

**4.3.3.3 Within group analysis for attention AA group**

**Table 4.13: Descriptive statistics for Attention subtest data (AA group)**

| Data      | n  | Median | M     | SD   | Min   | Max    |
|-----------|----|--------|-------|------|-------|--------|
| Pretest   | 12 | 82.00  | 81.83 | 8.28 | 67.00 | 94.00  |
| Posttest  | 12 | 84.00  | 84.42 | 8.07 | 71.00 | 98.00  |
| Follow up | 12 | 95.00  | 93.83 | 6.85 | 82.00 | 102.00 |

**Table 4.13.A: Pre, Post & Follow up intervention comparisons within (AA) group**

|                   | z     | p     | Effect size |
|-------------------|-------|-------|-------------|
| Pretest-Posttest  | -2.68 | .007* | -0.774      |
| Pretest-Follow up | -3.07 | .002* | -0.887      |
| Posttest-Follow up| -3.07 | .002* | -0.887      |

*significant at 0.05 level

There was a significant increase from pretest (median= 82.00) to posttest (median= 84.00), z=-2.68, p<0.001, r= -0.77, pretest (median=84.00) to follow up

(median=95.00)z=-3.07, p<0.001, r=-0.88 and posttest (median=84.00) to follow up

(median=95.00) z=-2.67, p<0.001 r= -0.88 in the scores of attention, and the increase

was large. This indicates that the group has significantly improved from AA

intervention in their attention and the improvement continued over a period of time

till the follow up assessment was made.

### 4.3.3.4 Within group analysis for attention C group

**Table 4.14: Descriptive statistics for Attention subtest data (C group)**

| Data | $n$ | Median | $M$ | $SD$ | Min | Max |
|---|---|---|---|---|---|---|
| Pretest | 15 | 75.00 | 76.93 | 10.10 | 59.00 | 98.00 |
| Posttest | 15 | 77.00 | 77.07 | 11.04 | 55.00 | 96.00 |
| Follow up | - | | - | - | - | - |

**Table 4.14.A: Pre, Post & Follow up intervention comparisons within (C) group**

| | $z$ | $p$ | Effect size |
|---|---|---|---|
| Pretest-Posttest | -.32 | .75 | -0.082 |

There was no increase from pretest (median= 75.00) to posttest (median=

77.00), z=-3.32, p<0.75.This indicates that the control group did not improve in their

attention

### 4.3.4 Between group analysis for attention post intervention data

**Table 4.15: Attention subtest data between groups analyses (Post-test data)**

| Groups | $n$ | Mean ranks | Chi sq | df | $p$ |
|---|---|---|---|---|---|
| Y&AA | 15 | 45.97 | | | |
| N&AA | 15 | 34.03 | 33.162 | 3 | .000* |
| C | 15 | 13.47 | | | |
| AA | 12 | 20.92 | | | |

*significant at 0.05 level

There was a statistically significant difference between the groups in attention

in the posttest data ($x^2(2) = 33.16$, $p= .00$) with a mean rank of 45.97 (Median= 84.00)

72

for Y&AA group, 34.03 (Median= 94.00) for N&AA group, 13.47 (Median= 77.00)

for C group and 20.92 (Median= 84.00) for AA group.

**4.3.4.A. Post-hoc analyses for Attention post intervention data**

**Table 4.15.A: Attention post intervention data Post-hoc analyses between Y&AA-N&AA**

| Groups | *n* | Mean ranks | U | *z* | *p* | Effect size |
|--------|-----|-----------|-------|--------|-------|-------------|
| Y&AA | 15 | 19.53 | 52.00 | -2.521 | .012* | -0.651 |
| N&AA | 15 | 11.47 | | | | |

*significant at 0.05 level

Descriptive statistics showed that Y&AA group (median= 108.00; mean rank = 19.53) had higher scores than that N&AA group (median= 94.00; mean rank = 11.47). Mann-Whitney U value was found to be statistically significant U= 52.00 (z = -2.52), p <0.001 and the difference between Y&AA and N&AA groups was moderate (r = -0.65).

**Table 4.15.B: Attention post intervention data Post-hoc analyses between Y&AA-AA**

| Groups | *n* | Mean ranks | U | *z* | *p* | Effect size |
|--------|-----|-----------|------|--------|-------|-------------|
| Y&AA | 15 | 19.67 | 5.00 | -4.164 | .000* | -1.075 |
| AA | 12 | 6.92 | | | | |

*significant at 0.05 level

Descriptive statistics showed that Y&AA group (median= 108.00; mean rank = 19.67) had higher scores than that AA group (median= 84.00; mean rank = 6.92). Mann-Whitney U value was found to be statistically significant U= 5.00 (z = -2.43), p <0.001 and the difference between Y&AA and AA groups was large (r = -1.07).

**Table 4.15.C: Attention post intervention data Post-hoc analyses between Y&AA-C**

| Groups | *n* | Mean ranks | U | *z* | *p* | Effect size |
|--------|-----|-----------|------|--------|-------|-------------|
| Y&AA | 15 | 22.77 | 3.50 | -4.539 | .000* | -1.172 |
| C | 15 | 8.23 | | | | |

*significant at 0.05 level

Descriptive statistics showed that Y&AA group (median= 108.00; mean rank = 22.77) had higer scores than that C group (median= 77.00; mean rank = 8.23). Mann-Whitney U value was found to be statistically significant U= 3.50 (z = -4.55), p <0.001 and the difference between Y&AA and C groups was large (r = -1.17).

**Table 4.15.D: Attention post intervention data Post-hoc analyses between N&AA-AA**

| Groups | $n$ | Mean ranks | U | $z$ | $p$ | Effect size |
|--------|-----|-----------|-------|--------|-------|-------------|
| N&AA | 15 | 17.27 | 41.00 | -2.399 | .016* | -0.619 |
| AA | 12 | 9.92 | | | | |

*significant at 0.05 level

Descriptive statistics showed that N&AA group (median= 94.00; mean rank = 17.27) had higher scores than that AA group (median= 84.00; mean rank = 9.92). Mann-Whitney U value was found to be statistically significant U= 41.00 (z = -2.39), p <0.001 and the difference between N&AA and AA groups was moderate (r = -0.62).

**Table 4.15.E: Attention post intervention data Post-hoc analyses betweenN&AA-C**

| Groups | $n$ | Mean ranks | U | $z$ | $p$ | Effect size |
|--------|-----|-----------|-------|--------|-------|-------------|
| N&AA | 15 | 21.30 | 25.50 | -3.622 | .000* | -0.935 |
| C | 15 | 9.70 | | | | |

*significant at 0.05 level

Descriptive statistics showed that N&AA group (median= 94.00; mean rank = 21.30) had higher scores than that C group (median= 77.00; mean rank = 9.70). Mann-Whitney U value was found to be statistically significant U= 25.50 (z = -3.62), p <0.001 and the difference between Y&AA and N&AA groups was large (r = -0.93).

**Table 4.15.F: Attention post intervention data Post-hoc analyses betweenAA-C**

| Groups | $n$ | Mean ranks | U | $z$ | $p$ | Effect size |
|--------|-----|-----------|-------|--------|------|-------------|
| AA | 12 | 17.08 | 53.00 | -1.814 | .070 | -0.524 |
| C | 15 | 11.53 | | | | |

Descriptive statistics showed that AA group (median= 84.00; mean rank = 17.08) had higher scores than that C group (median= 77.00; mean rank = 11.53). Mann-Whitney U value was found to be statistically non significant U= 53.00 (z = -1.81), p =0.07.

### 4.3.5 Between group analysis for attention follow up data

**Table 4.16: Attention subtest data between groups analyses (Follow up data)**

| Groups | $n$ | Mean ranks | Chi sq | df | p |
|--------|-----|-----------|--------|-----|-----|
| Y&AA | 15 | 26.77 | | | |
| N&AA | 15 | 23.03 | 8.898 | 2 | .012* |
| C | 15 | | | | |
| AA | 12 | 13.00 | | | |

*significant at 0.05 level

There was a statistically significant difference between the groups in attention in the posttest data ($x^2(2)$ = 8.89, $p$= .00) with a mean rank of 26.77 (Median= 102.00) for Y&AA group, 23.03 (Median= 100.00) for N&AA group, and 13.00 (Median= 95.00) for AA group.

### 4.3.5.A. Post-hoc analyses for Attention follow up data

**Table 4.16.A: Attention follow up data Post-hoc analyses Y&AA-N&AA**

| Groups | $n$ | Mean ranks | U | $z$ | p | Effect size |
|--------|-----|-----------|-------|-------|------|-------------|
| Y&AA | 15 | 16.87 | 90.00 | -.944 | .345 | -0.243 |
| N&AA | 15 | 14.13 | | | | |

Descriptive statistics showed that Y&AA group (median= 102.00; mean rank = 16.87) had higher scores than that N&AA group (median= 100.00; mean rank = 14.13). Mann-Whitney U value was found to be non statistically significant U= 90.00 (z = -.94), p =0.35.

### Table 4.16.B: Attention follow up data Post-hoc analyses Y&AA-AA

| Groups | n | Mean ranks | U | z | p | Effect size |
|--------|---|-----------|-----|-----|-----|------------|
| Y&AA | 15 | 17.77 | 33.50 | -2.771 | .006* | -0.716 |
| AA | 12 | 9.29 | | | | |

*significant at 0.05 level

Descriptive statistics showed that Y&AA group (median= 102.00; mean rank = 17.77) had higher scores than that AA group (median= 95.00; mean rank = 9.29). Mann-Whitney U value was found to be statistically significant U= 33.50 (z = -2.77), p <0.001 and the difference between Y&AA and AA groups was moderate (r = -0.72).

### Table 4.16.C: Attention follow up data Post-hoc analyses N&AA-AA

| Groups | n | Mean ranks | U | z | p | Effect size |
|--------|---|-----------|-----|-----|-----|------------|
| N&AA | 15 | 17.03 | 44.50 | -2.242 | .025* | -0.579 |
| AA | 12 | 10.21 | | | | |

*significant at 0.05 level

Descriptive statistics showed that N&AA group (median= 100.00; mean rank = 17.03) had higher scores than that AA group (median= 95.00; mean rank = 10.21). Mann-Whitney U value was found to be statistically significant U= 44.50 (z = -2.24), p <0.001 and the difference between Y&AA and N&AA groups was moderate (r = -0.58).

Graph 2

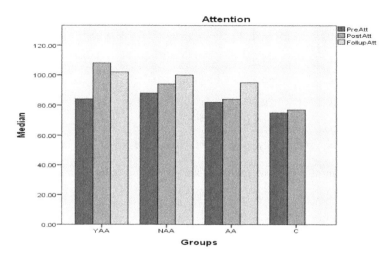

## 4.4 Testing Hypothesis 3: Practice of yoga will improve simultaneous process in children with LD

### 4.4.1 Homogeneity test for intervention subgroups for Simultaneous processing

**Table 4.17: Homogeneity test for intervention subgroups pre-interventiondata simultaneous process**

| Groups | n | Mean ranks | Chi sq | df | p |
|--------|---|-----------|--------|-----|------|
| Y&AA1 | 8 | 16.63 | | | |
| Y&AA2 | 7 | 22.71 | | | |
| N&AA1 | 7 | 26.21 | 2.43 | 5 | .787 |
| N&AA2 | 8 | 21.69 | | | |
| AA1 | 7 | 20.57 | | | |
| AA2 | 5 | 22.00 | | | |

There was no statistically significant difference ($p$=0.78) between the experimental sub groups carried out in two sessions in simultaneous processing subtest scores before the commencement of the intervention. Hence the groups Y&AA1 & Y&AA2, N&AA1 & N&AA2, AA1 & AA2 are merged respectively in further analysis

### 4.4.2 Homogeneity test for Simultaneous processing pre-intervention data

**Table 4.18: Homogeneity test for Simultaneous Processing pre-intervention data**

| Groups | n | Mean ranks | Chi sq | df | p |
|--------|----|-----------|--------|-----|------|
| Y&AA | 15 | 29.77 | | | |
| N&AA | 15 | 34.63 | 5.946 | 3 | .114 |
| C | 15 | 20.57 | | | |
| AA | 12 | 31.54 | | | |

There was no statistically significant difference ($p$=0.11) between the experimental and control groups in simultaneous processing before the start of the intervention.

### 4.4.3 Within group analysis for Simultaneous processing

#### 4.4.3.1 Within group analysis for Simultaneous processing Y&AA group

**Table 4.19: Descriptive statistics for Simultaneous Processing subtest data (Y&AA group)**

| Data | $n$ | Median | $M$ | $SD$ | Min | Max |
|---|---|---|---|---|---|---|
| Pretest | 15 | 92.00 | 93.20 | 9.26 | 81.00 | 110.00 |
| Posttest | 15 | 98.00 | 100.53 | 8.72 | 89.00 | 114.00 |
| Follow up | 15 | 102.00 | 102.67 | 4.82 | 96.00 | 112.00 |

**Table 4.19.A: Pre, Post & Follow up intervention comparisons within (Y&AA) group**

| | $z$ | $p$ | Effect size |
|---|---|---|---|
| Pretest-Posttest | -3.42 | .001* | -0.883 |
| Pretest-Follow up | -3.17 | .001* | -0.819 |
| Posttest-Follow up | -1.68 | .09 | -0.434 |

* significant at 0.05 level

There was a significant increase from pretest (median= 92.00) to posttest (median= 98.00), z=-3.42, p<0.001, r= -0.88, pretest (median=92.00) to follow up (median=102.00)z=-3.17, p<0.001, r=-0.82 and posttest (median=98.00) to follow up (median=102.00) z=-1.68, p=0.09 in the scores of successive processing, and the increase was large. This indicates that the group has significantly improved from Y&AA intervention in their successive processing.

#### 4.4.3.2 Within group analysis for Simultaneous processing N&AA group

**Table 4.20: Descriptive statistics for Simultaneous Processing subtest data (N&AA group)**

| Data | $n$ | Median | $M$ | $SD$ | Min | Max |
|---|---|---|---|---|---|---|
| Pretest | 15 | 98.00 | 94.67 | 10.73 | 67.00 | 110.00 |
| Posttest | 15 | 102.00 | 99.80 | 10.46 | 74.00 | 114.00 |
| Follow up | 15 | 102.00 | 102.37 | 5.55 | 92.00 | 112.00 |

**Table 4.20.A: Pre, Post & Follow up intervention comparisons within (N&AA) group**

|  | $z$ | $p$ | Effect size |
|---|---|---|---|
| Pretest-Posttest | -3.43 | .001* | -0.886 |
| Pretest-Follow up | -3.32 | .001* | -0.857 |
| Posttest-Follow up | -1.75 | .08 | -0.452 |

* significant at 0.05 level

There was a significant increase from pretest (median= 98.00) to posttest (median= 102.00), z=-3.43, p<0.001, r= -0.88, pretest (median=98.00) to follow up (median=102.00)z=-3.32, p<0.001, r=-0.86 in the scores of successive processing, and the increase was large. This indicates that the group has significantly improved from N&AA intervention in their successive processing.

**4.4.3.3 Within group analysis for Simultaneous processing AA group**

**Table 4.21: Descriptive statistics for Simultaneous Processing subtest data (AA group)**

| Data | $n$ | Median | $M$ | $SD$ | Min | Max |
|---|---|---|---|---|---|---|
| Pretest | 12 | 95.00 | 93.50 | 6.67 | 81.00 | 102.00 |
| Posttest | 12 | 98.00 | 96.58 | 8.62 | 81.00 | 112.00 |
| Follow up | 12 | 100.00 | 99.58 | 5.03 | 87.00 | 108.00 |

**Table 4.21.A: Pre, Post & Follow up intervention comparisons within (AA) group**

|  | $z$ | $p$ | Effect size |
|---|---|---|---|
| Pretest-Posttest | -2.46 | .01* | -0.710 |
| Pretest-Follow up | -2.82 | .005* | -0.815 |
| Posttest-Follow up | -1.97 | .05 | -0.569 |

* significant at 0.05 level

There was a significant increase from pretest (median= 95.00) to posttest (median= 98.00), z=-2.46, p<0.001, r= -0.71, pretest (median=95.00) to follow up (median=100.00)z=-2.82, p<0.001, r=-0.81 in the scores of successive processing, and the increase was large. This indicates that the group has significantly improved from AA intervention in their successive processing.

#### 4.4.3.4 Within group analysis for Simultaneous processing C group

**Table 4.22: Descriptive statistics for Simultaneous Processing subtest data (C group)**

| Data | $n$ | Median | $M$ | $SD$ | Min | Max |
|------|-----|--------|-----|------|-----|-----|
| Pretest | 15 | 87.00 | 81.00 | 17.49 | 56.00 | 104.00 |
| Posttest | 15 | 89.00 | 81.67 | 17.23 | 54.00 | 106.00 |
| Follow up | - | | - | - | - | - |

**Table 4.22.A: Pre, Post & Follow up intervention comparisons within (C) group**

| | $z$ | $p$ | Effect size |
|------|-----|-----|-------------|
| Pretest-Posttest | -1.18 | .238 | -0.304 |
| Pretest-Follow up | - | - | - |
| Posttest-Follow up | - | - | - |

There was no significant increase from pretest (median= 87.00) to posttest (median= 89.00), z=-1.18, p=0.24. This indicates that the control group has not improved in their successive processing.

#### 4.4.4 Between group analysis for Simultaneous processing post intervention data

**Table 4.23: Simultaneous Processing subtest data between groups analyses (Post-intervention data)**

| Groups | $n$ | Mean ranks | Chi sq | df | $p$ |
|--------|-----|-----------|--------|-----|-----|
| Y&AA | 15 | 34.87 | | | |
| N&AA | 15 | 35.30 | 12.562 | 3 | .006* |
| C | 15 | 16.53 | | | |
| AA | 12 | 29.38 | | | |

*significant at 0.05 level

There was a statistically significant difference between the groups on the levels of successive processing in the posttest data ($x^2(2)$ = 12.56, $p<0.001$) with a mean rank of 34.87 (Median= 98.00) for Y&AA group, 35.30 (Median= 102.00) for N&AA group, 16.53 (Median= 89.00) for C group and 29.38 (Median= 29.38) for AA group.

#### 4.4.4.A. Post-hoc analyses for Simultaneous processing post intervention data

**Table 4.23.A:Simultaneous processing post intervention data Post-hoc analyses between Y&AA-N&AA**

| Groups | n | Mean ranks | U | z | p | Effect size |
|--------|---|-----------|------|-------|------|-------------|
| Y&AA   | 15 | 15.40 | 111.00 | -.062 | .950 | -0.016 |
| N&AA   | 15 | 15.60 | | | | |

Descriptive statistics showed that Y&AA group (median= 98.00; mean rank = 15.40) had lower scores than that N&AA group (median= 102.00; mean rank = 15.60). Mann-Whitney U value was found to be statistically non significant U= 111.00 (z = -0.06), p =0.95.

**Table 4.23.B: Simultaneous processing post intervention data Post-hoc analyses between Y&AA-AA**

| Groups | n | Mean ranks | U | z | p | Effect size |
|--------|---|-----------|------|-------|------|-------------|
| Y&AA   | 15 | 15.40 | 69.00 | -1.030 | .303 | -0.266 |
| AA     | 12 | 12.25 | | | | |

Descriptive statistics showed that Y&AA group (median= 98.00; mean rank = 15.40) had equal scores as AA group (median= 98.00; mean rank = 12.25). Mann-Whitney U value was found to be statistically non significant U= 69.00 (z = -1.03), p =0.30.

**Table 4.23.C: Simultaneous processing post intervention data Post-hoc analyses between Y&AA-C**

| Groups | n | Mean ranks | U | z | p | Effect size |
|--------|---|-----------|------|-------|------|-------------|
| Y&AA   | 15 | 20.07 | 44.00 | -2.850 | .004* | -0.736 |
| C      | 15 | 10.93 | | | | |

* significant at 0.05 level

Descriptive statistics showed that Y&AA group (median= 98.00; mean rank = 20.07) had higher scores than that C group (median= 89.00; mean rank = 10.93). Mann-Whitney U value was found to be statistically significant U= 44.00 (z = -2.85), p <0.001 and the difference between Y&AA and C groups was moderate (r = -0.74).

**Table 4.23.D: Simultaneous processing post intervention data Post-hoc analyses between N&AA-AA**

| Groups | $n$ | Mean ranks | U | $z$ | $p$ | Effect size |
|--------|-----|------------|-------|--------|------|-------------|
| N&AA   | 15  | 15.50      | 67.50 | -1.105 | .269 | -0.285      |
| AA     | 12  | 12.13      |       |        |      |             |

Descriptive statistics showed that N&AA group (median= 102.00; mean rank = 15.50) had higher scores than that AA group (median= 98.00; mean rank = 12.13). Mann-Whitney U value was found to be statistically non significant U= 67.50 (z = -1.11), p = 0.27.

**Table 4.23.E: Simultaneous processing post intervention data Post-hoc analyses between N&AA-C**

| Groups | $n$ | Mean ranks | U | $z$ | $p$ | Effect size |
|--------|-----|------------|-------|--------|-------|-------------|
| N&AA   | 15  | 20.20      | 42.00 | -2.931 | .003* | -0.757      |
| C      | 15  | 10.80      |       |        |       |             |

*significant at 0.05 level

Descriptive statistics showed that N&AA group (median= 102.00; mean rank = 20.20) had higher scores than that C group (median= 89.00; mean rank = 10.80). Mann-Whitney U value was found to be statistically significant U= 42.00 (z = -2.93), p <0.001 and the difference between Y&AA and C groups was moderate (r = -0.76).

**Table 4.23.F: Simultaneous processing post intervention data Post-hoc analyses between AA-C**

| Groups | $n$ | Mean ranks | U | $z$ | $p$ | Effect size |
|--------|-----|------------|-------|--------|-------|-------------|
| AA     | 12  | 18.00      | 42.00 | -2.350 | .019* | -0.679      |
| C      | 15  | 10.80      |       |        |       |             |

*significant at 0.05 level

Descriptive statistics showed that AA group (median= 98.00; mean rank = 18.00) had higher scores than that C group (median= 89.00; mean rank = 10.80). Mann-Whitney U value was found to be statistically significant U= 42.00 (z = -2.35), p <0.001 and the difference between Y&AA and C groups was moderate (r = -0.68).

#### 4.4.5 Between group analysis for Simultaneous processing follow up data

**Table 4.24: Simultaneous Processing subtest data between groups analyses (Follow up data)**

| Groups | $n$ | Mean ranks | *Chi sq* | *df* | *p* |
|--------|-----|------------|----------|------|-----|
| Y&AA   | 15  | 23.07      |          |      |     |
| N&AA   | 15  | 23.33      | 2.070    | 2    | .355 |
| C      | 15  | -          |          |      |     |
| AA     | 12  | 17.25      |          |      |     |

There was no significant difference between the groups on the levels of successive processing in the posttest data ($x^2(2) = 2.07$, $p=0.35$) with a mean rank of 23.07 (Median= 102.00) for Y&AA group, 23.33 (Median= 102.00) for N&AA group, and 17.25 (Median= 100.00) for AA group. No further analysis was done.

Graph 3

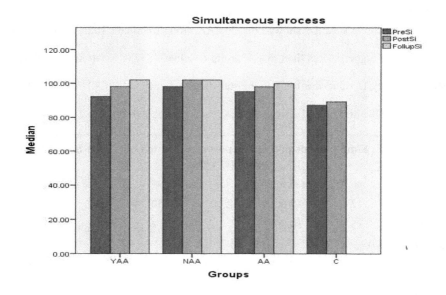

## 4.5 Testing Hypothesis 4: Practice of yoga will improve successive process in children with LD

### 4.5.1 Homogeneity test for intervention subgroups for Successive processing

Table 4.25: Homogeneity test for intervention subgroups pre-intervention data successive process

| Groups | $n$ | Mean ranks | Chi sq | df | p |
|--------|-----|------------|--------|-----|-----|
| Y&AA1 | 8 | 12.75 | | | |
| Y&AA2 | 7 | 18.79 | | | |
| N&AA1 | 7 | 18.43 | | | |
| N&AA2 | 8 | 24.63 | 9.84 | | |
| AA1 | 7 | 30.43 | | 5 | .080 |
| AA2 | 5 | 26.10 | | | |

There was no statistically significant difference ($p$=0.08) between the experimental groups carried out in two seasons in successive processing subtest scores before the commencement of the intervention. Hence the groups Y&AA1 & Y&AA2, N&AA1 & N&AA2, AA1 & AA2 are combined respectively in further analysis

### 4.5.2 Homogeneity test for Successive processing pre-intervention data

Table 4.26: Homogeneity test for Successive Processing preintervention data

| Groups | $n$ | Mean ranks | Chi sq | df | p |
|--------|-----|------------|--------|-----|-----|
| Y&AA | 15 | 21.77 | | | |
| N&AA | 15 | 29.93 | 7.61 | 3 | .05[*] |
| C | 15 | 27.17 | | | |
| AA | 12 | 39.17 | | | |

[*] significant at 0.05 level

There was statistically significant difference ($p$=0.05) between the experimental and control groups on successive processing before the start of the intervention.

84

### 4.5.3 Within group analysis for Successive processing

### 4.5.3.1 Within group analysis for Successive processing Y&AA group

**Table 4.27: Descriptive statistics for Successive Processing subtest data (Y&AA group)**

| Data | $n$ | Median | $M$ | $SD$ | Min | Max |
|---|---|---|---|---|---|---|
| Pretest | 15 | 77.00 | 79.73 | 9.48 | 65.00 | 94.00 |
| Posttest | 15 | 94.00 | 96.27 | 9.45 | 81.00 | 115.00 |
| Follow up | 15 | 100.00 | 98.40 | 6.73 | 90.00 | 112.00 |

**Table 4.27.A: Pre, Post & Follow up intervention comparisons within (Y&AA) group**

| | $z$ | $p$ | Effect size |
|---|---|---|---|
| Pretest-Posttest | -3.42 | .001* | -0.883 |
| Pretest-Follow up | -3.41 | .001* | -0.881 |
| Posttest-Follow up | -1.51 | .13 | -0.390 |

* significant at 0.05 level

There was a significant increase from pretest (median= 77.00) to posttest (median= 94.00), z=-3.42, p<0.001, r= -0.88, pretest (median=77.00) to follow up (median=100.00)z=-3.41, p<0.001, r=-0.88 but not in posttest (median=94.00) to follow up (median=100.00) z=-1.51, p=.13 and the increase was large. This indicates that the group has significantly improved from Y&AA intervention in their behavioral adjustment.

### 4.5.3.2 Within group analysis for Successive processing N&AA group

**Table 4.28: Descriptive statistics for Successive Processing subtest data (N&AA group)**

| Data | $n$ | Median | $M$ | $SD$ | Min | Max |
|---|---|---|---|---|---|---|
| Pretest | 15 | 86.00 | 85.00 | 12.26 | 63.00 | 104.00 |
| Posttest | 15 | 90.00 | 89.53 | 11.86 | 69.00 | 108.00 |
| Follow up | 15 | 98.00 | 96.53 | 6.56 | 84.00 | 106.00 |

**Table 4.28.A: Pre, Post & Follow up intervention comparisons within (N&AA) group**

|  | z | p | Effect size |
|---|---|---|---|
| Pretest-Posttest | -3.47 | .001* | -0.896 |
| Pretest-Follow up | -3.41 | .001* | -0.881 |
| Posttest-Follow up | -2.98 | .003* | -0.770 |

* significant at 0.05 level

There was a significant increase from pretest (median= 86.00) to posttest (median= 90.00), z=-3.47, p<0.001, r= -0.89, pretest (median=86.00) to follow up (median=98.00)z=-3.41, p<0.001, r=-0.88 and posttest (median=90.00) to follow up (median=98.00) z=-2.98, p<0.001 r= -0.77 in the scores of successive processing, and the increase was large. This indicates that the group has significantly improved from N&AA intervention in their successive processing and the improvement continued over a period of time till the follow up assessment was made.

### 4.5.3.3 Within group analysis for Successive processing AA group

**Table 4.29: Descriptive statistics for Successive Processing subtest data (AA group)**

| Data | n | Median | M | SD | Min | Max |
|---|---|---|---|---|---|---|
| Pretest | 12 | 90.00 | 91.50 | 6.72 | 84.00 | 110.00 |
| Posttest | 12 | 92.00 | 92.25 | 7.66 | 81.00 | 112.00 |
| Follow up | 12 | 100.00 | 100.42 | 4.81 | 92.00 | 113.00 |

**Table 4.29.A: Pre, Post & Follow up intervention comparisons within (AA) group**

|  | z | p | Effect size |
|---|---|---|---|
| Pretest-Posttest | -1.04 | .31 | -0.300 |
| Pretest-Follow up | -3.07 | .002* | -0.887 |
| Posttest-Follow up | -3.06 | .002* | -0.884 |

* significant at 0.05 level

There was no significant increase from pretest (median= 990.00) to posttest (median= 92.00), z=-1.04, p=0.31, but there is significant increase in pretest (median=90.00) to follow up (median=100.00)z=-3.07, p<0.001, r=-0.88 and posttest (median=92.00) to follow up (median=100.00) z=-3.06, p<0.001 r= -0.88 in the scores of successive processing, and the increase was large. This indicates that the group has significantly improved from AA intervention in their successive processing.

#### 4.5.3.4 Within group analysis for Successive processing C group

##### Table 4.30: Descriptive statistics for Successive Processing subtest data (C group)

| Data | $n$ | Median | $M$ | $SD$ | Min | Max |
|---|---|---|---|---|---|---|
| Pretest | 15 | 79.00 | 83.57 | 12.28 | 67.00 | 104.00 |
| Posttest | 15 | 81.00 | 83.20 | 12.45 | 65.00 | 104.00 |
| Follow up | - | | - | - | - | - |

##### Table 4.30.A: Pre, Post & Follow up intervention comparisons within (C) group

| | $z$ | $p$ | Effect size |
|---|---|---|---|
| Pretest-Posttest | -.31 | .75 | -0.080 |
| Pretest-Follow up | - | - | - |
| Posttest-Follow up | - | - | - |

There was no significant increase from pretest (median= 79.00) to posttest (median= 81.00), z=-.31, p=0.75. This indicates that the group has not improved in the control group

#### 4.5.4 Between group analysis for Successive processing post intervention data

##### Table 4.31: Successive processing subtest data between groups analyses (Post-intervention data)

| Groups | $n$ | Mean ranks | Chi sq | df | $p$ |
|---|---|---|---|---|---|
| Y&AA | 15 | 37.07 | | | |
| N&AA | 15 | 28.23 | 7.771 | 3 | .051[*] |
| C | 15 | 20.40 | | | |
| AA | 12 | 30.63 | | | |

[*] significant at 0.05 level

87

There was statistically significant difference between the groups on successive processing in the posttest data $(x^2(2) = 7.77, p= .05)$ with a mean rank of 37.07 (Median= 94.00) for Y&AA group, 28.23 (Median= 90.00) for N&AA group, 20.40 (Median= 81.00) for C group and 30.63 (Median= 92.00) for AA group.

**4.5.4.A. Post-hoc analyses for Successive processing post intervention data**

**Table 4.31.A: Successive processing post intervention data Post-hoc analyses between Y&AA-N&AA**

| Groups | $n$ | Mean ranks | U | $z$ | $p$ | Effect size |
|--------|-----|------------|-------|--------|------|-------------|
| Y&AA | 15 | 17.83 | 77.50 | -1.457 | .145 | -0.376 |
| N&AA | 15 | 13.17 | | | | |

Descriptive statistics showed that Y&AA group (median= 94.00; mean rank = 17.83) had higher scores than that of N&AA group (median= 90.00; mean rank = 13.17). Mann-Whitney U value was found to be statistically non significant U= 77.50 (z = -1.46), p =0.15.

**Table 4.31.B: Successive processing post intervention data Post-hoc analyses between Y&AA-AA**

| Groups | $n$ | Mean ranks | U | $z$ | $p$ | Effect size |
|--------|-----|------------|-------|--------|------|-------------|
| Y&AA | 15 | 15.63 | 65.50 | -1.204 | .228 | -0.311 |
| AA | 12 | 11.96 | | | | |

Descriptive statistics showed that Y&AA group (median= 94.00; mean rank = 15.63) had higher scores than that of AA group (median= 92.00; mean rank = 11.96). Mann-Whitney U value was found to be statistically non significant U= 65.50 (z = -1.20), p =0.23.

**Table 4.31.C: Successive processing post intervention data Post-hoc analyses between Y&AA-C**

| Groups | $n$ | Mean ranks | U | $z$ | $p$ | Effect size |
|--------|-----|------------|-------|--------|-------|-------------|
| Y&AA | 15 | 19.60 | 51.00 | -2.561 | .010* | -0.661 |
| C | 15 | 11.40 | | | | |

* significant at 0.05 level

Descriptive statistics showed that Y&AA group (median= 94.00; mean rank = 19.60) had higher scores than that of C group (median= 81.00; mean rank = 11.40). Mann-Whitney U value was found to be statistically significant U= 51.00 (z = -2.56), p <0.001 and the difference between Y&AA and C groups was moderate (r = -0.66).

**Table 4.31.D: Successive processing post intervention data Post-hoc analyses between N&AA-AA**

| Groups | n | Mean ranks | U | z | p | Effect size |
|--------|-----|-----------|-------|-------|------|------------|
| N&AA | 15 | 13.40 | 81.00 | -.441 | .659 | -0.113 |
| AA | 12 | 14.75 | | | | |

Descriptive statistics showed that N&AA group (median= 90.00; mean rank = 13.40) had lower scores than that of AA group (median= 92.00; mean rank = 14.75). Mann-Whitney U value was found to be statistically non significant U= 81.00 (z = -.44), p =0.66

**Table 4.31.E: Successive processing post intervention data Post-hoc analyses between N&AA-C**

| Groups | n | Mean ranks | U | z | p | Effect size |
|--------|-----|-----------|-------|--------|------|------------|
| N&AA | 15 | 17.67 | 80.00 | -1.353 | .176 | -0.349 |
| C | 15 | 13.33 | | | | |

Descriptive statistics showed that N&AA group (median= 90.00; mean rank = 17.67) had higher scores than that of C group (median= 81.00; mean rank = 13.33). Mann-Whitney U value was found to be statistically non significant U= 80.00 (z = -1.35), p =0.18.

**Table 4.31.F: Successive processing post intervention data Post-hoc analyses between AA-C**

| Groups | n | Mean ranks | U | z | p | Effect size |
|--------|-----|-----------|-------|--------|------|------------|
| AA | 12 | 16.92 | 55.00 | -1.713 | .087 | -0.495 |
| C | 15 | 11.67 | | | | |

Descriptive statistics showed that AA group (median= 92.00; mean rank = 16.92) had higher scores than that of C group (median= 81.00; mean rank = 11.67).

Mann-Whitney U value was found to be statistically non significant U= 55.00 (z = - 1.71), p =0.08.

## 4.5.5 Between group analysis for Successive processing follow up data

**Table 4.32: Successive Processing subtest data between groups analyses (Follow up data)**

| Groups | *n* | Mean ranks | *Chi sq* | *df* | *p* |
|--------|-----|-----------|----------|------|-----|
| Y&AA | 15 | 21.37 | | | |
| N&AA | 15 | 19.03 | 1.484 | 2 | .476 |
| C | 15 | - | | | |
| AA | 12 | 24.75 | | | |

There was no statistically significant difference between the groups on successive processing in the follow up data ($x^2(2)$ = 1.48, *p*= .47) with a mean rank of 21.37 (Median= 100.00) for Y&AA group, 19.03 (Median= 98.00) for N&AA group, and 24.75 (Median= 100.00) for AA group. Hence no further analysis was done.

Graph 4

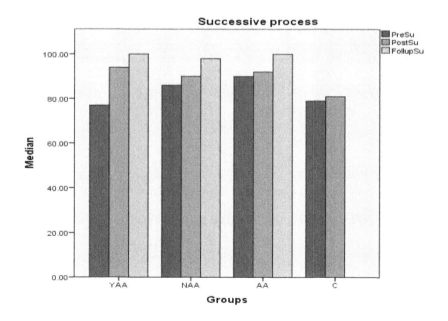

### 4.6 Testing Hypothesis 5: Practice of yoga will improve phonological process in children with LD

### 4.6.1 Elision

### 4.6.1.1 Homogeneity test for intervention subgroups for Elision

**Table 4.33:** Homogeneity test for intervention subgroups pre-intervention data Elision

| Groups | *n* | Mean ranks | *Chi sq* | *df* | *p* |
|--------|-----|-----------|----------|------|-----|
| Y&AA1  | 8   | 18.31     |          |      |     |
| Y&AA2  | 7   | 19.00     |          |      |     |
| N&AA1  | 7   | 14.64     | 8.29     |      |     |
| N&AA2  | 8   | 25.13     |          | 5    | .140 |
| AA1    | 7   | 22.57     |          |      |     |
| AA2    | 5   | 32.40     |          |      |     |

There was no statistically significant difference ($p=0.08$) between the experimental groups carried out in two seasons in elision subtest scores before the commencement of the intervention. Hence the groups Y&AA1 & Y&AA2, N&AA1 & N&AA2, AA1 & AA2 are combined respectively in further analysis

### 4.6.1.2 Homogeneity test for Elision pre-intervention data

**Table 4.34:** Homogeneity test for Elision pre-intervention data

| Groups | *n* | Mean ranks | *Chi sq* | *df* | *p* |
|--------|-----|-----------|----------|------|-----|
| Y&AA   | 15  | 25.33     |          |      |     |
| N&AA   | 15  | 27.57     | 3.48     | 3    | .32 |
| C      | 15  | 28.20     |          |      |     |
| AA     | 12  | 36.38     |          |      |     |

There was no statistically significant difference ($p=0.32$) between the experimental and control groups in elision task before the start of the intervention.

### 4.6.1.3 Within group analysis for Elision

### 4.6.1.3.1 Within group analysis for Elision Y&AA group

#### Table 4.35: Descriptive statistics for Elision subtest data (Y&AA group)

| Data | $n$ | Median | $M$ | $SD$ | Min | Max |
|------|-----|--------|-----|------|-----|-----|
| Pretest | 15 | 4.00 | 3.87 | .912 | 2.00 | 5.00 |
| Posttest | 15 | 12.00 | 12.13 | 2.92 | 7.00 | 16.00 |
| Follow up | 15 | 13.00 | 13.27 | 2.09 | 10.00 | 16.00 |

#### Table 4.35.A: Pre, Post & Follow up intervention comparisons within (Y&AA) group

| | $z$ | $p$ | Effect size |
|------|-----|-----|-------------|
| Pretest-Posttest | -3.41 | .001* | -0.881 |
| Pretest-Follow up | -3.43 | .001* | -0.886 |
| Posttest-Follow up | -2.03 | .042 | -0.524 |

* significant at 0.05 level

There was a significant increase from pretest (median= 4.00) to posttest (median= 12.00), z=-3.41, p<0.001, r= -0.88, pretest (median=4.00) to follow up (median=13.00)z=-3.43, p<0.001, r=-0.89 and the increase was large but not in posttest (median=12.00) to follow up (median=13.00) z=-2.03, p=0.04 r= -0.52 in the scores of elision. This indicates that the group has significantly improved from AA intervention in elision task and the improvement continued over a period of time till the follow up assessment was made.

### 4.6.1.3.2 Within group analysis for Elision N&AA group

#### Table 4.36: Descriptive statistics for Elision subtest data (N&AA group)

| Data | $n$ | Median | $M$ | $SD$ | Min | Max |
|------|-----|--------|-----|------|-----|-----|
| Pretest | 15 | 4.00 | 4.13 | 1.36 | 2.00 | 7.00 |
| Posttest | 15 | 12.00 | 11.40 | 2.38 | 7.00 | 15.00 |
| Follow up | 15 | 13.00 | 12.33 | 1.95 | 8.00 | 15.00 |

**Table 4.36.A: Pre, Post & Follow up intervention comparisons within (N&AA) group**

|  | z | p | Effect size |
|---|---|---|---|
| Pretest-Posttest | -3.41 | .001* | -0.881 |
| Pretest-Follow up | -3.41 | .001* | -0.881 |
| Posttest-Follow up | -2.21 | .027* | -0.571 |

* significant at 0.05 level

There was a significant increase from pretest (median= 4.00) to posttest (median= 12.00), z=-3.41, p<0.001, r= -0.88, pretest (median=4.00) to follow up (median=13.00)z=-3.41, p<0.001, r=-0.88 and posttest (median=12.00) to follow up (median=13.00) z=-2.21, p<0.001 r= -0.57 in the scores of elision, and the increase was moderate to large. This indicates that the group has significantly improved from N&AA intervention in elision task and the improvement continued over a period of time till the follow up assessment was made.

### 4.6.1.3.3 Within group analysis for Elision AA group

**Table 4.37: Descriptive statistics for Elision subtest data (AA group)**

| Data | n | Median | M | SD | Min | Max |
|---|---|---|---|---|---|---|
| Pretest | 12 | 5.00 | 4.77 | 1.073 | 3.00 | 6.00 |
| Posttest | 12 | 11.50 | 11.33 | 2.27 | 7.00 | 14.00 |
| Follow up | 12 | 13.50 | 13.50 | 1.24 | 12.00 | 16.00 |

**Table 4.37.A: Pre, Post & Follow up intervention comparisons within (AA) group**

|  | z | p | Effect size |
|---|---|---|---|
| Pretest-Posttest | -3.06 | .002* | -0.884 |
| Pretest-Follow up | -3.08 | .002* | -0.890 |
| Posttest-Follow up | -2.38 | .018* | -0.687 |

* significant at 0.05 level

There was a significant increase from pretest (median= 5.00) to posttest (median= 11.50), z=-3.06, p<0.001, r= -0.88, pretest (median=5.00) to follow up

(median=13.50)z=-3.08, p<0.001, r=-0.89 and posttest (median=11.50) to follow up (median=13.50) z=-2.38, p<0.001 r= -0.68 in the scores of elision, and the increase was large. This indicates that the group has significantly improved from AA intervention in elision task and the improvement continued over a period of time till the follow up assessment was made.

### 4.6.1.3.4 Within group analysis for Elision C group

**Table 4.38: Descriptive statistics for Elision subtest data (C group)**

| Data | $n$ | Median | $M$ | $SD$ | Min | Max |
|---|---|---|---|---|---|---|
| Pretest | 15 | 4.00 | 4.07 | 1.10 | 2.00 | 6.00 |
| Posttest | 15 | 4.00 | 4.00 | 1.36 | 2.00 | 6.00 |
| Follow up | - | | - | - | - | - |

**Table 4.38.A: Pre, Post & Follow up intervention comparisons within (C) group**

| | $z$ | $p$ | Effect size |
|---|---|---|---|
| Pretest-Posttest | -.09 | .93 | -0.023 |
| Pretest-Follow up | - | - | - |
| Posttest-Follow up | - | - | - |

There was no significant difference from pretest (median= 4.00) to posttest (median= 4.00), z=-.09, p=0.02 in the scores of elision. This indicates that the group has not improved in control condition.

### 4.6.1.4 Between group analyses for Elision post intervention data

**Table 4.39: Elision subtest data between groups analyses (Post-test data)**

| Groups | $n$ | Mean ranks | Chi sq | df | $p$ |
|---|---|---|---|---|---|
| Y&AA | 15 | 38.57 | | | |
| N&AA | 15 | 35.50 | 33.208 | 3 | .000* |
| C | 15 | 8.00 | | | |
| AA | 12 | 35.17 | | | |

* significant at 0.05 level

94

There was a statistically significant difference between the groups on the levels in elision sub test in the posttest data ($x^2(2) = 33.21$, $p= .00$) with a mean rank of 38.57 (Median= 12.00) for Y&AA group, 35.50 (Median= 12.00) for N&AA group, 8.00 (Median= 4.00) for C group and 35.17 (Median= 11.50) for AA group.

**4.6.1.4.A. Post-hoc analyses for Elision post intervention data**

**Table 4.39.A: Elision post intervention data Post-hoc analyses between Y&AA-N&AA**

| Groups | $n$ | Mean ranks | U | $z$ | $p$ | Effect size |
|--------|-----|------------|-------|-------|------|-------------|
| Y&AA | 15 | 16.60 | 96.00 | -.689 | .491 | -0.178 |
| N&AA | 15 | 14.40 | | | | |

Descriptive statistics showed that Y&AA group (median=12.00; mean rank = 16.60) had equal scores as N&AA group (median= 12.00; mean rank = 14.40). Mann-Whitney U value was found to be statistically non significant U= 96.00 ($z$ = -.68), p =0.49.

**Table 4. 39.B: Elision post intervention data Post-hoc analyses between Y&AA-AA**

| Groups | $n$ | Mean ranks | U | $z$ | $p$ | Effect size |
|--------|-----|------------|-------|-------|------|-------------|
| Y&AA | 15 | 14.97 | 75.50 | -.714 | .476 | -0.184 |
| AA | 12 | 12.79 | | | | |

Descriptive statistics showed that Y&AA group (median=12.00; mean rank = 14.97) had higher scores than that AA group (median= 11.50; mean rank = 12.79). Mann-Whitney U value was found to be statistically non significant U= 75.50 ($z$ = -4.43), p =0.48.

**Table 4. 39.C: Elision post intervention data Post-hoc analyses between Y&AA-C**

| Groups | $n$ | Mean ranks | U | $z$ | $p$ | Effect size |
|--------|-----|------------|------|--------|-------|-------------|
| Y&AA | 15 | 23.00 | .00 | -4.693 | .000* | -1.212 |
| C | 15 | 8.00 | | | | |

* significant at 0.05 level

Descriptive statistics showed that Y&AA group (median=12.00; mean rank = 23.00) had higher scores than that C group (median= 4.00; mean rank = 8.00). Mann-Whitney U value was found to be statistically significant U= .00 (z = -4.69), p <0.001 and the difference between Y&AA and C group was large (r = -1.21).

**Table 4. 39.D: Elision post intervention data Post-hoc analyses between N&AA-AA**

| Groups | $n$ | Mean ranks | U | $z$ | $p$ | Effect size |
|--------|-----|-----------|-------|-------|------|-------------|
| N&AA | 15 | 14.10 | 85.50 | -.074 | .941 | -0.019 |
| AA | 12 | 13.88 | | | | |

Descriptive statistics showed that N&AA group (median=12.00; mean rank = 14.10) had higher scores than that AA group (median= 11.50; mean rank = 13.88). Mann-Whitney U value was found to be statistically non significant U= 85.50 (z = -.07), p =0.94.

**Table 4. 39.E: Elision post intervention data Post-hoc analyses between N&AA-C**

| Groups | $n$ | Mean ranks | U | $z$ | $p$ | Effect size |
|--------|-----|-----------|------|--------|-------|-------------|
| N&AA | 15 | 23.00 | .00 | -4.692 | .000* | -1.212 |
| C | 15 | 8.00 | | | | |

* significant at 0.05 level

Descriptive statistics showed that N&AA group (median=12.00; mean rank = 23.00) had higher scores than that C group (median= 4.00; mean rank = 8.00). Mann-Whitney U value was found to be statistically significant U= .00 (z = -4.69), p <0.001 and the difference between N&AA and C group was large (r = -1.21).

**Table 4. 39.F: Elision post intervention data Post-hoc analyses between AA-C**

| Groups | $n$ | Mean ranks | U | $z$ | $p$ | Effect size |
|--------|-----|-----------|------|--------|-------|-------------|
| AA | 12 | 21.50 | .00 | -4.425 | .000* | -1.278 |
| C | 15 | 8.00 | | | | |

* significant at 0.05 level

Descriptive statistics showed that AA group (median=11.50; mean rank = 21.50) had higher scores than that C group (median= 4.00; mean rank = 8.00). Mann-

Whitney U value was found to be statistically significant U= .00 (z = -4.43), p <0.001 and the difference between AA and C group was large (r = -1.28).

**4.6.1.5 Between group analysis for Elision follow up data**

**Table 4.40: Elision subtest data between groups analyses (Follow up data)**

| Groups | $n$ | Mean ranks | *Chi sq* | *df* | *p* |
|---|---|---|---|---|---|
| Y&AA | 15 | 22.90 | | | |
| N&AA | 15 | 17.80 | 2.292 | 2 | .318 |
| C | 15 | - | | | |
| AA | 12 | 24.38 | | | |

There was a statistically non significant difference between the groups on the levels in elision sub test in the posttest data ($x^2(2)$ = 2.29, *p*= .00) with a mean rank of 22.90 (Median= 13.00) for Y&AA group, 17.80 (Median= 13.00) for N&AA group, and 24.38 (Median= 13.50) for AA group.

Graph 5

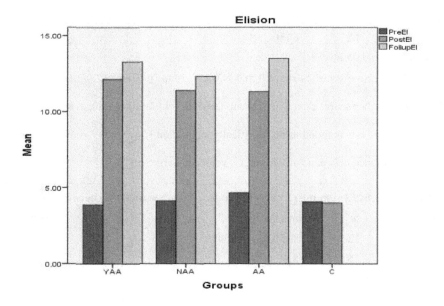

### 4.6.2 Blending Words

#### 4.6.2.1 Homogeneity test for intervention subgroups for Blending words

**Table 4.41:  Homogeneity test for intervention subgroups pre-intervention data Blending words**

| Groups | $n$ | Mean ranks | Chi sq | df | p |
|--------|-----|-----------|--------|-----|-----|
| Y&AA1 | 8 | 18.25 | | | |
| Y&AA2 | 7 | 20.29 | | | |
| N&AA1 | 7 | 24.64 | 8.50 | 5 | .131 |
| N&AA2 | 8 | 26.50 | | | |
| AA1 | 7 | 12.43 | | | |
| AA2 | 5 | 28.70 | | | |

There was no statistically significant difference ($p$=0.13) between the experimental groups carried out in two seasons in Blending words subtest scores before the commencement of the intervention. Hence the groups Y&AA1 & Y&AA2, N&AA1 & N&AA2, AA1 & AA2 are combined respectively in further analysis

#### 4.6.2.2 Homogeneity test for Blending words pre-intervention data

**Table 4.42:  Homogeneity test for Blending words pre-intervention data**

| Groups | $n$ | Mean ranks | Chi sq | df | p |
|--------|-----|-----------|--------|-----|-----|
| Y&AA | 15 | 24.77 | | | |
| N&AA | 15 | 33.00 | 3.52 | 3 | .32 |
| C | 15 | 32.63 | | | |
| AA | 12 | 24.75 | | | |

There was no statistically significant difference ($p$=0.32) between the experimental and control groups in blending words task before the start of the intervention.

98

### 4.6.2.3 Within group analysis for Blending words

### 4.6.2.3.1 Within group analysis for Blending words Y&AA group

**Table 4.43: Descriptive statistics for Blending Words subtest data (Y&AA group)**

| Data | $n$ | Median | $M$ | $SD$ | Min | Max |
|---|---|---|---|---|---|---|
| Pretest | 15 | 5.00 | 4.87 | 1.30 | 3.00 | 7.00 |
| Posttest | 15 | 13.00 | 12.60 | 2.16 | 9.00 | 17.00 |
| Follow up | 15 | 13.00 | 13.13 | 1.85 | 10.00 | 17.00 |

**Table 4.43.A: Pre, Post & Follow up intervention comparisons within (Y&AA) group**

| | $z$ | $p$ | Effect size |
|---|---|---|---|
| Pretest-Posttest | -3.42 | .001* | -0.883 |
| Pretest-Follow up | -3.42 | .001* | -0.883 |
| Posttest-Follow up | -1.60 | .109 | -0.413 |

* significant at 0.05 level

There was a significant increase from pretest (median= 5.00) to posttest (median= 13.00), z=-3.42, p<0.001, r= -0.88, pretest (median=5.00) to follow up (median=13.50)z=-3.42, p<0.001, r=-0.88 in the scores of blending words task, and the increase was large but not in posttest (median=13.00) to follow up (median=13.00) z=-1.60, p=0.109. This indicates that the group has significantly improved from Y&AA intervention in their blending words.

### 4.6.2.3.2 Within group analysis for Blending words N&AA group

**Table 4.44: Descriptive statistics for Blending Words subtest data (N&AA group)**

| Data | $n$ | Median | $M$ | $SD$ | Min | Max |
|---|---|---|---|---|---|---|
| Pretest | 15 | 5.00 | 5.53 | .99 | 4.00 | 7.00 |
| Posttest | 15 | 12.00 | 12.37 | 1.91 | 9.00 | 16.00 |
| Follow up | 15 | 13.00 | 12.77 | 1.88 | 10.00 | 16.00 |

**Table 4.44.A: Pre, Post & Follow up intervention comparisons within (N&AA) group**

|                    | z     | p     | Effect size |
|--------------------|-------|-------|-------------|
| Pretest-Posttest   | -3.42 | .001* | -0.883      |
| Pretest-Follow up  | -3.42 | .001* | -0.883      |
| Posttest-Follow up | -1.28 | .202  | 0.330       |

* significant at 0.05 level

There was a significant increase from pretest (median= 5.00) to posttest (median= 12.00), z=-3.42, p<0.001, r= -0.88, pretest (median=5.00) to follow up (median=13.00)z=-3.42, p<0.001, r=-0.88 in the scores of blending words task, and the increase was large but not in posttest (median=12.00) to follow up (median=13.00) z=-1.28, p=0.202. This indicates that the group has significantly improved from N&AA intervention in their blending words.

### 4.6.2.3.3 Within group analysis for Blending words AA group

**Table 4.45: Descriptive statistics for Blending Words subtest data (AA group)**

| Data      | n  | Median | M     | SD   | Min   | Max   |
|-----------|----|--------|-------|------|-------|-------|
| Pretest   | 12 | 5.00   | 4.77  | 1.56 | 2.00  | 7.00  |
| Posttest  | 12 | 13.00  | 12.92 | 1.88 | 10.00 | 16.00 |
| Follow up | 12 | 13.50  | 13.33 | 1.83 | 10.00 | 16.00 |

**Table 4.45.A: Pre, Post & Follow up intervention comparisons within (AA) group**

|                    | z     | p     | Effect size |
|--------------------|-------|-------|-------------|
| Pretest-Posttest   | -3.08 | .002* | -0.890      |
| Pretest-Follow up  | -3.08 | .002* | -0.890      |
| Posttest-Follow up | -1.63 | .102  | -0.471      |

* significant at 0.05 level

There was a significant increase from pretest (median= 5.00) to posttest (median= 13.00), z=-3.08, p<0.001, r= -0.89, pretest (median=5.00) to follow up (median=13.50)z=-3.08, p<0.001, r=-0.89 in the scores of blending words task, and the increase was large but not in posttest (median=13.00) to follow up (median=13.00) z=-1.63, p=0.102. This indicates that the group has significantly improved from AA intervention in their blending words.

**4.6.2.3.4 Within group analysis for Blending words C group**

**Table 4.46: Descriptive statistics for Blending Words subtest data (C group)**

| Data | $n$ | Median | $M$ | $SD$ | Min | Max |
|------|-----|--------|-----|------|-----|-----|
| Pretest | 15 | 6.00 | 5.53 | 1.73 | 2.00 | 8.00 |
| Posttest | 15 | 5.00 | 5.33 | 1.76 | 3.00 | 9.00 |
| Follow up | - | | - | - | - | - |

**Table 4.46.A: Pre, Post & Follow up intervention comparisons within (C) group**

| | $z$ | $p$ | Effect size |
|------|-----|-----|-------------|
| Pretest-Posttest | -.50 | .614 | -0.129 |

There was a non significant decrease from pretest (median= 6.00) to posttest (median= 5.00), z=-.50, p=0.61. This indicates that the group has not improved in control group in their blending words skills.

**4.6.2.4 Between group analysis for Blending words post intervention data**

**Table 4.47: Blending words subtest data between groups analyses (Post-test data)**

| Groups | $n$ | Mean ranks | $Chi\ sq$ | $df$ | $p$ |
|--------|-----|-----------|-----------|------|-----|
| Y&AA | 15 | 36.30 | | | |
| N&AA | 15 | 34.47 | 33.349 | 3 | .000* |
| C | 15 | 8.07 | | | |
| AA | 12 | 39.21 | | | |

* significant at 0.05 level

There was a statistically significant difference between the groups in blending words in the posttest data ($x^2(2) = 33.35$, $p= .00$) with a mean rank of 36.30 (Median= 13.00) for Y&AA group, 34.47 (Median= 12.00) for N&AA group, 8.07 (Median= 5.00) for C group and 39.21 (Median= 13.50) for AA group.

### 4.6.2.4.A. Post-hoc analyses for Blending words post intervention data

#### Table 4.47.A: Blending words post intervention data Post-hoc analyses between Y&AA-N&AA

| Groups | $n$ | Mean ranks | U | $z$ | $p$ | Effect size |
|--------|-----|------------|--------|-------|------|-------------|
| Y&AA | 15 | 16.17 | 102.50 | -.421 | .674 | -0.108 |
| N&AA | 15 | 14.83 | | | | |

Descriptive statistics showed that Y&AA group (median= 13.00; mean rank = 16.17) had higher scores than that N&AA group (median= 12.00; mean rank = 14.83). Mann-Whitney U value was found to be statistically non significant U= 102.50 (z = -.42), p =0.67.

#### Table 4. 47.B: Blending words post intervention data Post-hoc analyses between Y&AA-AA

| Groups | $n$ | Mean ranks | U | $z$ | $p$ | Effect size |
|--------|-----|------------|-------|-------|------|-------------|
| Y&AA | 15 | 13.17 | 77.50 | -.619 | .536 | -0.159 |
| AA | 12 | 15.04 | | | | |

Descriptive statistics showed that Y&AA group (median= 13.00; mean rank = 13.17) had higher scores than that AA group (median= 13.00; mean rank = 15.04). Mann-Whitney U value was found to be statistically non significant U= 77.50 (z = -.62), p =0.54.

#### Table 4. 47.C: Blending words post intervention data Post-hoc analyses between Y&AA-C

| Groups | $n$ | Mean ranks | U | $z$ | $p$ | Effect size |
|--------|-----|------------|-----|--------|-------|-------------|
| Y&AA | 15 | 22.97 | .50 | -4.668 | .000* | -1.206 |
| C | 15 | 8.03 | | | | |

\* significant at 0.05 level

Descriptive statistics showed that Y&AA group (median= 13.00; mean rank = 22.97) had higher scores than that C group (median= 5.00; mean rank = 8.03). Mann-Whitney U value was found to be statistically significant U= .50 (z = -4.66), p <0.001 and the difference between Y&AA and C groups was large (r = -1.21).

**Table 4. 47.D: Blending words post intervention data Post-hoc analyses between N&AA-AA**

| Groups | n | Mean ranks | U | z | p | Effect size |
|--------|---|-----------|------|-------|------|-------------|
| N&AA | 15 | 12.67 | 70.00 | -.990 | .322 | -0.255 |
| AA | 12 | 15.67 | | | | |

Descriptive statistics showed that N&AA group (median= 12.00; mean rank = 12.67) had lower scores than that AA group (median= 13.00; mean rank = 15.67). Mann-Whitney U value was found to be statistically non significant U= 70.00 (z = -.99), p =0.32.

**Table 4. 47.E: Blending words post intervention data Post-hoc analyses between N&AA-C**

| Groups | n | Mean ranks | U | z | p | Effect size |
|--------|---|-----------|-----|--------|-------|-------------|
| N&AA | 15 | 22.97 | .50 | -4.668 | .000* | -1.206 |
| C | 15 | 8.03 | | | | |

* significant at 0.05 level

Descriptive statistics showed that N&AA group (median= 12.00; mean rank = 22.97) had higher scores than that C group (median= 5.00; mean rank = 8.03). Mann-Whitney U value was found to be statistically significant U= .50 (z = -4.66), p <0.001 and the difference between N&AA and C groups was large (r = -1.21).

**Table 4. 47.F: Blending words post intervention data Post-hoc analyses between AA-C**

| Groups | n | Mean ranks | U | z | p | Effect size |
|--------|---|-----------|-----|--------|-------|-------------|
| AA | 12 | 21.50 | .00 | -4.415 | .000* | -1.276 |
| C | 15 | 8.00 | | | | |

* significant at 0.05 level

Descriptive statistics showed that AA group (median= 13.00; mean rank = 21.50) had higher scores than that C group (median= 5.00; mean rank = 8.00). Mann-Whitney U value was found to be statistically significant U= .00 (z = -4.42), p <0.001 and the difference between AA and C groups was large (r = -1.28).

**4.6.2.5 Between group analysis for Blending words follow up data**

**Table 4.48: Blending words subtest data between groups analyses (Follow up data)**

| Groups | $n$ | Mean ranks | Chi sq | df | p |
|--------|-----|-----------|--------|-----|-----|
| Y&AA | 15 | 21.90 | | | |
| N&AA | 15 | 19.23 | .987 | 2 | .611 |
| C | 15 | | | | |
| AA | 12 | 23.83 | | | |

There was no statistically significant difference between the groups in blending words in the posttest data ($x^2(2)$ = .98, $p$= .61) with a mean rank of 21.90 (Median= 13.00) for Y&AA group, 19.23 (Median= 13.00) for N&AA group, and 23.83 (Median= 13.50) for AA group.

Graph 6

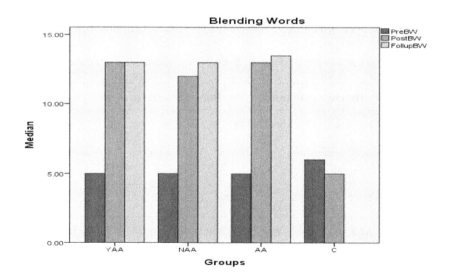

104

### 4.6.3 Blending nonwords

#### 4.6.3.1 Homogeneity test for intervention subgroups for Blending nonwords

**Table 4.49 :  Homogeneity test for intervention subgroups pre-intervention data Blending nonwords**

| Groups | n | Mean ranks | Chi sq | df | p |
|--------|---|-----------|--------|-----|-----|
| Y&AA1 | 8 | 15.13 | | | |
| Y&AA2 | 7 | 14.57 | | | |
| N&AA1 | 7 | 12.14 | 8.00 | | |
| N&AA2 | 8 | 21.13 | | 5 | .130 |
| AA1 | 7 | 23.14 | | | |
| AA2 | 5 | 22.80 | | | |

There was no statistically significant difference ($p$=0.13) between the experimental groups carried out in two seasons in Blending words subtest scores before the commencement of the intervention. Hence the groups Y&AA1 & Y&AA2, N&AA1 & N&AA2, AA1 & AA2 are combined respectively in further analysis

#### 4.6.3.2 Homogeneity test for Blending nonwords pre-intervention data

**Table 4.50:  Homogeneity test for Blending nonwords pre-intervention data**

| Groups | n | Mean ranks | Chi sq | df | p |
|--------|---|-----------|--------|-----|-----|
| Y&AA | 15 | 27.47 | | | |
| N&AA | 15 | 31.00 | 1.25 | 3 | .74 |
| C | 15 | 26.07 | | | |
| AA | 12 | 32.08 | | | |

There was no statistically significant difference ($p$=0.74) between the experimental and control groups in blending no words before the start of the intervention.

105

### 4.6.3.3 Within group analysis for Blending nonwords

#### 4.6.3.3.1 Within group analysis for Blending nonwords Y&AA group

**Table 4.51: Descriptive statistics for Blending nonwords subtest data (Y&AA group)**

| Data | *n* | Median | *M* | *SD* | Min | Max |
|---|---|---|---|---|---|---|
| Pretest | 15 | 6.00 | 6.77 | 1.91 | 4.00 | 11.00 |
| Posttest | 15 | 13.00 | 12.60 | 1.88 | 10.00 | 15.00 |
| Follow up | 15 | 13.00 | 12.80 | 1.86 | 10.00 | 15.00 |

**Table 4.51.A: Pre, Post & Follow up intervention comparisons within (Y&AA) group**

| | *z* | *p* | Effect size |
|---|---|---|---|
| Pretest-Posttest | -3.42 | .001* | -0.883 |
| Pretest-Follow up | -3.42 | .001* | -0.883 |
| Posttest-Follow up | -1.00 | .317 | -0.258 |

There was a significant increase from pretest (median= 6.00) to posttest (median= 13.00), z=-3.42, p<0.001, r= -0.88, pretest (median=6.00) to follow up (median=13.00)z=-3.42, p<0.001, r=-0.88 in blending non words, and the increase was large but not in posttest (median=13.00) to follow up (median=13.00) z=-1.00, p=0.32. r= -0.26. This indicates that the group has significantly improved from Y&AA intervention in blending non words.

#### 4.6.3.3.2 Within group analysis for Blending nonwords N&AA group

**Table 4.52: Descriptive statistics for Blending nonwords subtest data (N&AA group)**

| Data | *n* | Median | *M* | *SD* | Min | Max |
|---|---|---|---|---|---|---|
| Pretest | 15 | 7.00 | 3.00 | 13.00 | 7.60 | 3.33 |
| Posttest | 15 | 11.00 | 9.00 | 21.00 | 12.47 | 3.14 |
| Follow up | 15 | 12.00 | 10.00 | 21.00 | 13.20 | 3.09 |

**Table 4.52.A: Pre, Post & Follow up intervention comparisons within (N&AA) group**

|                  | z     | p     | Effect size |
|------------------|-------|-------|-------------|
| Pretest-Posttest | -3.05 | .002* | -0.788      |
| Pretest-Follow up | -3.33 | .001* | -0.860      |
| Posttest-Follow up | -1.34 | .180 | -0.346      |

There was a significant increase from pretest (median= 7.00) to posttest (median= 11.00), z=-3.05, p<0.001, r= -0.78, pretest (median=7.00) to follow up (median=12.00)z=-3.33, p<0.001, r=-0.86 in blending non words, and the increase was moderate but not in posttest (median=11.00) to follow up (median=12.00) z=-1.34, p=0.18. r= -0.77. This indicates that the group has significantly improved from N&AA intervention in blending non words.

**4.6.3.3.3 Within group analysis for Blending nonwords AA group**

**Table 4.53: Descriptive statistics for Blending nonwords subtest data (AA group)**

| Data | n | Median | M | SD | Min | Max |
|------|---|--------|---|----|----|-----|
| Pretest | 12 | 6.50 | 7.42 | 2.39 | 4.00 | 12.00 |
| Posttest | 12 | 10.00 | 10.75 | 2.14 | 7.00 | 15.00 |
| Follow up | 12 | 12.50 | 12.92 | 2.07 | 10.00 | 16.00 |

**Table 4.53.A: Pre, Post & Follow up intervention comparisons within (AA) group**

|                  | z     | p     | Effect size |
|------------------|-------|-------|-------------|
| Pretest-Posttest | -2.41 | .016* | -0.696      |
| Pretest-Follow up | -2.95 | .003* | -0.852      |
| Posttest-Follow up | -2.69 | .007* | -0.777      |

There was a significant increase from pretest (median= 6.50) to posttest (median= 10.00), z=-2.41, p<0.001, r= -0.69, pretest (median=6.50) to follow up (median=12.00)z=-2.95, p<0.001, r=-0.85 and posttest (median=10.00) to follow up (median=12.50) z=-2.69, p<0.001 r= -0.77 in blending non words, and the increase was moderate. This indicates that the group has significantly improved from AA intervention in blending non words and the improvement continued over a period of time till the follow up assessment was made.

#### 4.6.3.3.4 Within group analysis for Blending nonwords C group

**Table 4.54: Descriptive statistics for Blending nonwords subtest data (C group)**

| Data | $n$ | Median | $M$ | $SD$ | Min | Max |
|------|-----|--------|-----|------|-----|-----|
| Pretest | 15 | 6.00 | 6.47 | 2.07 | 4.00 | 10.00 |
| Posttest | 15 | 6.00 | 5.73 | 1.39 | 3.00 | 8.00 |
| Follow up | - | | | | | |

**Table 4.54.A: Pre, Post & Follow up intervention comparisons within (C) group**

| | $z$ | $p$ | Effect size |
|---|-----|-----|-------------|
| Pretest-Posttest | -.92 | .36 | -0.237 |
| Pretest-Follow up | - | - | - |
| Posttest-Follow up | - | - | - |

There was no significant increase from pretest (median= 6.00) to posttest (median= 6.00), z=-.92, p= .36. This indicates that the group has not improved in control group in blending nonwords

#### 4.6.3.4 Between group analyses for Blending nonwords post intervention data

**Table 4.55: Blending nonwords subtest data between groups analyses (Post-test data)**

| Groups | $n$ | Mean ranks | Chi sq | df | $p$ |
|--------|-----|------------|--------|-----|-----|
| Y&AA | 15 | 40.47 | | | |
| N&AA | 15 | 37.70 | 35.331 | 3 | .000* |
| C | 15 | 8.20 | | | |
| AA | 12 | 29.79 | | | |

There was a statistically significant difference between the groups in blending nonwords in the posttest data ($x^2(2) = 35.33$, $p= .00$) with a mean rank of 40.47

(Median= 13.00) for Y&AA group, 37.70 (Median= 11.00) for N&AA group, 8.20

(Median= 6.00) for C group and 29.79 (Median= 10.00) for AA group.

**4.6.3.4.A. Post-hoc analyses for Blending nonwords post intervention data**

**Table 4.55.A: Blending nonwords post intervention data Post-hoc analyses between Y&AA-N&AA**

| Groups | n | Mean ranks | U | z | p | Effect size |
|---|---|---|---|---|---|---|
| Y&AA | 15 | 16.50 | 97.50 | -.630 | .529 | -0.162 |
| N&AA | 15 | 14.50 | | | | |

Descriptive statistics showed that Y&AA group (median= 13.00; mean rank =

16.50) had higher scores than that N&AA group (median= 11.00; mean rank = 14.50).

Mann-Whitney U value was found to be statistically non significant U= 97.50 (z = -

.63), p =0.53.

**Table 4. 55.B: Blending nonwords post intervention data Post-hoc analyses between Y&AA-AA**

| Groups | n | Mean ranks | U | z | p | Effect size |
|---|---|---|---|---|---|---|
| Y&AA | 15 | 16.97 | 45.50 | -2.212 | .027* | -0.571 |
| AA | 12 | 10.29 | | | | |

Descriptive statistics showed that Y&AA group (median= 13.00; mean rank =

16.97) had higher scores than that AA group (median= 10.00; mean rank = 10.29).

Mann-Whitney U value was found to be statistically significant U= 45.00 (z = -2.21),

p <0.001 and the difference between Y&AA and AA groups was moderate (r = -0.57).

**Table 4. 55.C: Blending nonwords post intervention data Post-hoc analyses between Y&AA-C**

| Groups | n | Mean ranks | U | z | p | Effect size |
|---|---|---|---|---|---|---|
| Y&AA | 15 | 23.00 | .00 | -4.691 | .000* | -1.212 |
| C | 15 | 8.00 | | | | |

Descriptive statistics showed that Y&AA group (median= 13.00; mean rank =

23.00) had higher scores than that C group (median= 6.00; mean rank = 8.00). Mann-

Whitney U value was found to be statistically significant U= .00 (z = -4.69), p <0.001

and the difference between Y&AA and C groups was large (r = -1.21).

**Table 4.55.D: Blending nonwords post intervention data Post-hoc analyses between N&AA-AA**

| Groups | $n$ | Mean ranks | U | $z$ | $p$ | Effect size |
|--------|-----|-----------|-------|--------|------|-------------|
| N&AA | 15 | 16.20 | 57.00 | -1.643 | .100 | -0.424 |
| AA | 12 | 11.25 | | | | |

Descriptive statistics showed that N&AA group (median= 11.00; mean rank =

16.20) had higher scores than that AA group (median= 10.00; mean rank = 11.25).

Mann-Whitney U value was found to be statistically non significant U= 57.00 (z = -

1.64), p =0.10.

**Table 4. 55.E: Blending nonwords post intervention data Post-hoc analyses between N&AA-C**

| Groups | $n$ | Mean ranks | U | $z$ | $p$ | Effect size |
|--------|-----|-----------|-----|--------|-------|-------------|
| N&AA | 15 | 23.00 | .00 | -4.691 | .000* | -1.212 |
| C | 15 | 8.00 | | | | |

Descriptive statistics showed that N&AA group (median= 11.00; mean rank =

23.00) had higher scores than that C group (median= 6.00; mean rank = 8.00). Mann-

Whitney U value was found to be statistically significant U= .00 (z = -4.69), p <0.001

and the difference between N&AA and C groups was large (r = -1.21).

**Table 4. 55.F: Blending nonwords post intervention data Post-hoc analyses between AA-C**

| Groups | $n$ | Mean ranks | U | $z$ | $P$ | Effect size |
|--------|-----|-----------|------|--------|-------|-------------|
| AA | 12 | 21.25 | 3.00 | -4.282 | .000* | -1.106 |
| C | 15 | 8.20 | | | | |

Descriptive statistics showed that AA group (median= 13.00; mean rank =

21.25) had higher scores than that C group (median= 6.00; mean rank = 8.20). Mann-

Whitney U value was found to be statistically significant U= 3.00 (z = -4.28), p

<0.001 and the difference between AA and C groups was large (r = -1.11).

**4.6.3.5 Between group analyses for Blending nonwords follow up data**

**Table 4.56: Blending nonwords subtest data between groups analyses (Follow up data)**

| Groups | *n* | Mean ranks | *Chi sq* | *df* | *p* |
|--------|-----|------------|----------|------|-----|
| Y&AA | 15 | 20.90 | | | |
| N&AA | 15 | 21.80 | .058 | 2 | .972 |
| C | 15 | | | | |
| AA | 12 | 21.88 | | | |

There was a statistically significant difference between the groups in blending non words in the follow up data ($x^2(2)$ = .06, *p*= .97) with a mean rank of 20.90 (Median= 13.00) for Y&AA group, 21.80 (Median= 12.00) for N&AA group, and 21.88 (Median= 12.50) for AA group.

Graph 7

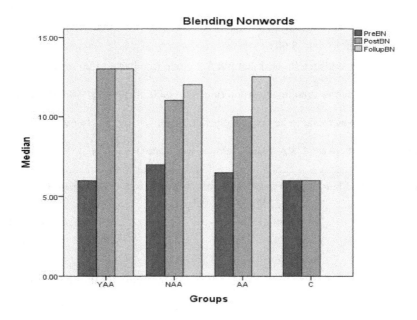

111

#### 4.6.4 Segmenting nonwords

#### 4.6.4.1 Homogeneity test for intervention subgroups for Segmenting nonwords

Table 4.57: Homogeneity test for intervention subgroups pre-intervention data Segmenting nonwords

| Groups | $n$ | Mean ranks | Chi sq | df | $p$ |
|--------|-----|-----------|--------|-----|-----|
| Y&AA1 | 8 | 18.25 | | | |
| Y&AA2 | 7 | 23.57 | | | |
| N&AA1 | 7 | 11.00 | 9.95 | | |
| N&AA2 | 8 | 23.13 | | 5 | .077 |
| AA1 | 7 | 24.86 | | | |
| AA2 | 5 | 31.20 | | | |

There was no statistically significant difference ($p$=0.07) between the experimental groups carried out in two seasons in Segmenting nonwords subtest scores before the commencement of the intervention. Hence the groups Y&AA1 & Y&AA2, N&AA1 & N&AA2, AA1 & AA2 are combined respectively in further analysis

#### 4.6.4.2 Homogeneity test for Segmenting nonwords pre-intervention data

Table 4.58: Homogeneity test for Segmenting nonwords pre-intervention data

| Groups | $n$ | Mean ranks | Chi sq | df | $p$ |
|--------|-----|-----------|--------|-----|-----|
| Y&AA | 15 | 27.17 | | | |
| N&AA | 15 | 22.37 | 5.63 | 3 | .13 |
| C | 15 | 31.23 | | | |
| AA | 12 | 36.79 | | | |

There was no statistically significant difference ($p$=0.13) between the experimental and control groups in segmenting nonwords before the start of the intervention.

#### 4.6.4.3 Within group analysis for Segmenting nonwords

#### 4.6.4.3.1 Within group analysis for Segmenting nonwords Y&AA group

**Table 4.59: Descriptive statistics for Segmenting nonwords subtest data (Y&AA group)**

| Data | $n$ | Median | $M$ | SD | Min | Max |
|---|---|---|---|---|---|---|
| Pretest | 15 | 5.00 | 5.73 | 2.60 | 1.00 | 11.00 |
| Posttest | 15 | 8.00 | 8.97 | 3.60 | 3.00 | 18.00 |
| Follow up | 15 | 11.00 | 11.47 | 2.70 | 8.00 | 18.00 |

**Table 4.59.A: Pre, Post & Follow up intervention comparisons within (Y&AA) group**

| | $z$ | $p$ | Effect size |
|---|---|---|---|
| Pretest-Posttest | -2.52 | .012* | -0.651 |
| Pretest-Follow up | -3.41 | .001* | -0.881 |
| Posttest-Follow up | -2.83 | .005* | --0.731 |

\* significant at 0.05 level

There was a significant increase from pretest (median= 5.00) to posttest (median= 8.00), z=-2.52, p<0.001, r= -0.65, pretest (median=5.00) to follow up (median=11.00)z=-3.41, p<0.001, r=-0.88 and posttest (median=8.00) to follow up (median=11.00) z=-2.83, p<0.001 r= -0.73 in segmenting nonwords, and the increase was large. This indicates that the group has significantly improved from Y&AA intervention in segmenting nonwords and the improvement continued over a period of time till the follow up assessment was made.

#### 4.6.4.3.2 Within group analysis for Segmenting nonwords N&AA group

**Table 4.60: Descriptive statistics for Segmenting nonwords subtest data (N&AA group)**

| Data | $n$ | Median | $M$ | SD | Min | Max |
|---|---|---|---|---|---|---|
| Pretest | 15 | 4.00 | 5.13 | 4.45 | .00 | 15.00 |
| Posttest | 15 | 8.00 | 9.00 | 2.70 | 4.00 | 15.00 |
| Follow up | 15 | 10.00 | 10.20 | 2.96 | 4.00 | 15.00 |

**Table 4.60.A: Pre, Post & Follow up intervention comparisons within (N&AA) group**

|  | $z$ | $p$ | Effect size |
|---|---|---|---|
| Pretest-Posttest | -3.15 | .002* | -0.813 |
| Pretest-Follow up | -3.31 | .001* | -0.855 |
| Posttest-Follow up | -2.39 | .017* | -0.617 |

* significant at 0.05 level

There was a significant increase from pretest (median= 4.00) to posttest (median= 8.00), z=-3.15, p<0.001, r= -0.81, pretest (median=4.00) to follow up (median=10.00)z=-3.31, p<0.001, r=-0.85 and posttest (median=8.00) to follow up (median=10.00) z=-2.39, p<0.001 r= -0.62 in segmenting nonwords, and the increase was moderate to large. This indicates that the group has significantly improved from N&AA intervention in segmenting nonwords and the improvement continued over a period of time till the follow up assessment was made.

**4.6.4.3.3 Within group analysis for Segmenting nonwords AA group**

**Table 4.61: Descriptive statistics for Segmenting nonwords subtest data (AA group)**

| Data | $n$ | Median | $M$ | $SD$ | Min | Max |
|---|---|---|---|---|---|---|
| Pretest | 12 | 8.00 | 7.75 | 3.05 | 4.00 | 12.00 |
| Posttest | 12 | 8.00 | 8.17 | 1.59 | 6.00 | 11.00 |
| Follow up | 12 | 13.00 | 13.00 | .00 | 13.00 | 13.00 |

**Table 4.61.A: Pre, Post & Follow up intervention comparisons within (AA) group**

|  | $z$ | $p$ | Effect size |
|---|---|---|---|
| Pretest-Posttest | -.49 | .622 | -0.141 |
| Pretest-Follow up | -3.07 | .002* | -0.887 |
| Posttest-Follow up | -3.08 | .002* | -0.890 |

* significant at 0.05 level

There was no significant difference from pretest (median= 8.00) to posttest (median= 8.00), z=-.49, p=0.62, but there is significant improvement in, pretest (median=8.00) to follow up (median=13.00)z=-3.07, p<0.001, r=-0.88 and posttest (median=8.00) to follow up (median=13.00) z=-3.08, p<0.001 r= -0.89 in segmenting nonwords, and the increase was large. This indicates that the group has significantly improved from AA intervention in segmenting nonwords and the improvement continued over a period of time till the follow up assessment was made.

**4.6.4.3.4 Within group analysis for Segmenting nonwords C group**

**Table 4.62: Descriptive statistics for Segmenting nonwords subtest data (C group)**

| Data | $n$ | Median | $M$ | $SD$ | Min | Max |
|------|-----|--------|-----|------|-----|-----|
| Pretest | 15 | 5.00 | 6.40 | 2.64 | 3.00 | 11.00 |
| Posttest | 15 | 4.00 | 3.27 | 1.39 | .00 | 5.00 |
| Follow up | - | | - | - | - | - |

**Table 4.62.A: Pre, Post & Follow up intervention comparisons within (C) group**

| | $z$ | $p$ | Effect size |
|---|-----|-----|-------------|
| Pretest-Posttest | -2.78 | .005* | -0.718 |

* significant at 0.05 level

There was a significant decrease from pretest (median= 5.00) to posttest (median= 4.00), z=-2.78, p<0.001, r= -0.72 in segmenting nonwords, and the decrease was moderate. This indicates that the group has significantly deteriorated in control groupin segmenting nonwords.

#### 4.6.4.4 Between group analyses for Segmenting nonwords post intervention data

**Table 4.63: Segmenting nonwords subtest data between groups analyses (Post-test data)**

| Groups | *n* | Mean ranks | *Chi sq* | *df* | *p* |
|--------|-----|-----------|---------|------|-----|
| Y&AA | 15 | 35.57 | | | |
| N&AA | 15 | 37.93 | 30.070 | 3 | .000* |
| C | 15 | 9.07 | | | |
| AA | 12 | 34.54 | | | |

* significant at 0.05 level

There was a statistically significant difference between the groups in segmenting nonwords in the posttest data ($x^2(2)$ = 30.57, *p*= .00) with a mean rank of 35.57 (Median= 8.00) for Y&AA group, 37.93 (Median= 8.00) for N&AA group, 9.07 (Median= 4.00) for C group and 34.54 (Median= 8.00) for AA group.

#### 4.6.4.4.A. Post-hoc analyses for Segmenting nonwords post intervention data

**Table 4. 63.A: Segmenting nonwords post intervention data Post-hoc analyses between Y&AA-N&AA**

| Groups | *n* | Mean ranks | U | *z* | *p* | Effect size |
|--------|-----|-----------|------|------|------|-------------|
| Y&AA | 15 | 14.87 | 103.00 | -.399 | .690 | -0.103 |
| N&AA | 15 | 16.13 | | | | |

Descriptive statistics showed that Y&AA group (median= 8.00; mean rank = 14.87) had equal scores as N&AA group (median= 8.00; mean rank = 16.13). Mann-Whitney U value was found to be statistically non significant U= 103.00 (z = -.39), p =0.69.

**Table 4. 63.B: Segmenting nonwords post intervention data Post-hoc analyses between Y&AA-AA**

| Groups | *n* | Mean ranks | U | *z* | *p* | Effect size |
|--------|-----|-----------|------|------|------|-------------|
| Y&AA | 15 | 14.43 | 83.50 | -.321 | .748 | -0.082 |
| AA | 12 | 13.46 | | | | |

Descriptive statistics showed that Y&AA group (median= 8.00; mean rank = 14.43) had equal scores as AA group (median= 8.00; mean rank = 13.46). Mann-Whitney U value was found to be statistically non significant U= 83.50 (z = -.32), p =0.75.

**Table 4. 63.C: Segmenting nonwords post intervention data Post-hoc analyses between Y&AA-C**

| Groups | n | Mean ranks | U | z | p | Effect size |
|--------|-----|-----------|-------|--------|-------|-------------|
| Y&AA | 15 | 22.27 | 11.00 | -4.244 | .000* | -1.096 |
| C | 15 | 8.73 | | | | |

* significant at 0.05 level

Descriptive statistics showed that Y&AA group (median= 8.00; mean rank = 22.27) had higher scores than that C group (median= 4.00; mean rank = 8.73). Mann-Whitney U value was found to be statistically significant U= 11.00 (z = -4.24), p <0.001 and the difference between Y&AA and C groups was large (r = -1.28).

**Table 4. 63.D: Segmenting nonwords post intervention data Post-hoc analyses between N&AA-AA**

| Groups | n | Mean ranks | U | z | p | Effect size |
|--------|-----|-----------|-------|--------|-------|-------------|
| N&AA | 15 | 15.13 | 73.00 | -.845 | .398 | -0.218 |
| AA | 12 | 12.58 | | | | |

Descriptive statistics showed that N&AA group (median= 8.00; mean rank = 15.13) had equal scores as AA group (median= 8.00; mean rank = 12.58). Mann-Whitney U value was found to be statistically non significant U= 73.00 (z = -.85), p =0.39.

**Table 4. 63.E: Segmenting nonwords post intervention data Post-hoc analyses between N&AA-C**

| Groups | n | Mean ranks | U | z | p | Effect size |
|--------|-----|-----------|-------|--------|-------|-------------|
| N&AA | 15 | 22.67 | 5.00 | -4.501 | .000* | -1.163 |
| C | 15 | 8.33 | | | | |

* significant at 0.05 level

Descriptive statistics showed that N&AA group (median= 8.00; mean rank = 22.67) had higher scores than that C group (median= 4.00; mean rank = 8.33). Mann-Whitney U value was found to be statistically significant U= 5.00 (z = -4.50), p <0.001 and the difference between N&AA and C groups was large (r = -1.16).

**Table 4. 63.F: Segmenting nonwords post intervention data Post-hoc analyses between AA-C**

| Groups | n | Mean ranks | U | z | p | Effect size |
|--------|-----|-----------|------|--------|-------|-------------|
| AA | 12 | 21.50 | .00 | -4.432 | .000* | -1.280 |
| C | 15 | 8.00 | | | | |

* significant at 0.05 level

Descriptive statistics showed that AA group (median= 8.00; mean rank = 21.50) had higher scores than that C group (median= 4.00; mean rank = 8.00). Mann-Whitney U value was found to be statistically significant U= .00 (z = -4.43), p <0.001 and the difference between AA and C groups was large (r = -1.28).

**4.6.4.5 Between group analysis for Segmenting nonwords follow up data**

**Table 4.64: Segmenting nonwords subtest data between groups analyses (Follow up data)**

| Groups | n | Mean ranks | Chi sq | df | p |
|--------|-----|-----------|--------|------|-------|
| Y&AA | 15 | 20.87 | | | |
| N&AA | 15 | 16.13 | 7.676 | 2 | .022* |
| C | 15 | | | | |
| AA | 12 | 29.00 | | | |

* significant at 0.05 level

There was a statistically significant difference between the groups in segmenting nonwords in the follow up data ($x^2(2)$ = 7.67, $p$= .02) with a mean rank of 20.87 (Median= 11.00) for Y&AA group, 16.13 (Median= 10.00) for N&AA group, and 29.00 (Median= 13.00) for AA group.

#### 4.6.4.5 A. Post-hoc analyses for Segmenting nonwords follow up data

**Table 4.64.A: Segmenting nonwords follow up data Post-hoc analyses between Y&AA-N&AA**

| Groups | $n$ | Mean ranks | U | $z$ | $p$ | Effect size |
|--------|-----|-----------|-------|--------|------|-------------|
| Y&AA | 15 | 17.27 | 86.00 | -1.110 | .267 | -0.286 |
| N&AA | 15 | 13.73 | | | | |

Descriptive statistics showed that Y&AA group (median= 11.00; mean rank = 17.27) had higher scores than that N&AA group (median= 10.00; mean rank = 13.57). Mann-Whitney U value was found to be statistically non significant U= 86.00 (z = -1.11), p =0.27.

**Table 4.64.B: Segmenting nonwords follow up data Post-hoc analyses between Y&AA-AA**

| Groups | $n$ | Mean ranks | U | $z$ | $p$ | Effect size |
|--------|-----|-----------|-------|--------|------|-------------|
| Y&AA | 15 | 11.60 | 54.00 | -1.867 | .062 | -0.482 |
| AA | 12 | 17.00 | | | | |

Descriptive statistics showed that Y&AA group (median= 11.00; mean rank = 11.60) had lower scores than that AA group (median= 13.00; mean rank = 17.00). Mann-Whitney U value was found to be statistically non significant U= 54.00 (z = -1.86), p =0.06.

**Table 4.64.C:Segmenting nonwords follow up data Post-hoc analyses between N&AA-AA**

| Groups | $n$ | Mean ranks | U | $z$ | $p$ | Effect size |
|--------|-----|-----------|-------|--------|-------|-------------|
| N&AA | 15 | 10.40 | 36.00 | -2.763 | .006* | -0.713 |
| AA | 12 | 18.50 | | | | |

* significant at 0.05 level

Descriptive statistics showed that N&AA group (median= 10.00; mean rank = 10.40) had lower scores than that AA group (median= 13.00; mean rank = 18.50). Mann-Whitney U value was found to be statistically significant U= 36.00 (z = -2.76), p <0.001 and the difference between N&AA and AA groups was moderate (r = -0.71).

Graph 8

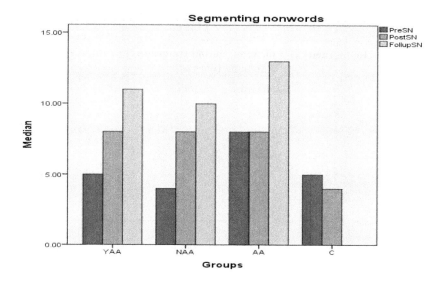

**4.6.5 Phoneme reversal**

**4.6.5.1 Homogeneity test for intervention subgroups for Phoneme reversal**

Table 4.65:  Homogeneity test for intervention subgroups pre-intervention data
Phoneme reversal

| Groups | *n* | Mean ranks | *Chi sq* | *df* | *p* |
|--------|-----|------------|----------|------|-----|
| Y&AA1 | 8 | 18.63 | | | |
| Y&AA2 | 7 | 22.86 | | | |
| N&AA1 | 7 | 17.64 | 4.83 | | |
| N&AA2 | 8 | 29.25 | | 5 | .437 |
| AA1 | 7 | 19.71 | | | |
| AA2 | 5 | 19.70 | | | |

There was no statistically significant difference (*p*=0.44) between the experimental groups carried out in two seasons in Phoneme reversal English subtest scores before the commencement of the intervention. Hence the groups Y&AA1 & Y&AA2, N&AA1 & N&AA2, AA1 & AA2 are combined respectively in further analysis

**4.6.5.2 Homogeneity test for Phoneme reversal pre-intervention data**

Table 4.66:  Homogeneity test for Phoneme reversal pre-intervention data

| Groups | *n* | Mean ranks | *Chi sq* | *df* | *p* |
|--------|-----|------------|----------|------|-----|
| Y&AA | 15 | 28.77 | | | |
| N&AA | 15 | 33.30 | 1.79 | 3 | .64 |
| C | 15 | 25.87 | | | |
| AA | 12 | 27.83 | | | |

There was no statistically significant difference (*p*=0.64) between the experimental and control groups in phoneme reversal task in english before the start of the intervention.

### 4.6.5.3 Within group analysis for Phoneme reversal

### 4.6.5.3.1 Within group analysis for Phoneme reversal Y&AA group

**Table 4.67: Descriptive statistics for Phoneme Reversal subtest data (Y&AA group)**

| Data | $n$ | Median | $M$ | $SD$ | Min | Max |
|------|-----|--------|-----|------|-----|-----|
| Pretest | 15 | 2.00 | 2.20 | 1.74 | .00 | 6.00 |
| Posttest | 15 | 9.00 | 8.93 | 2.31 | 5.00 | 14.00 |
| Follow up | 15 | 12.00 | 12.00 | .00 | 12.00 | 12.00 |

**Table 4.67.A: Pre, Post & Follow up intervention comparisons within (Y&AA) group**

| | $z$ | $p$ | Effect size |
|------|-----|-----|-------------|
| Pretest-Posttest | -3.42 | .001* | -0.883 |
| Pretest-Follow up | -3.43 | .001* | -0.886 |
| Posttest-Follow up | -3.12 | .002* | -0.806 |

* significant at 0.05 level

There was a significant increase from pretest (median= 2.00) to posttest (median= 9.00), z=-3.42, p<0.001, r= -0.88, pretest (median=2.00) to follow up (median=12.00)z=-3.43, p<0.001, r=-0.88 and posttest (median=9.00) to follow up (median=12.00) z=-3.12, p<0.001 r= -0.81 in the scores of phoneme reversal, and the increase was large. This indicates that the group has significantly improved from Y&AA intervention in their phoneme reversal skills and the improvement continued over a period of time till the follow up assessment was made.

### 4.6.5.3.2 Within group analysis for Phoneme reversal N&AA group

**Table 4.68: Descriptive statistics for Phoneme Reversal subtest data (N&AA group)**

| Data | $n$ | Median | $M$ | $SD$ | Min | Max |
|------|-----|--------|-----|------|-----|-----|
| Pretest | 15 | 2.00 | 2.77 | 1.84 | .00 | 6.00 |
| Posttest | 15 | 9.00 | 8.80 | 3.00 | 5.00 | 14.00 |
| Follow up | 15 | 12.00 | 12.00 | .00 | 12.00 | 12.00 |

### Table 4.68.A: Pre, Post & Follow up intervention comparisons within (N&AA) group

|  | z | p | Effect size |
|---|---|---|---|
| Pretest-Posttest | -3.305 | .001* | -0.854 |
| Pretest-Follow up | -3.418 | .001* | -0.883 |
| Posttest-Follow up | -2.855 | .004* | -0.737 |

* significant at 0.05 level

There was a significant increase from pretest (median= 2.00) to posttest (median= 9.00), z=-3.31, p<0.001, r= -0.85, pretest (median=2.00) to follow up (median=12.00)z=-3.42, p<0.001, r=-0.88 and posttest (median=9.00) to follow up (median=12.00) z=-2.85, p<0.001 r= -0.74 in the scores of phoneme reversal, and the increase was large. This indicates that the group has significantly improved from N&AA intervention in their phoneme reversal skills and the improvement continued over a period of time till the follow up assessment was made.

#### 4.6.5.3.3 Within group analysis for Phoneme reversal AA group

### Table 4.69: Descriptive statistics for Phoneme Reversal subtest data (AA group)

| Data | n | Median | M | SD | Min | Max |
|---|---|---|---|---|---|---|
| Pretest | 12 | 2.00 | 2.00 | 2.41 | 3.00 | 10.00 |
| Posttest | 12 | 5.50 | 6.16 | 1.78 | 5.00 | 11.00 |
| Follow up | 12 | 7.50 | 7.58 | | | |

### Table 4.69.A: Pre, Post & Follow up intervention comparisons within (AA) group

|  | z | p | Effect size |
|---|---|---|---|
| Pretest-Posttest | -3.07 | .002* | -0.887 |
| Pretest-Follow up | -3.07 | .002* | -0.887 |
| Posttest-Follow up | -2.70 | .007* | -0.780 |

* significant at 0.05 level

There was a significant increase from pretest (median= 2.00) to posttest (median= 5.50), z=-3.07, p<0.001, r= -0.88, pretest (median=2.00) to follow up

(median=5.50)z=-3.07, p<0.001, r=-0.88 and posttest (median=5.50) to follow up (median=7.50) z=-2.70, p<0.001 r= -0.78 in the scores of phoneme reversal, and the increase was large. This indicates that the group has significantly improved from AA intervention in their phoneme reversal skills and the improvement continued over a period of time till the follow up assessment was made.

### 4.6.5.3.4 Within group analysis for Phoneme reversal C group

**Table 4.70: Descriptive statistics for Phoneme Reversal subtest data (C group)**

| Data | $n$ | Median | $M$ | $SD$ | Min | Max |
|------|-----|--------|-----|------|-----|-----|
| Pretest | 15 | 2.00 | 1.80 | .94 | .00 | 3.00 |
| Posttest | 15 | 2.00 | 1.60 | .99 | .00 | 3.00 |
| Follow up | - | | | | | |

**Table 4.70.A: Pre, Post & Follow up intervention comparisons within (C) group**

| | $z$ | $p$ | Effect size |
|------|-----|-----|-------------|
| Pretest-Posttest | -.49 | .62 | -0.126 |
| Pretest-Follow up | - | - | - |
| Posttest-Follow up | - | - | - |

There was no significant difference from pretest (median= 2.00) to posttest (median= 2.00), z=-.49, p=0.62. This indicates that the control group did not improve.

### 4.6.5.4 Between group analysis for Phoneme reversal post intervention data

**Table 4.71: Phoneme reversal subtest data between groups analyses (Post-test data)**

| Groups | $n$ | Mean ranks | $Chi\ sq$ | $df$ | $p$ |
|--------|-----|------------|-----------|------|-----|
| Y&AA | 15 | 40.20 | | | |
| N&AA | 15 | 39.33 | 36.723 | 3 | .000* |
| C | 15 | 8.13 | | | |
| AA | 12 | 28.17 | | | |

* significant at 0.05 level

There was a statistically significant difference between the groups in phoneme reversal task in the posttest data ($x^2(2) = 36.72$, $p = .00$) with a mean rank of 40.20 (Median= 9.00) for Y&AA group, 39.33 (Median= 9.00) for N&AA group, 8.13 (Median= 2.00) for C group and 28.17 (Median= 5.50) for AA group.

**4.6.5.4.A. Post-hoc analyses for Phoneme reversal post intervention data**

**Table 4. 71.A: Phoneme reversal post intervention data Post-hoc analyses between Y&AA-N&AA**

| Groups | n | Mean ranks | U | z | p | Effect size |
|--------|---|-----------|-----|------|------|-------------|
| Y&AA   | 15 | 15.73 | 109.00 | -.146 | .884 | -0.037 |
| N&AA   | 15 | 15.27 | | | | |

Descriptive statistics showed that Y&AA group (median= 9.00; mean rank = 15.73) had equal scores as N&AA group (median= 9.00; mean rank = 15.27). Mann-Whitney U value was found to be statistically non significant U= 109.00 ($z = -.15$), p =0.88.

**Table 4. 71.B: Phoneme reversal post intervention data Post-hoc analyses between Y&AA-AA**

| Groups | n | Mean ranks | U | z | p | Effect size |
|--------|---|-----------|-----|------|------|-------------|
| Y&AA   | 15 | 17.47 | 38.00 | -2.561 | .010* | -0.661 |
| AA     | 12 | 9.67 | | | | |

* significant at 0.05 level

Descriptive statistics showed that Y&AA group (median= 9.00; mean rank = 17.47) had higher scores than that AA group (median= 5.50; mean rank = 9.67). Mann-Whitney U value was found to be statistically significant U= 38.00 ($z = -2.56$), p <0.001 and the difference between Y&AA and AA groups was moderate ($r = -0.66$).

**Table 4. 71.C: Phoneme reversal post intervention data Post-hoc analyses between Y&AA-C**

| Groups | n | Mean ranks | U | z | p | Effect size |
|--------|---|-----------|-----|------|------|-------------|
| Y&AA   | 15 | 23.00 | .00 | -4.721 | .000* | -1.219 |
| C      | 15 | 8.00 | | | | |

* significant at 0.05 level

Descriptive statistics showed that Y&AA group (median= 9.00; mean rank = 23.00) had higher scores than that C group (median= 2.00; mean rank = 8.00). Mann-Whitney U value was found to be statistically significant U= 00.00 (z = -4.72), p <0.001 and the difference between Y&AA and C groups was large (r = -1.23).

**Table 4. 71.D: Phoneme reversal post intervention data Post-hoc analyses between N&AA-AA**

| Groups | $n$ | Mean ranks | U | $z$ | $p$ | Effect size |
|--------|-----|-----------|-------|--------|-------|------------|
| N&AA | 15 | 17.07 | 44.00 | -2.265 | .024* | -0.585 |
| AA | 12 | 10.17 | | | | |

* significant at 0.05 level

Descriptive statistics showed that N&AA group (median= 9.00; mean rank = 17.07) had higher scores than that AA group (median= 5.50; mean rank = 10.17). Mann-Whitney U value was found to be statistically significant U= 44.00 (z = -2.26), p <0.001 and the difference between N&AA and AA groups was moderate (r = -1.58).

**Table 4. 71.E: Phoneme reversal post intervention data Post-hoc analyses between N&AA-C**

| Groups | $n$ | Mean ranks | U | $z$ | $p$ | Effect size |
|--------|-----|-----------|-----|--------|-------|------------|
| N&AA | 15 | 23.00 | .00 | -4.720 | .000* | -1.219 |
| C | 15 | 8.00 | | | | |

* significant at 0.05 level

Descriptive statistics showed that N&AA group (median= 9.00; mean rank = 23.00) had higher scores than that C group (median= 2.00; mean rank = 8.00). Mann-Whitney U value was found to be statistically significant U= 00.00 (z = -4.72), p <0.001 and the difference between N&AA and C groups was large (r = -1.23).

**Table 4. 71.F: Phoneme reversal post intervention data Post-hoc analyses between AA-C**

| Groups | $n$ | Mean ranks | U | $z$ | $p$ | Effect size |
|--------|-----|-----------|------|--------|-------|------------|
| AA | 12 | 21.33 | 2.00 | -4.364 | .000* | -1.261 |
| C | 15 | 8.13 | | | | |

* significant at 0.05 level

Descriptive statistics showed that AA group (median= 5.50; mean rank = 21.33) had higher scores than that C group (median= 2.00; mean rank = 8.13). Mann-Whitney U value was found to be statistically significant U= 2.00 (z = -4.36), p <0.001 and the difference between AA and C groups was large (r = -1.26).

**4.6.5.5 Between group analysis for Phoneme reversal follow up data**

**Table 4.72: Phoneme reversal subtest data between groups analyses (Follow up data)**

| Groups | $n$ | Mean ranks | Chi sq | df | p |
|--------|-----|-----------|--------|-----|-----|
| Y&AA | 15 | 27.50 | | | |
| N&AA | 15 | 27.50 | 39.556 | 2 | .000* |
| C | 15 | | | | |
| AA | 12 | 6.50 | | | |

* significant at 0.05 level

There was a statistically significant difference between the groups in phoneme reversal task in the posttest data ($x^2(2)$ = 39.55, $p$= .00) with a mean rank of 27.50 (Median= 12.00) for Y&AA group, 27.50 (Median= 12.00) for N&AA group, and 6.50 (Median= 7.50) for AA group.

**4.6.5.5 A. Post-hoc analyses for Phoneme reversal follow up data**

**Table 4.72.A: Phoneme reversal follow up data Post-hoc analyses between Y&AA-N&AA**

| Groups | $n$ | Mean ranks | U | $z$ | p | Effect size |
|--------|-----|-----------|--------|------|-------|-------------|
| Y&AA | 15 | 15.50 | 112.50 | .000 | 1.000 | 0 |
| N&AA | 15 | 15.50 | | | | |

Descriptive statistics showed that Y&AA group (median= 12.00; mean rank = 15.50) had equal scores as N&AA group (median= 12.00; mean rank = 15.50). Mann-Whitney U value was found to be statistically non significant U= 112.50 (z = -.00), p =1.00.

**Table 4.72.B: Phoneme reversal follow up data Post-hoc analyses between Y&AA-AA**

| Groups | $n$ | Mean ranks | U | $z$ | $p$ | Effect size |
|---|---|---|---|---|---|---|
| Y&AA | 15 | 20.00 | .00 | -4.832 | .000* | -1.248 |
| AA | 12 | 6.50 | | | | |

* significant at 0.05 level

Descriptive statistics showed that Y&AA group (median= 12.00; mean rank = 20.00) had higher scores than that AA group (median= 7.50; mean rank = 6.50). Mann-Whitney U value was found to be statistically significant U= 00.00 (z = -4.83), p <0.001 and the difference between Y&AA and AA groups was large (r = -1.25).

**Table 4.72.C: Phoneme reversal follow up data Post-hoc analyses between N&AA-AA**

| Groups | $n$ | Mean ranks | U | $z$ | $p$ | Effect size |
|---|---|---|---|---|---|---|
| N&AA | 15 | 20.00 | .00 | -4.832 | .000* | -1.248 |
| AA | 12 | 6.50 | | | | |

* significant at 0.05 level

Descriptive statistics showed that N&AA group (median= 12.00; mean rank = 20.00) had higher scores than that AA group (median= 7.50; mean rank = 6.50). Mann-Whitney U value was found to be statistically significant U= 00.00 (z = -4.83), p <0.001 and the difference between N&AA and AA groups was large (r = -1.25).

Graph 9

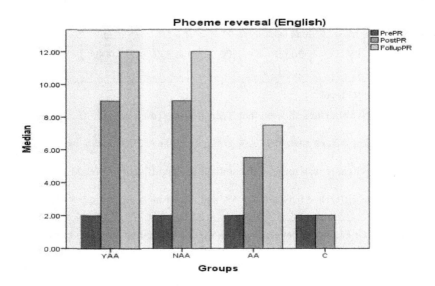

### 4.6.6 Phoneme oddity

#### 4.6.6.1 Homogeneity test for intervention subgroups for Phoneme oddity

**Table 4.73: Homogeneity test for intervention subgroups pre-intervention data Phoneme oddity**

| Groups | $n$ | Mean ranks | Chi sq | df | p |
|--------|-----|------------|--------|----|----|
| Y&AA1 | 8 | 17.88 | | | |
| Y&AA2 | 7 | 25.21 | | | |
| N&AA1 | 7 | 27.57 | 4.86 | 5 | .433 |
| N&AA2 | 8 | 19.81 | | | |
| AA1 | 7 | 18.50 | | | |
| AA2 | 5 | 20.50 | | | |

There was no statistically significant difference ($p$=0.44) between the experimental groups carried out in two seasons in Phoneme oddity subtest scores before the commencement of the intervention. Hence the groups Y&AA1 & Y&AA2, N&AA1 & N&AA2, AA1 & AA2 are combined respectively in further analysis

#### 4.6.6.2 Homogeneity test for Phoneme oddity pre-intervention data

**Table 4.74: Homogeneity test for Phoneme oddity pre-intervention data**

| Groups | $n$ | Mean ranks | Chi sq | df | p |
|--------|-----|------------|--------|----|----|
| Y&AA | 15 | 31.37 | | | |
| N&AA | 15 | 33.60 | 6.167 | 3 | .104 |
| C | 15 | 22.17 | | | |
| AA | 12 | 28.83 | | | |

There was no statistically significant difference ($p$=0.104) between the experimental and control groups in phoneme oddity task before the start of the intervention.

### 4.6.6.3 Within group analysis for Phoneme oddity

### 4.6.6.3.1 Within group analysis for Phoneme oddity Y&AA group

**Table 4.75: Descriptive statistics for Phoneme oddity subtest data (Y&AA group)**

| Data | $n$ | Median | $M$ | $SD$ | Min | Max |
|---|---|---|---|---|---|---|
| Pretest | 15 | .00 | .53 | .74 | .00 | 2.00 |
| Posttest | 15 | 3.00 | 3.00 | 1.41 | .00 | 5.00 |
| Follow up | 15 | 4.00 | 3.47 | 1.06 | 1.00 | 5.00 |

**Table 4.75.A: Pre, Post & Follow up intervention comparisons within (Y&AA) group**

| | $z$ | $p$ | Effect size |
|---|---|---|---|
| Pretest-Posttest | -3.324 | .001* | -0.858 |
| Pretest-Follow up | -3.426 | .001* | -0.885 |
| Posttest-Follow up | -1.811 | .070 | -0.467 |

* significant at 0.05 level

There was a significant increase from pretest (median= .00) to posttest (median= 3.00), z=-3.32, p<0.001, r= -0.86, pretest (median=.00) to follow up (median=4.00)z=-3.43, p<0.001, r=-0.88 in the scores of behavioral adjustment, and the decrease was large but not in posttest (median=3.00) to follow up (median=4.00) z=-1.81, p=0.07. This indicates that the group has significantly improved from Y&AA intervention in phoneme oddity task.

### 4.6.6.3.2 Within group analysis for Phoneme oddity N&AA group

**Table 4.76: Descriptive statistics for Phoneme oddity subtest data (N&AA group)**

| Data | $n$ | Median | $M$ | $SD$ | Min | Max |
|---|---|---|---|---|---|---|
| Pretest | 15 | .00 | 1.00 | 1.36 | .00 | 3.00 |
| Posttest | 15 | 1.00 | 1.53 | 1.29 | .00 | 4.00 |
| Follow up | 15 | 2.00 | 1.73 | 1.22 | .00 | 4.00 |

**Table 4.76.A: Pre, Post & Follow up intervention comparisons within (N&AA) group**

|  | $z$ | $p$ | Effect size |
|---|---|---|---|
| Pretest-Posttest | -1.153 | .249 | -0.297 |
| Pretest-Follow up | -1.489 | .136 | -0.384 |
| Posttest-Follow up | -1.732 | .083 | -0.447 |

There was no significant increase from pretest (median= .00) to posttest (median= 1.00), z=-1.15, p=0.25, pretest (median=.00) to follow up (median=2.00)z=-1.48, p=0.13, posttest (median=1.00) to follow up (median=2.00) z=-1.73, p=0.08 in the scores of phoneme oddity task. This indicates that the group has snot improved from N&AA intervention in phoneme oddity task.

**4.6.6.3.3 Within group analysis for Phoneme oddity AA group**

**Table 4.77: Descriptive statistics for Phoneme oddity subtest data (AA group)**

| Data | $n$ | Median | $M$ | $SD$ | Min | Max |
|---|---|---|---|---|---|---|
| Pretest | 12 | .00 | .33 | .49 | .00 | 1.00 |
| Posttest | 12 | 1.00 | .83 | .72 | .00 | 2.00 |
| Follow up | 12 | 1.00 | .92 | .77 | .00 | 2.00 |

**Table 4.77.A: Pre, Post & Follow up intervention comparisons within (AA) group**

|  | $z$ | $p$ | Effect size |
|---|---|---|---|
| Pretest-Posttest | -1.897 | .058 | -0.548 |
| Pretest-Follow up | -2.111 | .035* | -0.610 |
| Posttest-Follow up | -1.000 | .317 | -0.289 |

* significant at 0.05 level

There was a significant increase from pretest (median=.00) to follow up (median=1.00)z=-2.11, p<0.001, r=-0.61 but not in pretest (median= .00) to posttest (median= 1.00), z=-1.89, p=0.55, posttest (median=1.00) to follow up (median=1.00) z=-1.00, p=0.32.

#### 4.6.6.3.4 Within group analysis for Phoneme oddity C group

##### Table 4.78: Descriptive statistics for Phoneme oddity subtest data (C group)

| Data | $n$ | Median | $M$ | $SD$ | Min | Max |
|---|---|---|---|---|---|---|
| Pretest | 15 | .00 | .07 | .26 | .00 | 1.00 |
| Posttest | 15 | .00 | .57 | .92 | .00 | 3.00 |
| Follow up | - | | | | | |

##### Table 4.78.A: Pre, Post & Follow up intervention comparisons within (C) group

| | $z$ | $p$ | Effect size |
|---|---|---|---|
| Pretest-Posttest | -1.511 | .131 | -0.390 |

There was no significant increase from pretest (median= .00) to posttest (median= .00), z=-1.51, p=0.13 in the scores of phoneme oddity task. This indicates that the group has not improved in control condition in phoneme oddity task.

#### 4.6.6.4 Between group analysis for Phoneme oddity post intervention data

##### Table 4.79: Phoneme oddity subtest data between groups analyses (Post-test data)

| Groups | $n$ | Mean ranks | Chi sq | $df$ | $p$ |
|---|---|---|---|---|---|
| Y&AA | 15 | 44.33 | | | |
| N&AA | 15 | 30.90 | 24.437 | 3 | .000* |
| C | 15 | 16.57 | | | |
| AA | 12 | 23.00 | | | |

* significant at 0.05 level

There was a statistically significant difference between the groups in phoneme oddity task in the posttest data ($x^2(2) = 24.43$, $p= .00$) with a mean rank of 44.33 (Median= 4.00) for Y&AA group, 30.90 (Median= 1.00) for N&AA group, 16.57 (Median= .00) for C group and 23.00 (Median= 1.00) for AA group.

#### 4.6.6.4.A. Post-hoc analyses for Phoneme oddity post intervention data

**Table 4. 79.A: Phoneme oddity post intervention data Post-hoc analyses between Y&AA-N&AA**

| Groups | n | Mean ranks | U | z | p | Effect size |
|--------|---|-----------|-----|------|------|------------|
| Y&AA | 15 | 19.80 | 48.00 | -2.723 | .006* | -0.703 |
| N&AA | 15 | 11.20 | | | | |

* significant at 0.05 level

Descriptive statistics showed that Y&AA group (median= 3.00; mean rank = 19.80) had higher scores than that N&AA group (median= 1.00; mean rank = 11.20). Mann-Whitney U value was found to be statistically significant U= 48.00 (z = -2.72), p <0.001 and the difference between Y&AA and N&AA groups was large (r = -0.70).

**Table 4. 79.B: Phoneme oddity post intervention data Post-hoc analyses between Y&AA-AA**

| Groups | n | Mean ranks | U | z | p | Effect size |
|--------|---|-----------|-----|------|------|------------|
| Y&AA | 15 | 18.80 | 18.00 | -3.578 | .000* | -0.924 |
| AA | 12 | 8.00 | | | | |

* significant at 0.05 level

Descriptive statistics showed that Y&AA group (median= 3.00; mean rank = 18.80) had higher scores than that AA group (median= 1.00; mean rank = 8.00). Mann-Whitney U value was found to be statistically significant U= 18.00 (z = -3.58), p <0.001 and the difference between Y&AA and AA groups was large (r = -0.92).

**Table 4. 79.C: Phoneme oddity post intervention data Post-hoc analyses between Y&AA-C**

| Groups | n | Mean ranks | U | z | p | Effect size |
|--------|---|-----------|-----|------|------|------------|
| Y&AA | 15 | 21.73 | 19.00 | -4.029 | .000* | -1.041 |
| C | 15 | 9.27 | | | | |

* significant at 0.05 level

Descriptive statistics showed that Y&AA group (median= 3.00; mean rank = 21.73) had higher scores than that C group (median= 1.00; mean rank = 9.27). Mann-Whitney U value was found to be statistically significant U= 19.00 (z = -4.03), p <0.001 and the difference between Y&AA and C groups was large (r = -1.04).

**Table 4.79.D: Phoneme oddity post intervention data Post-hoc analyses between N&AA-AA**

| Groups | $n$ | Mean ranks | U | $z$ | $p$ | Effect size |
|---|---|---|---|---|---|---|
| N&AA | 15 | 16.07 | 59.00 | -1.590 | .112 | -0.410 |
| AA | 12 | 11.42 | | | | |

Descriptive statistics showed that N&AA group (median= 1.00; mean rank = 16.07) had equal scores as AA group (median= 1.00; mean rank = 11.42). Mann-Whitney U value was found to be statistically non significant U= 59.00 (z = -1.59), p =0.11.

**Table 4. 79.E:Phoneme oddity post intervention data Post-hoc analyses between N&AA-C**

| Groups | $n$ | Mean ranks | U | $z$ | $p$ | Effect size |
|---|---|---|---|---|---|---|
| N&AA | 15 | 19.63 | 50.00 | -2.740 | .006* | -0.708 |
| C | 15 | 11.37 | | | | |

* significant at 0.05 level

Descriptive statistics showed that N&AA group (median= 1.00; mean rank = 19.63) had higher scores than that C group (median= .00; mean rank = 11.37). Mann-Whitney U value was found to be statistically significant U= 50.00 (z = -2.74), p <0.001 and the difference between N&AA and C groups was moderate (r = -0.71).

**Table 4. 79.F: Phoneme oddity post intervention data Post-hoc analyses between AA-C**

| Groups | $n$ | Mean ranks | U | $z$ | $p$ | Effect size |
|---|---|---|---|---|---|---|
| AA | 12 | 16.58 | 59.00 | -1.689 | .091 | -0.488 |
| C | 15 | 11.93 | | | | |

Descriptive statistics showed that AA group (median= 1.00; mean rank = 16.58) had higher scores than that C group (median= .00; mean rank = 11.93). Mann-Whitney U value was found to be statistically non significant U= 59.00 (z = -1.68), p =0.09

#### 4.6.6.5 Between group analysis for Phoneme oddity follow up data

**Table 4.80: Phoneme oddity subtest data between groups analyses (Follow up data)**

| Groups | $n$ | Mean ranks | Chi sq | df | p |
|--------|-----|------------|--------|-----|------|
| Y&AA   | 15  | 32.27      |        |     |      |
| N&AA   | 15  | 18.73      | 21.305 | 2   | .000* |
| C      | 15  |            |        |     |      |
| AA     | 12  | 11.50      |        |     |      |

* significant at 0.05 level

There was a statistically significant difference between the groups in phoneme oddity task in the follow up data ($x^2(2)$ = 21.31, $p$= .00) with a mean rank of 32.27 (Median= 4.00) for Y&AA group, 18.73 (Median= 2.00) for N&AA group, and 11.50 (Median= 1.00) for AA group.

#### 4.6.6.5 A. Post-hoc analyses for Phoneme oddity follow up data

**Table 4.81.A: Phoneme oddity follow up data Post-hoc analyses between Y&AA-N&AA**

| Groups | $n$ | Mean ranks | U | $z$ | p | Effect size |
|--------|-----|------------|------|--------|-------|-------------|
| Y&AA   | 15  | 20.70      | 34.50 | -3.306 | .001* | -0.854      |
| N&AA   | 15  | 10.30      |      |        |       |             |

* significant at 0.05 level

Descriptive statistics showed that Y&AA group (median= 4.00; mean rank = 20.70) had higher scores than that N&AA group (median= 2.00; mean rank = 10.30). Mann-Whitney U value was found to be statistically significant U= 34.50 (z = -3.31), p <0.001 and the difference between Y&AA and N&AA groups was large (r = -0.85).

**Table 4.81.B: Phoneme oddity follow up data Post-hoc analyses between Y&AA-AA**

| Groups | $n$ | Mean ranks | U | $z$ | p | Effect size |
|--------|-----|------------|------|--------|-------|-------------|
| Y&AA   | 15  | 19.57      | 6.50 | -4.170 | .000* | -1.077      |
| AA     | 12  | 7.04       |      |        |       |             |

* significant at 0.05 level

Descriptive statistics showed that Y&AA group (median= 4.00; mean rank = 19.57) had higher scores than that AA group (median= 1.00; mean rank = 7.04). Mann-Whitney U value was found to be statistically significant U= 6.50 (z = -4.17), p <0.001 and the difference between Y&AA and AA groups was large (r = -1.07).

**Table 4.81.C: Phoneme oddity follow up data Post-hoc analyses between N&AA-AA**

| Groups | n | Mean ranks | U | z | p | Effect size |
|--------|----|-----------|-------|--------|------|-------------|
| N&AA | 15 | 16.43 | 53.50 | -1.889 | .059 | -0.488 |
| AA | 12 | 10.96 | | | | |

Descriptive statistics showed that N&AA group (median= 2.00; mean rank = 16.43) had higher scores than that AA group (median= 1.00; mean rank = 10.96). Mann-Whitney U value was found to be statistically non significant U= 53.50 (z = -1.88), p =0.06

Graph 10

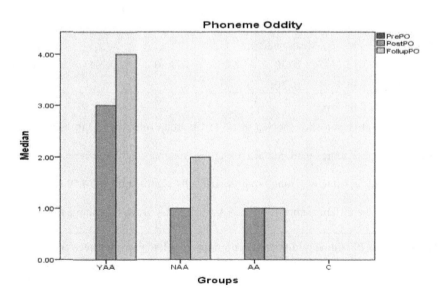

### 4.6.7 Phoneme deletion

#### 4.6.7.1 Homogeneity test for intervention subgroups for Phoneme deletion

Table 4.82: Homogeneity test for intervention subgroups pre-intervention data Phoneme deletion

| Groups | $n$ | Mean ranks | Chi sq | df | p |
|--------|-----|------------|--------|----|----|
| Y&AA1 | 8 | 16.60 | | | |
| Y&AA2 | 7 | 24.57 | | | |
| N&AA1 | 7 | 24.57 | 4.18 | | |
| N&AA2 | 8 | 22.50 | | | .52 |
| AA1 | 7 | 18.71 | | 5 | |
| AA2 | 5 | 23.90 | | | |

There was no statistically significant difference ($p$=0.52) between the experimental groups carried out in two seasons in Phoneme deletion subtest scores before the commencement of the intervention. Hence the groups Y&AA1 & Y&AA2, N&AA1 & N&AA2, AA1 & AA2 are combined respectively in further analysis

#### 4.6.7.2 Homogeneity test for Phoneme deletion pre-intervention data

Table 4.83: Homogeneity test for Phoneme deletion pre-intervention data

| Groups | $n$ | Mean ranks | Chi sq | df | p |
|--------|-----|------------|--------|----|----|
| Y&AA | 15 | 28.53 | | | |
| N&AA | 15 | 33.00 | 3.048 | 3 | .384 |
| C | 15 | 24.60 | | | |
| AA | 12 | 30.08 | | | |

There was no statistically significant difference ($p$=0.38) between the experimental and control groups in phoneme deletion before the start of the intervention.

### 4.6.7.3 Within group analysis for Phoneme deletion

### 4.6.7.3.1 Within group analysis for Phoneme deletion Y&AA group

**Table 4.84: Descriptive statistics for Phoneme deletion subtest data (Y&AA group)**

| Data | *n* | Median | *M* | *SD* | Min | Max |
|------|-----|--------|-----|------|-----|-----|
| Pretest | 15 | .00 | .77 | 1.29 | .00 | 4.00 |
| Posttest | 15 | 5.00 | 5.93 | 2.29 | 3.00 | 10.00 |
| Follow up | 15 | 6.00 | 6.77 | 2.059 | 4.00 | 12.00 |

**Table 4.84.A: Pre, Post & Follow up intervention comparisons within (Y&AA) group**

| | *z* | *p* | Effect size |
|------|-----|-----|-------------|
| Pretest-Posttest | -3.417 | .001* | -0.882 |
| Pretest-Follow up | -3.426 | .001* | -0.885 |
| Posttest-Follow up | -2.114 | .034* | -0.546 |

* significant at 0.05 level

There was a significant increase from pretest (median= .00) to posttest (median= 5.00), z=-3.42, p<0.001, r= -0.88, pretest (median=.00) to follow up (median=6.00)z=-3.43, p<0.001, r=-0.88 and posttest (median=5.00) to follow up (median=6.00) z=-2.11, p<0.001 r= -0.55 in phoneme deletion task, and the increase was medium to large. This indicates that the group has significantly improved from Y&AA intervention in phoneme deletion task and the improvement continued over a period of time till the follow up assessment was made.

### 4.6.7.3.2 Within group analysis for Phoneme deletion N&AA group

**Table 4.85: Descriptive statistics for Phoneme deletion subtest data (N&AA group)**

| Data | *n* | Median | *M* | *SD* | Min | Max |
|------|-----|--------|-----|------|-----|-----|
| Pretest | 15 | .00 | 1.17 | 1.44 | .00 | 4.00 |
| Posttest | 15 | 1.00 | 1.00 | 1.17 | .00 | 3.00 |
| Follow up | 15 | 1.00 | 1.13 | 1.06 | .00 | 3.00 |

**Table 4.85.A: Pre, Post & Follow up intervention comparisons within (N&AA) group**

|  | $z$ | $p$ | Effect size |
|---|---|---|---|
| Pretest-Posttest | -.105 | .917 | -0.027 |
| Pretest-Follow up | -.367 | .713 | -0.094 |
| Posttest-Follow up | -1.414 | .157 | -0.365 |

There was no significant increase from pretest (median= .00) to posttest (median= 1.00), z=-.105, p=0.92, pretest (median=.00) to follow up (median=1.00)z=-.37, p=0.71 and posttest (median=1.00) to follow up (median=1.00) z=-1.41, p=0.16 in phoneme deletion task. This indicates that the group has not improved from N&AA intervention in phoneme deletion task.

**4.6.7.3.3 Within group analysis for Phoneme deletion AA group**

**Table 4.86: Descriptive statistics for Phoneme deletion subtest data (AA group)**

| Data | $n$ | Median | $M$ | $SD$ | Min | Max |
|---|---|---|---|---|---|---|
| Pretest | 12 | .00 | .42 | .51 | .00 | 1.00 |
| Posttest | 12 | 1.50 | 1.50 | 1.27 | .00 | 3.00 |
| Follow up | 12 | 1.50 | 1.77 | .98 | .00 | 3.00 |

**Table 4.86.A: Pre, Post & Follow up intervention comparisons within (AA) group**

|  | $z$ | $p$ | Effect size |
|---|---|---|---|
| Pretest-Posttest | -2.392 | .017* | -0.691 |
| Pretest-Follow up | -2.719 | .007* | -0.785 |
| Posttest-Follow up | -1.414 | .157 | -0.408 |

* significant at 0.05 level

There was a significant increase from pretest (median= .00) to posttest (median= 1.50), z=-2.39, p<0.001, r= -0.69, pretest (median=.00) to follow up (median=1.50)z=-2.72, p<0.001, r=-0.88 in phoneme deletion task, and the increase was medium. But no significant difference in posttest (median=1.50) to follow up (median=1.50) z=-1.41, p=0.16 This indicates that the group has significantly improved from AA intervention in phoneme deletion task.

#### 4.6.7.3.4 Within group analysis for Phoneme deletion C group

**Table 4.87: Descriptive statistics for Phoneme deletion subtest data (C group)**

| Data | *n* | Median | *M* | *SD* | Min | Max |
|------|-----|--------|-----|------|-----|-----|
| Pretest | 15 | .00 | .33 | .91 | .00 | 3.00 |
| Posttest | 15 | 1.00 | .97 | .83 | .00 | 2.00 |
| Follow up | - | | | | | |

**Table 4.87.A: Pre, Post & Follow up intervention comparisons within (C) group**

| | *z* | *p* | Effect size |
|--|-----|-----|-------------|
| Pretest-Posttest | -1.628 | .103 | -0.420 |

There was no significant increase from pretest (median= .00) to posttest (median= 1.00), z=-1.63, p=0.10, in phoneme deletion task. This indicates that the group has not improved in control group in phoneme deletion task.

#### 4.6.7.4 Between group analysis for Phoneme deletion post intervention data

**Table 4.88: Phoneme deletion subtest data between groups analyses (Post-test data)**

| Groups | *n* | Mean ranks | *Chi sq* | *df* | *p* |
|--------|-----|-----------|----------|------|-----|
| Y&AA | 15 | 49.83 | | | |
| N&AA | 15 | 20.33 | 34.457 | 3 | .000* |
| C | 15 | 19.33 | | | |
| AA | 12 | 25.88 | | | |

* significant at 0.05 level

There was a statistically significant difference between the groups in phoneme deletion task in the posttest data ($x^2(2)$ = 34.46, *p*= .00) with a mean rank of 49.83 (Median= 5.00) for Y&AAgroup, 20.33 (Median= 1.00) for N&AA group, 19.33 (Median= 1.00) for C group and 25.88 (Median= 1.50) for AA group.

141

### 4.6.7.4.A. Post-hoc analyses for Phoneme deletion post intervention data

**Table 4.88.A: Phoneme deletion post intervention data Post-hoc analyses between Y&AA-N&AA**

| Groups | $n$ | Mean ranks | U | $z$ | $p$ | Effect size |
|--------|-----|-----------|------|--------|-------|-------------|
| Y&AA | 15 | 22.93 | 1.00 | -4.664 | .000* | -1.205 |
| N&AA | 15 | 8.07 | | | | |

* significant at 0.05 level

Descriptive statistics showed that Y&AA group (median= 5.00; mean rank = 22.93) had higher scores than that N&AA group (median= 1.00; mean rank = 8.07). Mann-Whitney U value was found to be statistically significant U= 1.00 ($z$ = -4.66), p <0.001 and the difference between Y&AA and N&AA groups was large ($r$ = -1.21).

**Table 4.88.B: Phoneme deletion post intervention data Post-hoc analyses between Y&AA-AA**

| Groups | $n$ | Mean ranks | U | $z$ | $p$ | Effect size |
|--------|-----|-----------|------|--------|-------|-------------|
| Y&AA | 15 | 19.90 | 1.50 | -4.344 | .000* | -1.122 |
| AA | 12 | 6.63 | | | | |

* significant at 0.05 level

Descriptive statistics showed that Y&AA group (median= 5.00; mean rank = 19.90) had higher scores than that AA group (median= 1.50; mean rank = 6.63). Mann-Whitney U value was found to be statistically significant U= 1.50 ($z$ = -4.34), p <0.001 and the difference between Y&AA and N&AA groups was large ($r$ = -1.12).

**Table 4. 88.C: Phoneme deletion post intervention data Post-hoc analyses between Y&AA-C**

| Groups | $n$ | Mean ranks | U | $z$ | $p$ | Effect size |
|--------|-----|-----------|------|--------|-------|-------------|
| Y&AA | 15 | 23.00 | .00 | -4.709 | .000* | -1.216 |
| C | 15 | 8.00 | | | | |

* significant at 0.05 level

Descriptive statistics showed that Y&AA group (median= 5.00; mean rank = 23.00) had higher scores than that C group (median= 1.00; mean rank = 8.00). Mann-

Whitney U value was found to be statistically significant U= .00 (z = -4.71), p <0.001 and the difference between Y&AA and C groups was large (r = -1.22).

**Table 4. 88.D: Phoneme deletion post intervention data Post-hoc analyses between N&AA-AA**

| Groups | n | Mean ranks | U | z | p | Effect size |
|--------|-----|-----------|-------|--------|------|------------|
| N&AA | 15 | 12.50 | 67.50 | -1.141 | .254 | -0.294 |
| AA | 12 | 15.88 | | | | |

Descriptive statistics showed that N&AA group (median= 1.00; mean rank = 12.50) had lower scores than that AA group (median= 1.50; mean rank = 15.88). Mann-Whitney U value was found to be statistically non significant U= 67.00 (z = -1.14), p =0.25.

**Table 4. 88.E: Phoneme deletion post intervention data Post-hoc analyses between N&AA-C**

| Groups | n | Mean ranks | U | z | p | Effect size |
|--------|-----|-----------|--------|--------|------|------------|
| N&AA | 15 | 15.77 | 108.50 | -.176 | .861 | -0.045 |
| C | 15 | 15.23 | | | | |

Descriptive statistics showed that N&AA group (median= 1.00; mean rank = 15.77) had same scores as C group (median= 1.00; mean rank = 15.23). Mann-Whitney U value was found to be statistically significant U= 108.50 (z = -.18), p =0.86.

**Table 4. 88.F: Phoneme deletion post intervention data Post-hoc analyses between AA-C**

| Groups | n | Mean ranks | U | z | p | Effect size |
|--------|-----|-----------|-------|--------|------|------------|
| AA | 12 | 16.38 | 61.50 | -1.450 | .147 | -0.419 |
| C | 15 | 12.10 | | | | |

Descriptive statistics showed that AA group (median= 1.50; mean rank = 16.38) had higher scores than that C group (median= 1.00; mean rank = 12.10). Mann-Whitney U value was found to be statistically non significant U= 61.50 (z = -1.45), p =0.15.

#### 4.6.7.5 Between group analysis for Phoneme deletion follow up data

**Table 4.89: Phoneme deletion subtest data between groups analyses (Follow up data)**

| Groups | $n$ | Mean ranks | Chi sq | df | $p$ |
|--------|-----|------------|--------|-----|-----|
| Y&AA | 15 | 35.00 | | | |
| N&AA | 15 | 12.23 | 29.635 | 2 | .000* |
| C | 15 | | | | |
| AA | 12 | 16.21 | | | |

* significant at 0.05 level

There was a statistically significant difference between the groups in phoneme deletion task in the posttest data ($x^2(2)$ = 29.64, $p$= .00) with a mean rank of 35.00 (Median= 6.00) for Y&AA group, 12.23 (Median= 1.00) for N&AA group, and 16.21 (Median= 1.50) for AA group.

#### 4.6.7.5 A. Post-hoc analyses for Phoneme deletion follow up data

**Table 4.89.A: Phoneme deletion follow up data Post-hoc analyses between Y&AA-N&AA**

| Groups | $n$ | Mean ranks | U | $z$ | $p$ | Effect size |
|--------|-----|------------|-----|-----|-----|-------------|
| Y&AA | 15 | 23.00 | .00 | -4.705 | .000* | -1.215 |
| N&AA | 15 | 8.00 | | | | |

* significant at 0.05 level

Descriptive statistics showed that Y&AA group (median= 6.00; mean rank = 23.00) had higher scores than that N&AA group (median= 1.00; mean rank = 8.00). Mann-Whitney U value was found to be statistically significant U= .00 (z = -4.71), p <0.001 and the difference between Y&AA and N&AA groups was large (r = -1.21).

**Table 4.89.B: Phoneme deletion follow up data Post-hoc analyses between Y&AA-AA**

| Groups | $n$ | Mean ranks | U | $z$ | $p$ | Effect size |
|--------|-----|------------|-----|-----|-----|-------------|
| Y&AA | 15 | 20.00 | .00 | -4.430 | .000* | -1.144 |
| AA | 12 | 6.50 | | | | |

* significant at 0.05 level

Descriptive statistics showed that Y&AA group (median= 6.00; mean rank = 20.00) had higher scores than that AA group (median= 1.50; mean rank = 6.50). Mann-Whitney U value was found to be statistically significant U= .00 (z = -4.43), p <0.001 and the difference between Y&AA and AA groups was large (r = -1.14).

**Table 4.89.C: Phoneme deletion follow up data Post-hoc analyses between N&AA-AA**

| Groups | n | Mean ranks | U | z | p | Effect size |
|--------|-----|-----------|-------|--------|------|-------------|
| N&AA | 15 | 12.23 | 63.50 | -1.347 | .178 | -0.348 |
| AA | 12 | 16.21 | | | | |

Descriptive statistics showed that N&AA group (median= 1.00; mean rank = 12.23) had lower scores than that AA group (median= 1.50; mean rank = 16.21). Mann-Whitney U value was found to be non statistically significant U= 63.50 (z = -1.35), p =0.18.

Graph 11

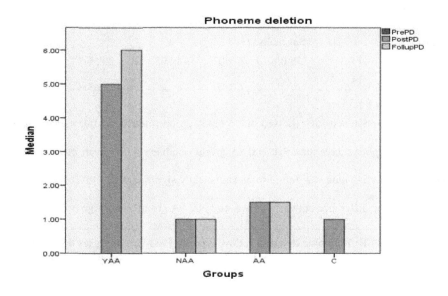

145

### 4.6.8 Spoonerism

### 4.6.8.1 Homogeneity test for intervention subgroups for Spoonerism

**Table4.90:Homogeneity test for intervention subgroups pre-intervention data Spoonerism**

| Groups | $n$ | Mean ranks | Chi sq | df | p |
|--------|-----|------------|--------|-----|-----|
| Y&AA1 | 8 | 18.50 | | | |
| Y&AA2 | 7 | 25.07 | | | |
| N&AA1 | 7 | 21.36 | 6.31 | 5 | .276 |
| N&AA2 | 8 | 21.00 | | | |
| AA1 | 7 | 18.50 | | | |
| AA2 | 5 | 26.50 | | | |

There was no statistically significant difference ($p=0.28$) between the experimental groups carried out in two seasons in spoonerism subtest scores before the commencement of the intervention. Hence the groups Y&AA1 & Y&AA2, N&AA1 & N&AA2, AA1 & AA2 are combined respectively in further analysis

### 4.6.8.2 Homogeneity test for Spoonerism pre-intervention data

**Table 4.91: Homogeneity test for Spoonerism pre-intervention data**

| Groups | $n$ | Mean ranks | Chi sq | df | p |
|--------|-----|------------|--------|-----|-----|
| Y&AA | 15 | 28.77 | | | |
| N&AA | 15 | 28.03 | .352 | 3 | .950 |
| C | 15 | 30.27 | | | |
| AA | 12 | 28.92 | | | |

There was no statistically significant difference ($p=0.95$) between the experimental and control groups in spoonerism before the start of the intervention.

### 4.6.8.3 Within group analysis for Spoonerism

#### 4.6.8.3.1 Within group analysis for Spoonerism Y&AA group

**Table 4.92: Descriptive statistics for Spoonerism subtest data (Y&AA group)**

| Data | $n$ | Median | $M$ | $SD$ | Min | Max |
|------|-----|--------|-----|------|-----|-----|
| Pretest | 15 | .00 | .45 | 1.25 | .00 | 4.00 |
| Posttest | 15 | 5.00 | 5.17 | 1.59 | 3.00 | 8.00 |
| Follow up | 15 | 6.00 | 5.80 | 1.37 | 4.00 | 9.00 |

**Table 4.92.A: Pre, Post & Follow up intervention comparisons within (Y&AA) group**

| | $z$ | $p$ | Effect size |
|---|---|---|---|
| Pretest-Posttest | -3.309 | .001* | -0.855 |
| Pretest-Follow up | -3.320 | .001* | -0.857 |
| Posttest-Follow up | -2.021 | .043* | -0.522 |

\* significant at 0.05 level

There was a significant increase from pretest (median= .00) to posttest (median= 5.00), $z$=-3.31, $p$<0.001, $r$= -0.86, pretest (median=.00) to follow up (median=6.00)$z$=-3.32, $p$<0.001, $r$=-0.86 and posttest (median=5.00) to follow up (median=6.00) $z$=-2.02, $p$<0.001 $r$= -0.52 in the scores of spoonerism, and the increase was large. This indicates that the group has significantly improved from Y&AA intervention spoonerism and the improvement continued over a period of time till the follow up assessment was made.

#### 4.6.8.3.2 Within group analysis for Spoonerism N&AA group

**Table 4.93: Descriptive statistics for Spoonerism subtest data (N&AA group)**

| Data | $n$ | Median | $M$ | $SD$ | Min | Max |
|------|-----|--------|-----|------|-----|-----|
| Pretest | 15 | .00 | .13 | .35 | .00 | 1.00 |
| Posttest | 15 | .00 | .80 | 1.01 | .00 | 3.00 |
| Follow up | 15 | 1.00 | .93 | 1.11 | .00 | 3.00 |

**Table 4.93.A: Pre, Post & Follow up intervention comparisons within (N&AA) group**

| | z | p | Effect size |
|---|---|---|---|
| Pretest-Posttest | -2.058 | .040* | -0.531 |
| Pretest-Follow up | -2.203 | .028* | -0.569 |
| Posttest-Follow up | -1.414 | .157 | -0.365 |

* significant at 0.05 level

There was a significant increase from pretest (median= .00) to posttest (median= .00), z=-2.05, p<0.001, r= -0.53, pretest (median=.00) to follow up (median=1.00)z=-2.20, p<0.001, r=-0.56 in the scores of spoonerism, and the increase was large and there was no significant improvement in posttest (median=.00) to follow up (median=1.00) z=-1.41, p=0.16. This indicates that the group has significantly improved from N&AA intervention spoonerism.

### 4.6.8.3.3 Within group analysis for Spoonerism AA group

**Table 4.94: Descriptive statistics for Spoonerism subtest data (AA group)**

| Data | n | Median | M | SD | Min | Max |
|---|---|---|---|---|---|---|
| Pretest | 12 | .00 | .27 | .49 | .00 | 1.00 |
| Posttest | 12 | 1.00 | .92 | .77 | .00 | 2.00 |
| Follow up | 12 | 1.00 | 1.08 | .67 | .00 | 2.00 |

**Table 4.94.A: Pre, Post & Follow up intervention comparisons within (AA) group**

| | z | p | Effect size |
|---|---|---|---|
| Pretest-Posttest | -2.460 | .014* | -0.710 |
| Pretest-Follow up | -2.598 | .009* | -0.750 |
| Posttest-Follow up | -1.414 | .157 | -0.408 |

* significant at 0.05 level

There was a significant increase from pretest (median= .00) to posttest (median= 1.00), z=-2.46, p<0.001, r= -0.71, pretest (median=1.00) to follow up (median=1.00)z=-2.59, p<0.001, r=-0.75 in the scores of spoonerism, and the increase was large and there was no significant improvement in posttest (median=1.00) to follow up (median=1.00) z=-1.41, p=0.16. This indicates that the group has significantly improved from AA intervention spoonerism.

#### 4.6.8.3.4 Within group analysis for Spoonerism C group

**Table 4.95: Descriptive statistics for Spoonerism subtest data (C group)**

| Data | $n$ | Median | $M$ | $SD$ | Min | Max |
|---|---|---|---|---|---|---|
| Pretest | 15 | .00 | .33 | .72 | .00 | 2.00 |
| Posttest | 15 | .00 | .77 | .98 | .00 | 3.00 |
| Follow up | - | | | | | |

**Table 4.95.A: Pre, Post & Follow up intervention comparisons within (C) group**

| | $z$ | $p$ | Effect size |
|---|---|---|---|
| Pretest-Posttest | -.844 | .399 | -0.218 |

There was no significant increase from pretest (median= .00) to posttest (median= .00), z=-.84, p=.39. This indicates that the group has not improved in control group.

#### 4.6.8.4 Between group analyses for Spoonerism post intervention data

**Table 4.96: Spoonerism subtest data between groups analyses (Post-test data)**

| Groups | $n$ | Mean ranks | $Chi\ sq$ | $df$ | $p$ |
|---|---|---|---|---|---|
| Y&AA | 15 | 49.80 | | | |
| N&AA | 15 | 21.27 | 34.600 | 3 | .000* |
| C | 15 | 19.50 | | | |
| AA | 12 | 24.54 | | | |

* significant at 0.05 level

There was a statistically significant difference between the groups in spoonerism in the posttest data ($x^2(2) = 34.60$, $p= .00$) with a mean rank of 49.80 (Median= 5.00) for Y&AA group, 21.27 (Median= .00) for N&AA group, 19.50 (Median= .00) for C group and 24.54 (Median= 1.00) for AA group.

#### 4.6.8.4.A. Post-hoc analyses for Spoonerism post intervention data

**Table 4. 96.A: Spoonerism post intervention data Post-hoc analyses between Y&AA-N&AA**

| Groups | n | Mean ranks | U | z | p | Effect size |
|--------|----|-----------|------|--------|-------|-----------|
| Y&AA | 15 | 22.90 | 1.50 | -4.668 | .000* | -1.206 |
| N&AA | 15 | 8.10 | | | | |

* significant at 0.05 level

Descriptive statistics showed that Y&AA group (median= 5.00; mean rank = 22.90) had higher scores than that N&AA group (median= .00; mean rank = 8.10). Mann-Whitney U value was found to be statistically significant U= 1.50 ($z$ = -4.66), p <0.001 and the difference between Y&AA and N&AA groups was moderate ($r$ = -1.26).

**Table 4. 96.B: Spoonerism post intervention data Post-hoc analyses between Y&AA-AA**

| Groups | n | Mean ranks | U | z | p | Effect size |
|--------|----|-----------|------|--------|-------|-----------|
| Y&AA | 15 | 20.00 | .00 | -4.450 | .000* | -1.149 |
| AA | 12 | 6.50 | | | | |

* significant at 0.05 level

Descriptive statistics showed that Y&AA group (median= 5.00; mean rank = 20.00) had higher scores than that AA group (median= 1.00; mean rank = 6.50). Mann-Whitney U value was found to be statistically significant U= .00 ($z$ = -4.45), p <0.001 and the difference between Y&AA and AA groups was moderate ($r$ = -1.15).

**Table 4. 96.C: Spoonerism post intervention data Post-hoc analyses between Y&AA-C**

| Groups | n | Mean ranks | U | z | p | Effect size |
|--------|----|-----------|------|--------|-------|-----------|
| Y&AA | 15 | 22.90 | 1.50 | -4.686 | .000* | -1.210 |
| C | 15 | 8.10 | | | | |

* significant at 0.05 level

Descriptive statistics showed that Y&AA group (median= 5.00; mean rank = 22.90) had higher scores than that C group (median= .00; mean rank = 8.10). Mann-

Whitney U value was found to be statistically significant U= 1.50 (z = -4.68), p <0.001 and the difference between Y&AA and C groups was moderate (r = -1.21).

**Table 4. 96.D: Spoonerism post intervention data Post-hoc analyses between N&AA-AA**

| Groups | *n* | Mean ranks | U | *z* | *p* | Effect size |
|--------|-----|------------|-------|-------|------|-------------|
| N&AA | 15 | 13.10 | 76.50 | -.704 | .482 | -0.181 |
| AA | 12 | 15.13 | | | | |

Descriptive statistics showed that N&AA group (median= .00; mean rank = 13.10) had lower scores than that AA group (median= 1.00; mean rank = 15.13). Mann-Whitney U value was found to be statistically non significant U= 76.50 (z = -.70), p =0.48.

**Table 4. 96.E: Spoonerism post intervention data Post-hoc analyses between N&AA-C**

| Groups | *n* | Mean ranks | U | *z* | *p* | Effect size |
|--------|-----|------------|--------|-------|------|-------------|
| N&AA | 15 | 16.07 | 104.00 | -.393 | .695 | -0.101 |
| C | 15 | 14.93 | | | | |

Descriptive statistics showed that N&AA group (median= .00; mean rank = 16.07) had equal scores than that C group (median= .00; mean rank = 14.93). Mann-Whitney U value was found to be statistically non significant U= 104.00 (z = -.39), p =0.69.

**Table 4. 96.F: Spoonerism post intervention data Post-hoc analyses between AA-C**

| Groups | *n* | Mean ranks | U | *z* | *p* | Effect size |
|--------|-----|------------|-------|--------|------|-------------|
| AA | 12 | 15.92 | 67.00 | -1.211 | .226 | -0.35 |
| C | 15 | 12.47 | | | | |

Descriptive statistics showed that AA group (median= 1.00; mean rank = 15.92) had higher scores than that C group (median= .00; mean rank = 12.47). Mann-Whitney U value was found to be statistically non significant U= 67.00 (z = -1.21), p =0.23.

#### 4.6.8.5 Between group analysis for Spoonerism follow up data

**Table 4.97: Spoonerism subtest data between groups analyses (Follow up data)**

| Groups | $n$ | Mean ranks | *Chi sq* | *df* | *p* |
|---|---|---|---|---|---|
| Y&AA | 15 | 35.00 | | | |
| N&AA | 15 | 12.93 | 29.471 | 2 | .000* |
| C | 15 | | | | |
| AA | 12 | 15.33 | | | |

* significant at 0.05 level

There was a statistically significant difference between the groups in spoonerism in the posttest data ($x^2$(2) = 35.00, $p$= .00) with a mean rank of 35.00 (Median= 6.00) for Y&AA group, 12.93 (Median= 1.00) for N&AA group, and 15.33 (Median= 1.00) for AA group.

#### 4.6.8.5 A. Post-hoc analyses for Spoonerism follow up data

**Table 4.98.A: Spoonerism follow up data Post-hoc analyses between Y&AA-N&AA**

| Groups | $n$ | Mean ranks | U | $z$ | $p$ | Effect size |
|---|---|---|---|---|---|---|
| Y&AA | 15 | 23.00 | .00 | -4.724 | .000* | -1.220 |
| N&AA | 15 | 8.00 | | | | |

* significant at 0.05 level

Descriptive statistics showed that Y&AA group (median= 5.00; mean rank = 23.00) had higher scores than that N&AA group (median= .00; mean rank = 8.00). Mann-Whitney U value was found to be statistically significant U= .00 (z = -4.72), p <0.001 and the difference between Y&AA and N&AA groups was moderate (r = -1.22).

**Table 4.98.B: Spoonerism follow up data Post-hoc analyses between Y&AA-AA**

| Groups | $n$ | Mean ranks | U | $z$ | $p$ | Effect size |
|---|---|---|---|---|---|---|
| Y&AA | 15 | 20.00 | .00 | -4.462 | .000* | -1.152 |
| AA | 12 | 6.50 | | | | |

* significant at 0.05 level

Descriptive statistics showed that Y&AA group (median= 6.00; mean rank = 20.00) had higher scores than that AA group (median= 1.00; mean rank = 6.50). Mann-Whitney U value was found to be statistically significant U= .00 (z = -4.46), p <0.001 and the difference between Y&AA and AA groups was moderate (r = -1.15).

**Table 4.98.C: Spoonerism follow up data Post-hoc analyses between N&AA-AA**

| Groups | *n* | Mean ranks | U | *z* | *p* | Effect size |
|--------|-----|-----------|------|------|------|-------------|
| N&AA | 15 | 12.93 | 74.00 | -.828 | .408 | -0.213 |
| AA | 12 | 15.33 | | | | |

Descriptive statistics showed that N&AA group (median= 1.00; mean rank = 12.93) had equal scores than that AA group (median= 1.00; mean rank = 15.33). Mann-Whitney U value was found to be statistically non significant U= 74.00 (z = -.83), p =0.41.

Graph 12

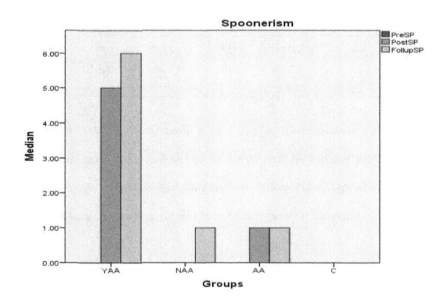

### 4.6.9 Phoneme reversal Kannada

**4.6.9.1 Homogeneity test for intervention subgroups for Phoneme reversal Kannada**

**Table 4.99: Homogeneity test for intervention subgroups pre-intervention data Phoneme reversal Kannada**

| Groups | $n$ | Mean ranks | Chi sq | df | p |
|--------|-----|-----------|--------|----|----|
| Y&AA1 | 8 | 20.50 | | | |
| Y&AA2 | 7 | 20.50 | | | |
| N&AA1 | 7 | 23.50 | 3.71 | 5 | .591 |
| N&AA2 | 8 | 23.13 | | | |
| AA1 | 7 | 20.50 | | | |
| AA2 | 5 | 20.50 | | | |

There was no statistically significant difference ($p$=0.59) between the experimental groups carried out in two seasons in phoneme reversal Kannada subtest scores before the commencement of the intervention. Hence the groups Y&AA1 & Y&AA2, N&AA1 & N&AA2, AA1 & AA2 are combined respectively in further analysis

**4.6.9.2 Homogeneity test for Phoneme reversal Kannada pre-intervention data**

**Table 4.100: Homogeneity test for Phoneme reversal Kannada pre-intervention data**

| Groups | $n$ | Mean ranks | Chi sq | df | p |
|--------|-----|-----------|--------|----|----|
| Y&AA | 15 | 28.00 | | | |
| N&AA | 15 | 31.80 | 5.702 | 3 | .127 |
| C | 15 | 28.00 | | | |
| AA | 12 | 28.00 | | | |

There was no statistically significant difference ($p$=0.13) between the experimental and control groups on Kannada phoneme reversal before the start of the intervention.

### 4.6.9.3 Within group analysis for Phoneme reversal Kannada

### 4.6.9.3.1 Within group analysis for Phoneme reversal Kannada Y&AA group

**Table 4.101: Descriptive statistics for Phoneme Reversal Kannada subtest data (Y&AA group)**

| Data | $n$ | Median | $M$ | $SD$ | Min | Max |
|------|-----|--------|-----|------|-----|-----|
| Pretest | 15 | 1.00 | .00 | .00 | .00 | .00 |
| Posttest | 15 | 2.00 | 2.17 | .96 | 1.00 | 4.00 |
| Follow up | 15 | 3.00 | 2.80 | .86 | 1.00 | 4.00 |

**Table 4.101.A: Pre, Post & Follow up intervention comparisons within (Y&AA) group**

| | $z$ | $p$ | Effect size |
|---|-----|-----|-------------|
| Pretest-Posttest | -3.443 | .001* | -0.889 |
| Pretest-Follow up | -3.457 | .001* | -0.893 |
| Posttest-Follow up | -2.161 | .031* | -0.558 |

\* significant at 0.05 level

There was a significant increase from pretest (median= 1.00) to posttest (median= 2.00), z=-3.44, p<0.001, r= -0.88, pretest (median=1.00) to follow up (median=3.00)z=-3.46, p<0.001, r=-0.89 and posttest (median=2.00) to follow up (median=3.00) z=-2.16, p<0.001 r= -0.56 in the scores Kannada phoneme reversal, and the decrease was large. This indicates that the group has significantly improved from Y&AA intervention in their Kannada phoneme reversal and the improvement continued over a period of time till the follow up assessment was made.

### 4.6.9.3.2 Within group analysis for Phoneme reversal Kannada N&AA group

**Table 4.102: Descriptive statistics for Phoneme Reversal Kannada subtest data (N&AA group)**

| Data | $n$ | Median | $M$ | $SD$ | Min | Max |
|------|-----|--------|-----|------|-----|-----|
| Pretest | 15 | .00 | .13 | .35 | .00 | 1.00 |
| Posttest | 15 | .00 | .37 | .59 | .00 | 2.00 |
| Follow up | 15 | .00 | .47 | .92 | .00 | 3.00 |

**Table 4.102.A: Pre, Post & Follow up intervention comparisons within (N&AA) group**

|  | $z$ | $p$ | Effect size |
|---|---|---|---|
| Pretest-Posttest | -.707 | .480 | -0.182 |
| Pretest-Follow up | -1.289 | .197 | -0.333 |
| Posttest-Follow up | -1.732 | .083 | -0.447 |

There was no significant difference from pretest (median= .00) to posttest (median= .00), z=-.71, p=0.18, pretest (median=.00) to follow up (median=.00)z=-1.29, p=0.33, and posttest (median=.00) to follow up (median=.00) z=-1.73, p=0.08 in the scores Kannada phoneme reversal, and the decrease was large. This indicates that the group has not improved from N&AA intervention in their Kannada phoneme reversal skills.

**4.6.9.3.3 Within group analysis for Phoneme reversal Kannada AA group**

**Table 4.103: Descriptive statistics for Phoneme Reversal Kannada subtest data (AA group)**

| Data | $n$ | Median | $M$ | $SD$ | Min | Max |
|---|---|---|---|---|---|---|
| Pretest | 12 | .00 | .00 | .00 | .00 | .00 |
| Posttest | 12 | 1.00 | .50 | .78 | .00 | 2.00 |
| Follow up | 12 | 1.00 | .67 | .65 | .00 | 2.00 |

**Table 4.103.A: Pre, Post & Follow up intervention comparisons within (AA) group**

|  | $z$ | $p$ | Effect size |
|---|---|---|---|
| Pretest-Posttest | -2.121 | .034* | -0.613 |
| Pretest-Follow up | -2.530 | .011* | -0.731 |
| Posttest-Follow up | -1.414 | .157 | -0.408 |

* significant at 0.05 level

There was a significant increase from pretest (median= .00) to posttest (median= .00), z=-2.12, p<0.001, r= -0.61, pretest (median=.00) to follow up (median=1.00)z=-2.53, p<0.001, r=-0.73 but not in posttest (median=.00) to follow up

156

(median=1.00) z=-1.41, p=0.16 in the scores Kannada phoneme reversal, and the decrease was large. This indicates that the group has significantly improved from AA intervention in their Kannada phoneme reversal.

**4.6.9.3.4 Within group analysis for Phoneme reversal Kannada C group**

**Table 4.104: Descriptive statistics for Phoneme Reversal Kannada subtest data (C group)**

| Data | $n$ | Median | $M$ | $SD$ | Min | Max |
|---|---|---|---|---|---|---|
| Pretest | 15 | .00 | .00 | .00 | .00 | .00 |
| Posttest | 15 | .00 | .00 | .00 | .00 | .00 |
| Follow up | - | | | | | |

**Table 4.104.A: Pre, Post & Follow up intervention comparisons within (C) group**

| | $z$ | $p$ | Effect size |
|---|---|---|---|
| Pretest-Posttest | .000 | 1.000 | 0 |

There was no significant decrease from pretest (median= .00) to posttest (median= .00), z=-.00, p=1.00. This indicates that the group has not improved in control group in their Kannada phoneme reversal skills

**4.6.9.4 Between group analysis for Phoneme reversal Kannada post intervention**

**Table 4.105: Phoneme reversal Kannada subtest data between groups analyses (Post-test data)**

| Groups | $n$ | Mean ranks | $Chi\ sq$ | $df$ | $p$ |
|---|---|---|---|---|---|
| Y&AA | 15 | 48.00 | | | |
| N&AA | 15 | 22.60 | 37.462 | 3 | .000* |
| C | 15 | 17.50 | | | |
| AA | 12 | 27.63 | | | |

* significant at 0.05 level

There was a statistically significant difference between the groups on the levels of Kannada phoneme reversal skill in the posttest data ($x^2(2) = 37.46$, $p= .00$) with a mean rank of 48.00 (Median= 2.00) for Y&AA group, 22.60 (Median= .00) for

N&AA group, 17.50 (Median= .00) for C group and 27.63 (Median= .00) for AA group.

### 4.6.9.4.A. Post-hoc analyses for Phoneme reversal Kannada post intervention

**Table 4. 105.A: Phoneme reversal Kannada post intervention data Post-hoc analyses between Y&AA-N&AA**

| Groups | $n$ | Mean ranks | U | $z$ | $p$ | Effect size |
|--------|-----|-----------|-------|--------|-------|-------------|
| Y&AA | 15 | 22.17 | 12.50 | -4.339 | .000* | -1.121 |
| N&AA | 15 | 8.83 | | | | |

* significant at 0.05 level

Descriptive statistics showed that Y&AA group (median= 2.00; mean rank = 22.17) had higher scores than that N&AA group (median= .00; mean rank = 8.83). Mann-Whitney U value was found to be statistically significant U= 12.50 (z = -4.34), p <0.001 and the difference between Y&AA and N&AA groups was large (r = -1.12).

**Table 4. 105.B: Phoneme reversal Kannada post intervention data Post-hoc analyses between Y&AA-AA**

| Groups | $n$ | Mean ranks | U | $z$ | $p$ | Effect size |
|--------|-----|-----------|-------|--------|-------|-------------|
| Y&AA | 15 | 18.83 | 17.50 | -3.663 | .000* | -0.946 |
| AA | 12 | 7.96 | | | | |

* significant at 0.05 level

Descriptive statistics showed that Y&AA group (median= 2.00; mean rank = 18.83) had higher scores than that AA group (median= .00; mean rank = 7.96). Mann-Whitney U value was found to be statistically significant U= 17.50 (z = -3.66), p <0.001 and the difference between Y&AA and AA groups was large (r = -0.95).

**Table 4. 105.C: Phoneme reversal Kannada post intervention data Post-hoc analyses between Y&AA-C**

| Groups | $n$ | Mean ranks | U | $z$ | $p$ | Effect size |
|--------|-----|-----------|-----|--------|-------|-------------|
| Y&AA | 15 | 23.00 | .00 | -5.019 | .000* | -1.296 |
| C | 15 | 8.00 | | | | |

* significant at 0.05 level

Descriptive statistics showed that Y&AA group (median= 2.00; mean rank = 23.00) had higher scores than that C group (median= .00; mean rank = 8.00). Mann-Whitney U value was found to be statistically significant U= .00 (z = -5.02), p <0.001 and the difference between Y&AA and C groups was large (r = -1.29).

**Table 4. 105.D: Phoneme reversal Kannada post intervention data Post-hoc analyses between N&AA-AA**

| Groups | *n* | Mean ranks | U | *z* | *p* | Effect size |
|--------|-----|------------|------|--------|------|-------------|
| N&AA | 15 | 12.77 | 71.50 | -1.127 | .260 | -0.291 |
| AA | 12 | 15.54 | | | | |

Descriptive statistics showed that N&AA group (median= .00; mean rank = 12.77) had equal scores as AA group (median= .00; mean rank = 15.54). Mann-Whitney U value was found to be statistically significant U= 71.50 (z = -4.34), p =0.26.

**Table 4. 105.E: Phoneme reversal Kannada post intervention data Post-hoc analyses between N&AA-C**

| Groups | *n* | Mean ranks | U | *z* | *p* | Effect size |
|--------|-----|------------|-------|--------|------|-------------|
| N&AA | 15 | 17.00 | 90.00 | -1.793 | .073 | -0.463 |
| C | 15 | 14.00 | | | | |

Descriptive statistics showed that N&AA group (median= .00; mean rank = 17.00) had equal scores as C group (median= .00; mean rank = 14.00). Mann-Whitney U value was found to be statistically significant U= 90.00 (z = -1.79), p =0.07.

**Table 4. 105.F: Phoneme reversal Kannada post intervention data Post-hoc analyses between AA-C**

| Groups | *n* | Mean ranks | U | *z* | *p* | Effect size |
|--------|-----|------------|-------|--------|-------|-------------|
| AA | 12 | 17.13 | 52.50 | -2.709 | .007* | -0.782 |
| C | 15 | 11.50 | | | | |

* significant at 0.05 level

Descriptive statistics showed that AA group (median= .00; mean rank = 17.13) had equal cores as C group (median= .00; mean rank = 11.50). But Mann-Whitney U value was found to be statistically significant U= 52.50 (z = -4.34), p <0.001 and the difference between AA and C groups was large (r = -0.78).

**4.6.9.5 Between group analyses for Phoneme reversal Kannada follow up data**

**Table 4.106: Phoneme reversal Kannada subtest data between groups analyses (Follow up data)**

| Groups | $n$ | Mean ranks | $Chi\ sq$ | $df$ | $p$ |
|--------|-----|------------|-----------|------|-----|
| Y&AA | 15 | 33.77 | | | |
| N&AA | 15 | 13.30 | 25.680 | 2 | .000* |
| C | 15 | | | | |
| AA | 12 | 16.42 | | | |

* significant at 0.05 level

There was a statistically significant difference between the groups on the levels of Kannada phoneme reversal skill in the follow up data ($x^2(2)$ = 25.68, $p$= .00) with a mean rank of 33.77 (Median= 3.00) for Y&AA group, 12.30 (Median= .00) for N&AA group, and 16.42 (Median= 1.00) for AA group.

**4.6.9.5 A. Post-hoc analyses for Phoneme reversal Kannada follow up data**

**Table 4.106.A: Phoneme reversal Kannada follow up data Post-hoc analyses between Y&AA-N&AA**

| Groups | $n$ | Mean ranks | U | $z$ | $p$ | Effect size |
|--------|-----|------------|-------|--------|-------|-------------|
| Y&AA | 15 | 22.17 | 12.50 | -4.310 | .000* | -1.113 |
| N&AA | 15 | 8.83 | | | | |

* significant at 0.05 level

Descriptive statistics showed that Y&AA group (median= 3.00; mean rank = 22.17) had higher scores than that N&AA group (median= .00; mean rank = 8.83). Mann-Whitney U value was found to be statistically significant U= 12.50 (z = -4.31), p <0.001 and the difference between Y&AA and N&AA groups was large (r = -1.11).

**Table 4.106.B: Phoneme reversal Kannada follow up data Post-hoc analyses between Y&AA-AA**

| Groups | n | Mean ranks | U | z | p | Effect size |
|--------|-----|------------|------|--------|-------|-------------|
| Y&AA | 15 | 19.60 | 6.00 | -4.200 | .000* | -1.085 |
| AA | 12 | 7.00 | | | | |

* significant at 0.05 level

Descriptive statistics showed that Y&AA group (median= 3.00; mean rank = 19.60) had higher scores than that N&AA group (median= .00; mean rank = 7.00). Mann-Whitney U value was found to be statistically significant U= 6.00 (z = -4.20), p <0.001 and the difference between Y&AA and N&AA groups was large (r = -1.09).

**Table 4.106.C: Phoneme reversal Kannada follow up data Post-hoc analyses between N&AA-AA**

| Groups | n | Mean ranks | U | z | p | Effect size |
|--------|-----|------------|-------|--------|------|-------------|
| N&AA | 15 | 12.47 | 67.00 | -1.282 | .200 | -0.331 |
| AA | 12 | 15.92 | | | | |

Descriptive statistics showed that N&AA group (median= .00; mean rank 12.47) had equal scores as N&AA group (median= .00; mean rank = 15.92). Mann-Whitney U value was found to be statistically non significant U= 67.00 (z = -1.28), p <0.001 and the difference between Y&AA and N&AA groups was large (r = -0.33).

Graph 13

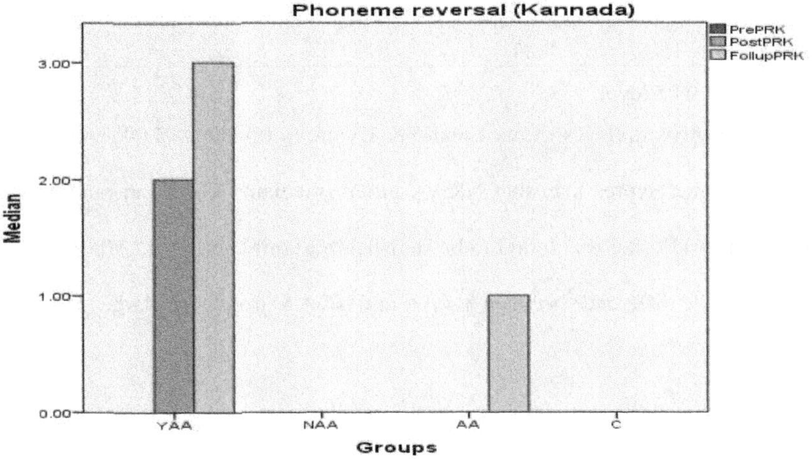

Phoneme reversal (Kannada)

161

## 4.7 Testing Hypothesis 6: Practice of yoga will improve word reading efficiency in children with LD

### 4.7.1 Sight word reading Eng

#### 4.7.1.1 Homogeneity test for intervention subgroups for Sight word reading Eng

Table 4.107 : Homogeneity test for intervention subgroups pre-intervention data Sight word reading Eng

| Groups | n | Mean ranks | Chi sq | df | p |
|--------|---|-----------|--------|----|----|
| Y&AA1 | 8 | 17.31 | | | |
| Y&AA2 | 7 | 16.50 | | | |
| N&AA1 | 7 | 11.86 | | | |
| N&AA2 | 8 | 17.44 | 10.59 | 5 | .06 |
| AA1 | 7 | 23.64 | | | |
| AA2 | 5 | 24.00 | | | |

There was no statistically significant difference ($p=0.01$) between the experimental groups carried out in two seasons in sight word English subtest scores before the commencement of the intervention. Hence the groups Y&AA1 & Y&AA2, N&AA1 & N&AA2, AA1 & AA2 are combined respectively in further analysis

#### 4.7.1.2 Homogeneity test for Sight word reading Eng pre-intervention data

Table 4.108: Homogeneity test for Sight word reading Eng pre-intervention data

| Groups | n | Mean ranks | Chi sq | df | p |
|--------|----|-----------|--------|----|----|
| Y&AA | 15 | 31.50 | | | |
| N&AA | 15 | 20.33 | 8.386 | 3 | .09 |
| C | 15 | 27.67 | | | |
| AA | 12 | 38.38 | | | |

There was no statistically significant difference ($p=0.09$) between the experimental and control groups on levels of English sight word reading before the start of the intervention.

**4.7.1.3 Within group analysis for Sight word reading Eng**

**4.7.1.3.1 Within group analysis for Sight word reading Eng Y&AA group**

**Table 4.109: Descriptive statistics for Sight Word Reading English subtest data (Y&AA group)**

| Data | $n$ | Median | $M$ | $SD$ | Min | Max |
|------|-----|--------|-----|------|-----|-----|
| Pretest | 15 | 19.00 | 19.40 | 5.59 | 10.00 | 28.00 |
| Posttest | 15 | 29.00 | 27.80 | 5.86 | 16.00 | 39.00 |
| Follow up | 15 | 31.00 | 30.13 | 6.16 | 20.00 | 42.00 |

**Table 4.109.A: Pre, Post & Follow up intervention comparisons within (Y&AA) group**

|  | $z$ | $p$ | Effect size |
|--|-----|-----|-------------|
| Pretest-Posttest | -3.07 | .002* | -0.793 |
| Pretest-Follow up | -3.15 | .002* | -0.813 |
| Posttest-Follow up | -2.79 | .007* | -0.720 |

There was a significant increase from pretest (median= 19.00) to posttest (median= 29.00), z=-3.07, p<0.001, r= -0.79, pretest (median=19.00) to follow up (median=31.00)z=-3.15, p<0.001, r=-0.81 and posttest (median=29.00) to follow up (median=31.00) z=-2.79, p<0.001 r= -0.72 in the scores of English sight word reading, and the increase was large. This indicates that the group has significantly improved from Y&AA intervention in their English sight word reading skills and the improvement continued over a period of time till the follow up assessment was made.

**4.7.1.3.2 Within group analysis for Sight word reading Eng N&AA group**

**Table 4.110: Descriptive statistics for Sight Word Reading English subtest data (N&AA group)**

| Data | $n$ | Median | $M$ | $SD$ | Min | Max |
|------|-----|--------|-----|------|-----|-----|
| Pretest | 15 | 16.00 | 15.73 | 2.52 | 11.00 | 21.00 |
| Posttest | 15 | 16.00 | 16.77 | 2.55 | 13.00 | 23.00 |
| Follow up | 15 | 20.00 | 21.97 | 4.19 | 17.00 | 30.00 |

**Table 4.110.A: Pre, Post & Follow up intervention comparisons within (N&AA) group**

|  | $z$ | $p$ | Effect size |
|---|---|---|---|
| Pretest-Posttest | -2.58 | .010* | -0.666 |
| Pretest-Follow up | -3.41 | .001* | -0.881 |
| Posttest-Follow up | -3.41 | .001* | -0.881 |

There was a significant increase from pretest (median= 16.00) to posttest (median= 16.00), z=-2.58, p<0.001, r= -0.66, pretest (median=16.00) to follow up (median=20.00)z=-3.41, p<0.001, r=-0.88 and posttest (median=16.00) to follow up (median=20.00) z=-3.41, p<0.001 r= -0.88 in the scores of English sight word reading, and the increase was large. This indicates that the group has significantly improved from N&AA intervention in their English sight word reading skills and the improvement continued over a period of time till the follow up assessment was made.

### 4.7.1.3.3 Within group analysis for Sight word reading Eng AA group

**Table 4.111: Descriptive statistics for Sight Word Reading English subtest data (AA group)**

| Data | $n$ | Median | $M$ | $SD$ | Min | Max |
|---|---|---|---|---|---|---|
| Pretest | 12 | 23.00 | 21.75 | 5.56 | 13.00 | 29.00 |
| Posttest | 12 | 25.00 | 23.08 | 5.99 | 14.00 | 30.00 |
| Follow up | 12 | 27.50 | 27.27 | 3.61 | 21.00 | 32.00 |

**Table 4.111.A: Pre, Post & Follow up intervention comparisons within (AA) group**

|  | $z$ | $p$ | Effect size |
|---|---|---|---|
| Pretest-Posttest | -1.253 | .210 | -0.362 |
| Pretest-Follow up | -3.086 | .002* | -0.891 |
| Posttest-Follow up | -2.807 | .005* | -0.811 |

There was no significant difference from pretest (median= 23.00) to posttest (median= 25.00), z=-.21, p=-0.36, But there was significant increase in pretest (median=23.00) to follow up (median=27.00)z=-3.08, p<0.001, r=-0.89 and posttest (median=25.00) to follow up (median=27.00) z=-2.80, p<0.001 r= -0.81 in the scores of English sight word reading, and the increase was large. This indicates that the group has significantly improved from AA intervention in their English sight word reading skills and the improvement continued over a period of time till the follow up assessment was made.

**4.7.1.3.4 Within group analysis for Sight word reading Eng C group**

**Table 4.112: Descriptive statistics for Sight Word Reading English subtest data (C group)**

| Data | *n* | Median | *M* | *SD* | Min | Max |
|------|-----|--------|-----|------|-----|-----|
| Pretest | 15 | 20.00 | 18.13 | 5.38 | 10.00 | 27.00 |
| Posttest | 15 | 17.00 | 17.73 | 5.15 | 10.00 | 28.00 |
| Follow up | - | | | | | |

**Table 4.112.A: Pre, Post & Follow up intervention comparisons within (C) group**

| | *z* | *p* | Effect size |
|---|-----|-----|-------------|
| Pretest-Posttest | -.315 | .753 | -0.081 |
| Pretest-Follow up | - | - | - |
| Posttest-Follow up | - | - | - |

There was no significant difference from pretest (median= 20.00) to posttest (median= 17.00), z=-3.15, p=0.75. This indicates that the group has not improved in control group.

**4.7.1.4 Between group analyses for Sight word reading Eng post intervention data**

**Table 4.113: Sight word reading Eng subtest data between groups analyses (Post-test data)**

| Groups | *n* | Mean ranks | *Chi sq* | *df* | *p* |
|--------|-----|-----------|----------|------|-----|
| Y&AA | 15 | 44.37 | | | |
| N&AA | 15 | 18.07 | 24.523 | 3 | .000* |
| C | 15 | 20.53 | | | |
| AA | 12 | 34.04 | | | |

165

There was a statistically significant difference between the groups on the levels of English sight word reading skills in the posttest data ($x^2(2) = 24.52$, $p = .00$) with a mean rank of 44.37 (Median= 29.00) for Y&AA group, 18.07 (Median= 16.00) for N&AA group, 20.53 (Median= 17.00) for C group and 34.04 .(Median= 25.00) for AA group.

**4.7.1.4.A. Post-hoc analyses for Sight word reading Eng post intervention**

**Table 4. 113.A: Sight word reading Eng post intervention data Post-hoc analyses between Y&AA-N&AA**

| Groups | $n$ | Mean ranks | U | $z$ | $p$ | Effect size |
|--------|-----|-----------|-------|--------|-------|-------------|
| Y&AA | 15 | 22.33 | 10.00 | -4.275 | .000* | -1.104 |
| N&AA | 15 | 8.67 | | | | |

Descriptive statistics showed that Y&AA group (median= 29.00; mean rank = 22.33) had higher scores than that N&AA group (median= 16.00; mean rank = 8.67). Mann-Whitney U value was found to be statistically significant U= 10.00 (z = -4.28), p <0.001 and the difference between Y&AA and N&AA groups was large (r = -1.10).

**Table 4. 113.B: Sight word reading Eng post intervention data Post-hoc analyses between Y&AA-AA**

| Groups | $n$ | Mean ranks | U | $z$ | $p$ | Effect size |
|--------|-----|-----------|-------|--------|------|-------------|
| Y&AA | 15 | 16.53 | 52.00 | -1.859 | .063 | -0.480 |
| AA | 12 | 10.83 | | | | |

Descriptive statistics showed that Y&AA group (median= 29.00; mean rank = 16.53) had higher scores than that AA group (median= 25.00; mean rank = 10.83). Mann-Whitney U value was found to be statistically non significant U= 52.00 (z = -1.86), p = .06.

**Table 4. 113.C: Sight word reading Eng post intervention data Post-hoc analyses between Y&AA-C**

| Groups | $n$ | Mean ranks | U | $z$ | $p$ | Effect size |
|--------|-----|-----------|-------|--------|-------|-------------|
| Y&AA | 15 | 21.50 | 22.50 | -3.738 | .000* | -0.965 |
| C | 15 | 9.50 | | | | |

Descriptive statistics showed that Y&AA group (median= 29.00; mean rank = 2150) had higher scores than that C group (median= 17.00; mean rank = 9.50). Mann-Whitney U value was found to be statistically significant U= 22.50 (z = -3.74), p <0.001 and the difference between Y&AA and C groups was large (r = -.97).

**Table 4. 113.D: Sight word reading Eng post intervention data Post-hoc analyses between N&AA-AA**

| Groups | *n* | Mean ranks | U | *z* | *p* | Effect size |
|--------|-----|-----------|-----|-----|-----|-------------|
| N&AA | 15 | 10.37 | 35.50 | -2.681 | .007* | -0.692 |
| AA | 12 | 18.54 | | | | |

Descriptive statistics showed that N&AA group (median= 16.00; mean rank = 10.37) had lower scores than that AA group (median= 25.00; mean rank = 18.54). Mann-Whitney U value was found to be statistically significant U= 35.50 (z = -2.68), p <0.001 and the difference between N&AA and AA groups was large (r = -.69).

**Table 4. 113.E: Sight word reading Eng post intervention data Post-hoc analyses between N&AA-C**

| Groups | *n* | Mean ranks | U | *z* | *p* | Effect size |
|--------|-----|-----------|--------|-------|------|-------------|
| N&AA | 15 | 15.03 | 105.50 | -.293 | .769 | -0.075 |
| C | 15 | 15.97 | | | | |

Descriptive statistics showed that N&AA group (median= 16.00; mean rank = 15.03) had lower scores than that C group (median= 16.00; mean rank = 15.97). Mann-Whitney U value was found to be statistically non significant U= 105.50 (z = -.29), p =0.77.

**Table 4. 113.F: Sight word reading Eng post intervention data Post-hoc analyses between AA-C**

| Groups | *n* | Mean ranks | U | *z* | *p* | Effect size |
|--------|-----|-----------|-------|--------|-------|-------------|
| AA | 12 | 17.67 | 46.00 | -2.157 | .031* | -0.623 |
| C | 15 | 11.07 | | | | |

Descriptive statistics showed that AA group (median= 25.00; mean rank = 17.67) had higher scores than that C group (median= 17.00; mean rank = 11.07).

Mann-Whitney U value was found to be statistically significant U= 46.00 (z = -2.16), p <0.001 and the difference between AA and C groups was large (r = -0.62).

**4.7.1.5 Between group analyses for Sight word reading Eng follow up data**

**Table 4.114: Sight word reading Eng subtest data between groups analyses (Follow up data)**

| Groups | $n$ | Mean ranks | Chi sq | df | p |
|--------|-----|------------|--------|-----|-----|
| Y&AA | 15 | 29.33 | | | |
| N&AA | 15 | 11.77 | 16.100 | 2 | .000* |
| C | | | | | |
| AA | 12 | 23.88 | | | |

There was a statistically significant difference between the groups on the levels of English sight word reading skills in the follow up data ($x^2(2) = 16.10$, $p= .00$) with a mean rank of 29.33 (Median= 31.00) for Y&AA group, 11.77 (Median= 20.00) for N&AA group, and 23.88 (Median= 27.50) for AA group.

**4.7.1.5. A. Post-hoc analyses for Sight word reading Eng follow up data**

**Table 4.114.A: Sight word reading Engfollow up data Post-hoc analyses between Y&AA-N&AA**

| Groups | $n$ | Mean ranks | U | $z$ | p | Effect size |
|--------|-----|------------|-------|--------|-------|-------------|
| Y&AA | 15 | 21.13 | 28.00 | -3.517 | .000* | -0.908 |
| N&AA | 15 | 9.87 | | | | |

Descriptive statistics showed that Y&AA group (median= 31.00; mean rank = 21.13) had higher scores than that N&AA group (median= 20.00; mean rank = 9.87). Mann-Whitney U value was found to be statistically significant U= 28.00 (z = -3.52), p <0.001 and the difference between Y&AA and N&AA groups was large (r = -0.91).

**Table 4.114.B: Sight word reading Eng follow up data Post-hoc analyses between Y&AA-AA**

| Groups | $n$ | Mean ranks | U | $z$ | p | Effect size |
|--------|-----|------------|-------|--------|------|-------------|
| Y&AA | 15 | 16.20 | 57.00 | -1.617 | .106 | -0.417 |
| AA | 12 | 11.25 | | | | |

Descriptive statistics showed that Y&AA group (median= 31.00; mean rank = 16.20) had higher scores than that AA group (median= 27.50; mean rank = 11.25). Mann-Whitney U value was found to be statistically non significant U= 57.00 (z = -1.62), p =0.11.

**Table 4.114.C: Sight word reading Eng follow up data Post-hoc analyses between N&AA-AA**

| Groups | *n* | Mean ranks | U | *z* | *p* | Effect size |
|--------|-----|------------|-------|--------|-------|-------------|
| N&AA | 15 | 9.90 | 28.50 | -3.011 | .003* | -0.778 |
| AA | 12 | 19.13 | | | | |

Descriptive statistics showed that N&AA group (median= 20.00; mean rank = 9.90) had lower scores than that AA group (median= 27.50; mean rank = 19.13). Mann-Whitney U value was found to be statistically significant U= 28.50 (z = -3.01), p <0.001 and the difference between N&AA and AA groups was large (r = -0.77).

Graph 14

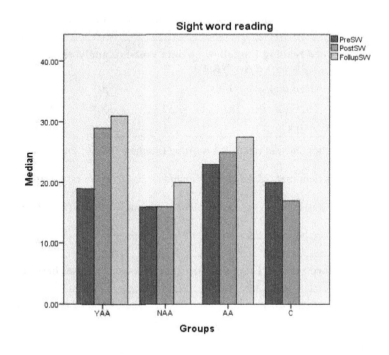

169

### 4.7.2 Decoding English

#### 4.7.2.1 Homogeneity test for intervention subgroups for Decoding Eng

**Table 4.115: Homogeneity test for intervention subgroups pre-intervention data Decoding Eng**

| Groups | $n$ | Mean ranks | Chi sq | df | p |
|--------|-----|------------|--------|-----|-----|
| Y&AA1 | 8 | 22.81 | | | |
| Y&AA2 | 7 | 24.86 | | | |
| N&AA1 | 7 | 15.14 | | | |
| N&AA2 | 8 | 19.19 | 4.59 | 5 | .47 |
| AA1 | 7 | 20.50 | | | |
| AA2 | 5 | 28.70 | | | |

There was no statistically significant difference ($p$=0.47) between the experimental groups carried out in two seasons in decoding English subtest scores before the commencement of the intervention. Hence the groups Y&AA1 & Y&AA2, N&AA1 & N&AA2, AA1 & AA2 are combined respectively in further analysis

#### 4.7.2.2 Homogeneity test for Decoding Eng pre-intervention data

**Table 4.116: Homogeneity test for Decoding Eng pre-intervention data**

| Groups | $n$ | Mean ranks | Chi sq | df | p |
|--------|-----|------------|--------|-----|-------|
| Y&AA | 15 | 31.90 | | | |
| N&AA | 15 | 23.43 | 2.580 | 3 | .461 |
| C | 15 | 29.20 | | | |
| AA | 12 | 32.08 | | | |

There was no statistically significant difference ($p$=0.46) between the experimental and control groups on levels of behavioral adjustment before the start of the intervention.

170

### 4.7.2.3 Within group analysis for Decoding Eng

### 4.7.2.3.1 Within group analysis for Decoding Eng Y&AA group

**Table 4.117: Descriptive statistics for Decoding English subtest data (Y&AA group)**

| Data | $n$ | Median | $M$ | $SD$ | Min | Max |
|------|-----|--------|-----|------|-----|-----|
| Pretest | 15 | 11.00 | 13.80 | 6.05 | 6.00 | 24.00 |
| Posttest | 15 | 30.00 | 26.33 | 7.31 | 12.00 | 35.00 |
| Follow up | 15 | 30.00 | 28.93 | 5.13 | 19.00 | 37.00 |

**Table 4.117.A: Pre, Post & Follow up intervention comparisons within (Y&AA) group**

| | $z$ | $p$ | Effect size |
|------|-----|-----|-------------|
| Pretest-Posttest | -2.201 | .003* | -0.568 |
| Pretest-Follow up | -3.414 | .001* | -0.882 |
| Posttest-Follow up | -2.687 | .028* | -0.694 |

* significant at 0.05 level

There was a significant increase from pretest (median= 11.00) to posttest (median= 30.00), z=-2.20, p<0.001, r= -0.57, pretest (median=11.00) to follow up (median=30.00)z=-3.41, p<0.001, r=-0.88 and posttest (median=11.00) to follow up (median=30.00) z=-2.69, p<0.001 r= -0.69 English decoding scores, and the increase was moderate to large. This indicates that the group has significantly improved from Y&AA intervention in their English decoding skills and the improvement continued over a period of time till the follow up assessment was made.

### 4.7.2.3.2 Within group analysis for Decoding Eng N&AA group

**Table 4.118: Descriptive statistics for Decoding English subtest data (N&AA group)**

| Data | $n$ | Median | $M$ | $SD$ | Min | Max |
|------|-----|--------|-----|------|-----|-----|
| Pretest | 15 | 10.00 | 10.73 | 3.65 | 6.00 | 19.00 |
| Posttest | 15 | 11.00 | 12.57 | 3.18 | 9.00 | 20.00 |
| Follow up | 15 | 20.00 | 21.33 | 3.71 | 16.00 | 30.00 |

**Table 4.118.A: Pre, Post & Follow up intervention comparisons within (N&AA) group**

|  | z | p | Effect size |
|---|---|---|---|
| Pretest-Posttest | -2.983 | .003* | -0.770 |
| Pretest-Follow up | -3.414 | .001* | -0.882 |
| Posttest-Follow up | -3.305 | .001* | -0.854 |

* significant at 0.05 level

There was a significant increase from pretest (median= 10.00) to posttest (median= 11.00), z=-2.98, p<0.001, r= -0.77, pretest (median=10.00) to follow up (median=20.00)z=-3.41, p<0.001, r=-0.88 and posttest (median=11.00) to follow up (median230.00) z=-3.31, p<0.001 r= -0.85 English decoding scores, and the increase was large. This indicates that the group has significantly improved from N&AA intervention in their English decoding skills and the improvement continued over a period of time till the follow up assessment was made.

### 4.7.2.3.3 Within group analysis for Decoding Eng AA group

**Table 4.119: Descriptive statistics for Decoding English subtest data (AA group)**

| Data | n | Median | M | SD | Min | Max |
|---|---|---|---|---|---|---|
| Pretest | 12 | 12.50 | 14.00 | 5.59 | 8.00 | 21.00 |
| Posttest | 12 | 30.00 | 25.92 | 7.73 | 10.00 | 33.00 |
| Follow up | 12 | 30.00 | 27.08 | 5.63 | 15.00 | 34.00 |

**Table 4.119.A: Pre, Post & Follow up intervention comparisons within (AA) group**

|  | z | p | Effect size |
|---|---|---|---|
| Pretest-Posttest | -2.669 | .008* | -0.771 |
| Pretest-Follow up | -2.903 | .004* | -0.839 |
| Posttest-Follow up | -1.439 | .150 | -0.415 |

* significant at 0.05 level

There was a significant increase from pretest (median= 12.00) to posttest (median= 30.00), z=-2.66, p<0.001, r= -0.77, pretest (median=12.00) to follow up

(median=30.00)z=-2.90, p<0.001, r=-0.84 English decoding scores, and the increase was large. But there was no difference in posttest (median=30.00) to follow up (median 30.00) z=-1.43, p=0.41 This indicates that the group has significantly improved from AA intervention in their English decoding skills.

**4.7.2.3.4 Within group analysis for Decoding Eng C group**

**Table 4.120: Descriptive statistics for Decoding English subtest data (C group)**

| Data | $n$ | Median | $M$ | $SD$ | Min | Max |
|------|-----|--------|-----|------|-----|-----|
| Pretest | 15 | 11.00 | 13.13 | 6.53 | 5.00 | 28.00 |
| Posttest | 15 | 10.00 | 11.20 | 3.98 | 7.00 | 20.00 |
| Follow up | - | | | | | |

**Table 4.120.A: Pre, Post & Follow up intervention comparisons within (C) group**

| | $z$ | $p$ | Effect size |
|---|-----|-----|-------------|
| Pretest-Posttest | -.787 | .431 | -0.203 |

There was a no significant difference from pretest (median= 11.00) to posttest (median= 10.00), z=-.78, p<0.001.This indicates that the group has not improved in control group in their English decoding skills

**4.7.2.4 Between group analyses for Decoding Eng post intervention data**

**Table 4.121: Decoding Eng subtest data between groups analyses (Post-test data)**

| Groups | $n$ | Mean ranks | Chi sq | df | $p$ |
|--------|-----|------------|--------|-----|-----|
| Y&AA | 15 | 42.87 | | | |
| N&AA | 15 | 19.60 | 32.989 | 3 | .000* |
| C | 15 | 14.77 | | | |
| AA | 12 | 41.21 | | | |

* significant at 0.05 level

There was a statistically significant difference between the groups on the levels of English decoding skills in the posttest data $(x^2(2) = 32.98, p= .00)$ with a mean rank of **42.87** (Median= 30.00) for Y&AA group, 19.60 (Median= 11.00) for

173

N&AA group, 14.77 (Median= 10.00) for C group and 41.21 (Median= 30.00) for AA group.

### 4.7.2.4. A. Post-hoc analyses for Decoding Eng post intervention

**Table 4. 121.A: Decoding Eng post intervention data Post-hoc analyses between Y&AA-N&AA**

| Groups | *n* | Mean ranks | U | *z* | *p* | Effect size |
|--------|-----|-----------|-------|--------|-------|-------------|
| Y&AA | 15 | 22.13 | 13.00 | -4.139 | .000* | -1.069 |
| N&AA | 15 | 8.87 | | | | |

* significant at 0.05 level

Descriptive statistics showed that Y&AA group (median= 30.00; mean rank = 22.13) had higher scores than that of N&AA group (median= 11.00; mean rank = 8.87). Mann-Whitney U value was found to be statistically significant U= 13.00 (z = -4.14), p <0.001 and the difference between Y&AA and N&AA groups was large (r = -1.06).

**Table 4. 121.B: Decoding Eng post intervention data Post-hoc analyses between Y&AA-AA**

| Groups | *n* | Mean ranks | U | *z* | *p* | Effect size |
|--------|-----|-----------|-------|-------|------|-------------|
| Y&AA | 15 | 14.37 | 84.50 | -.272 | .785 | -0.070 |
| AA | 12 | 13.54 | | | | |

Descriptive statistics showed that Y&AA group (median= 30.00; mean rank = 14.37) had equal scores as of AA group (median= 30.00; mean rank = 13.54). Mann-Whitney U value was found to be statistically non significant U= 84.50 (z = -.27), p = 0.78.

**Table 4. 121.C: Decoding Eng post intervention data Post-hoc analyses between Y&AA-C**

| Groups | *n* | Mean ranks | U | *z* | *p* | Effect size |
|--------|-----|-----------|------|--------|-------|-------------|
| Y&AA | 15 | 22.37 | 9.50 | -4.282 | .000* | -1.106 |
| C | 15 | 8.63 | | | | |

* significant at 0.05 level

Descriptive statistics showed that Y&AA group (median= 30.00; mean rank = 22.37) had higher scores than that of C group (median= 10.00; mean rank = 8.63). Mann-Whitney U value was found to be statistically significant U= 9.50 (z = -4.28), p <0.001 and the difference between Y&AA and C groups was large (r = -1.10).

**Table 4. 121.D: Decoding Eng post intervention data Post-hoc analyses between N&AA-AA**

| Groups | *n* | Mean ranks | U | *z* | *p* | Effect size |
|--------|-----|------------|------|--------|-------|-------------|
| N&AA | 15 | 9.10 | 16.50 | -3.602 | .000* | -0.930 |
| AA | 12 | 20.13 | | | | |

* significant at 0.05 level

Descriptive statistics showed that N&AA group (median= 11.00; mean rank = 9.10) had lower scores than that of AA group (median= 30.00; mean rank = 20.13). Mann-Whitney U value was found to be statistically significant U= 16.50 (z = -3.60), p <0.001 and the difference between N&AA and AA groups was large (r = -0.93).

**Table 4. 121.E: Decoding Eng post intervention data Post-hoc analyses between N&AA-C**

| Groups | *n* | Mean ranks | U | *z* | *p* | Effect size |
|--------|-----|------------|------|--------|------|-------------|
| N&AA | 15 | 17.63 | 80.50 | -1.336 | .182 | -0.345 |
| C | 15 | 13.37 | | | | |

Descriptive statistics showed that N&AA group (median= 11.00; mean rank = 17.40) had equal scores as of C group (median= 10.00; mean rank = 12.25). Mann-Whitney U value was found to be statistically non significant U= 80.50 (z = -1.34), p = 0.18.

**Table 4. 121.F: Decoding Eng post intervention data Post-hoc analyses between AA-C**

| Groups | *n* | Mean ranks | U | *z* | *p* | Effect size |
|--------|-----|------------|------|--------|-------|-------------|
| AA | 12 | 20.54 | 11.50 | -3.842 | .000* | -1.110 |
| C | 15 | 8.77 | | | | |

* significant at 0.05 level

Descriptive statistics showed that AA group (median= 30.00; mean rank = 20.54) had higher scores than that of C group (median= 10.00; mean rank = 8.77). Mann-Whitney U value was found to be statistically significant U= 11.50 (z = -3.84), p <0.001 and the difference between AA and C groups was large (r = -1.11).

### 4.7.2.5 Between group analyses for Decoding Eng follow up data

**Table 4.122: Decoding Eng subtest data between groups analyses (Follow up data)**

| Groups | $n$ | Mean ranks | $Chi\ sq$ | $df$ | $p$ |
|--------|-----|------------|-----------|------|-----|
| Y&AA | 15 | 28.53 | | | |
| N&AA | 15 | 12.13 | 14.544 | 2 | .001* |
| C | 15 | | | | |
| AA | 12 | 24.42 | | | |

* significant at 0.05 level

There was a statistically significant difference between the groups on the levels of English decoding skills in the posttest data ($x^2(2)$ = 14.54, $p$= .00) with a mean rank of 28.53 (Median= 30.00) for Y&AA group, 12.13 (Median= 20.00) for N&AA group, and 24.42 (Median= 30.00) for AA group.

### 4.7.2.5. A. Post-hoc analyses for Decoding Eng follow up data

**Table 4.122.A: Decoding Engfollow up data Post-hoc analyses between Y&AA-N&AA**

| Groups | $n$ | Mean ranks | U | $z$ | $p$ | Effect size |
|--------|-----|------------|-------|--------|-------|-------------|
| Y&AA | 15 | 21.13 | 28.00 | -3.519 | .000* | -0.909 |
| N&AA | 15 | 9.87 | | | | |

* significant at 0.05 level

Descriptive statistics showed that Y&AA group (median= 30.00; mean rank = 21.13) had higher scores than that of N&AA group (median= 20.00; mean rank = 9.87). Mann-Whitney U value was found to be statistically significant U= 28.00 (z = -3.51), p <0.001 and the difference between Y&AA and N&AA groups was large (r = -0.91).

**Table 4.122.B: Decoding Eng follow up data Post-hoc analyses between Y&AA-AA**

| Groups | n | Mean ranks | U | z | p | Effect size |
|--------|---|-----------|------|--------|------|------------|
| Y&AA | 15 | 15.40 | 69.00 | -1.039 | .299 | -0.268 |
| AA | 12 | 12.25 | | | | |

Descriptive statistics showed that Y&AA group (median= 30.00; mean rank = 15.40) had equal scores as of AA group (median= 30.00; mean rank = 12.25). Mann-Whitney U value was found to be statistically non significant U= 69.00 (z = -1.04), p = 0.29.

**Table 4.122.C: Decoding Eng follow up data Post-hoc analyses between N&AA-AA**

| Groups | n | Mean ranks | U | z | p | Effect size |
|--------|---|-----------|------|--------|-------|------------|
| N&AA | 15 | 10.27 | 34.00 | -2.754 | .006* | -0.711 |
| AA | 12 | 18.67 | | | | |

* significant at 0.05 level

Descriptive statistics showed that N&AA group (median= 20.00; mean rank = 10.27) had lower scores than that of AA group (median= 30.00; mean rank = 18.67). Mann-Whitney U value was found to be statistically significant U= 34.00 (z = -2.75), p <0.001 and the difference between N&AA and AA groups was large (r = -0.71).

Graph 15

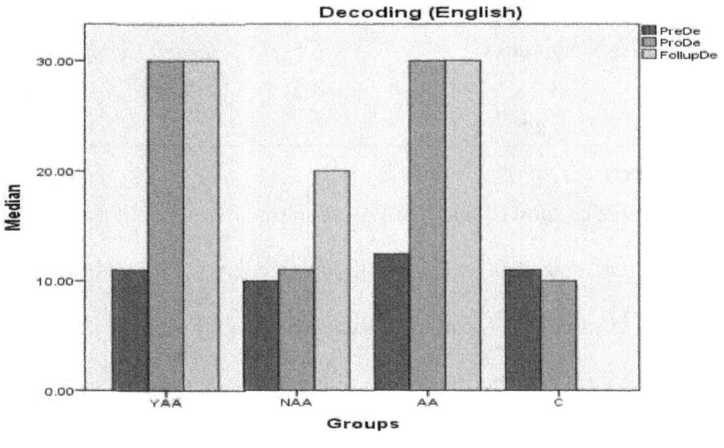

Decoding (English)

177

### 4.7.3 Sight word reading- Kannada

#### 4.7.3.1 Homogeneity test for intervention subgroups for Sight word Kan

**Table 4.123: Homogeneity test for intervention subgroups pre-intervention data Sight word Kan**

| Groups | $n$ | Mean ranks | Chi sq | df | p |
|--------|-----|-----------|--------|-----|-----|
| Y&AA1 | 8 | 26.75 | | | |
| Y&AA2 | 7 | 21.86 | | | |
| N&AA1 | 7 | 26.57 | | | |
| N&AA2 | 8 | 16.44 | 5.26 | 5 | .39 |
| AA1 | 7 | 18.57 | | | |
| AA2 | 5 | 17.70 | | | |

There was no statistically significant difference ($p=0.39$) between the experimental groups carried out in two seasons in Sight word Kan subtest scores before the commencement of the intervention. Hence the groups Y&AA1 & Y&AA2, N&AA1 & N&AA2, AA1 & AA2 are combined respectively in further analysis

#### 4.7.3.2 Homogeneity test for Sight word Kan pre-intervention data

**Table 4.124: Homogeneity test for Sight word Kan pre-intervention data**

| Groups | $n$ | Mean ranks | Chi sq | df | p |
|--------|-----|-----------|--------|-----|-----|
| Y&AA | 15 | 32.90 | | | |
| N&AA | 15 | 28.40 | 1.986 | 3 | .575 |
| C | 15 | 29.50 | | | |
| AA | 12 | 24.25 | | | |

There was no statistically significant difference ($p=0.57$) between the experimental and control groups on levels of behavioral adjustment before the start of the intervention.

### 4.7.3.3 Within group analysis for Sight word Kan

### 4.7.3.3.1 Within group analysis for Sight word Kan Y&AA group

**Table 4.125: Descriptive statistics for Sight Word Reading Kannada subtest data (Y&AA group)**

| Data | $n$ | Median | $M$ | $SD$ | Min | Max |
|---|---|---|---|---|---|---|
| Pretest | 15 | 5.00 | 4.97 | 1.06 | 3.00 | 7.00 |
| Posttest | 15 | 8.00 | 8.13 | 1.55 | 6.00 | 11.00 |
| Follow up | 15 | 11.00 | 10.86 | 1.77 | 8.00 | 15.00 |

**Table 4.125.A: Pre, Post & Follow up intervention comparisons within (Y&AA) group**

| | $z$ | $p$ | Effect size |
|---|---|---|---|
| Pretest-Posttest | -3.432 | .001* | -0.886 |
| Pretest-Follow up | -3.438 | .001* | -0.888 |
| Posttest-Follow up | -3.324 | .001* | -0.858 |

* significant at 0.05 level

There was a significant increase from pretest (median= 5.00) to posttest (median= 8.00), $z$=-3.43, $p<0.001$, $r$= -0.88, pretest (median=5.00) to follow up (median=11.00)$z$=-3.44, $p<0.001$, $r$=-0.88 and posttest (median=8.00) to follow up (median=11.00) $z$=-3.32, $p<0.001$ $r$= -0.86 in Kannada sight word reading scores, and the increase was large. This indicates that the group has significantly improved from Y&AA intervention in their Kannada sight word reading and the improvement continued over a period of time till the follow up assessment was made.

### 4.7.3.3.2 Within group analysis for Sight word Kan N&AA group

**Table 4.126: Descriptive statistics for Sight Word Reading Kannada subtest data (N&AA group)**

| Data | $n$ | Median | $M$ | $SD$ | Min | Max |
|---|---|---|---|---|---|---|
| Pretest | 15 | 4.00 | 4.53 | 1.46 | 2.00 | 7.00 |
| Posttest | 15 | 5.00 | 5.37 | 1.22 | 3.00 | 8.00 |
| Follow up | 15 | 6.00 | 6.00 | 1.17 | 4.00 | 8.00 |

**Table 4.126.A: Pre, Post & Follow up intervention comparisons within (N&AA) group**

|  | $z$ | $p$ | Effect size |
|---|---|---|---|
| Pretest-Posttest | -2.072 | .038* | -0.535 |
| Pretest-Follow up | -2.887 | .004* | -0.745 |
| Posttest-Follow up | -2.392 | .017* | -0.618 |

* significant at 0.05 level

There was a significant increase from pretest (median= 4.00) to posttest (median= 5.00), z=-2.07, p<0.001, r= -0.56, pretest (median=4.00) to follow up (median=6.00)z=-2.88, p<0.001, r=-0.76 and posttest (median=5.00) to follow up (median=6.00) z=-2.39, p<0.001 r= -0.62 in Kannada sight word reading scores, and the increase was moderate. This indicates that the group has significantly improved from N&AA intervention in their Kannada sight word reading and the improvement continued over a period of time till the follow up assessment was made.

**4.7.3.3.3 Within group analysis for Sight word Kan AA group**

**Table 4.127: Descriptive statistics for Sight Word Reading Kannada subtest data (AA group)**

| Data | $n$ | Median | $M$ | $SD$ | Min | Max |
|---|---|---|---|---|---|---|
| Pretest | 12 | 4.00 | 4.25 | .97 | 3.00 | 6.00 |
| Posttest | 12 | 5.00 | 5.42 | .99 | 4.00 | 7.00 |
| Follow up | 12 | 6.00 | 6.27 | .83 | 5.00 | 8.00 |

**Table 4.127.A: Pre, Post & Follow up intervention comparisons within (AA) group**

|  | $z$ | $p$ | Effect size |
|---|---|---|---|
| Pretest-Posttest | -2.739 | .006* | -0.791 |
| Pretest-Follow up | -2.877 | .004* | -0.831 |
| Posttest-Follow up | -1.706 | .088 | -0.493 |

* significant at 0.05 level

There was a significant increase from pretest (median= 4.00) to posttest (median= 5.00), $z$=-2.74, p<0.001, r= -0.79, pretest (median=4.00) to follow up (median=6.00)$z$=-2.87, p<0.001, r=-0.83 but not in posttest (median=5.00) to follow up (median=6.00) $z$=-1.71, p=.08. in Kannada sight word reading scores, and the increase was large. This indicates that the group has significantly improved from AA intervention in their Kannada sight word reading.

### 4.7.3.3.4 Within group analysis for Sight word Kan C group

Table 4.128: Descriptive statistics for Sight word Kan subtest data (C group)

| Data | $n$ | Median | $M$ | $SD$ | Min | Max |
|------|-----|--------|-----|------|-----|-----|
| Pretest | 15 | 5.00 | 4.60 | .98 | 3.00 | 6.00 |
| Posttest | 15 | 5.00 | 4.77 | 1.45 | 2.00 | 7.00 |
| Follow up | - | | | | | |

Table 4.128.A: Pre, Post & Follow up intervention comparisons within (C) group

| | $z$ | $p$ | Effect size |
|---|-----|-----|-------------|
| Pretest-Posttest | -.081 | .935 | -0.020 |
| Pretest-Follow up | | | |
| Posttest-Follow up | | | |

There was a no significant increase from pretest (median= 5.00) to posttest (median= 5.00), $z$=-.08, p=0.96, r= -0.02. This indicates that the group has not improved from pretest to posttest assessment in the control group.

### 4.7.3.4 Between group analyses for Sight word Kan post intervention data

Table 4.129: Sight word Kan subtest data between groups analyses (Post-test data)

| Groups | $n$ | Mean ranks | Chi sq | df | $p$ |
|--------|-----|------------|--------|-----|-----|
| Y&AA | 15 | 48.03 | | | |
| N&AA | 15 | 23.33 | 28.869 | 3 | .000* |
| C | 15 | 18.80 | | | |
| AA | 12 | 25.04 | | | |

* significant at 0.05 level

181

There was a statistically significant difference between the groups on the levels of Kannada sight word reading skills in the posttest data $(x^2(2) = 26.87, p= .00)$ with a mean rank of 48.03 (Median= 8.00) for Y&AA group, 23.33 (Median= 5.00) for N&AA group, 18.80 (Median= 5.00) for C group and 25.04 (Median= 5.00) for AA group.

**4.7.3.4. A. Post-hoc analyses for Sight word Kan post intervention**

**Table 4. 129.A: Sight word Kan post intervention data Post-hoc analyses between Y&AA-N&AA**

| Groups | $n$ | Mean ranks | U | $z$ | $p$ | Effect size |
|--------|-----|-----------|------|--------|-------|-------------|
| Y&AA | 15 | 22.07 | 14.00 | -4.148 | .000* | -1.071 |
| N&AA | 15 | 8.93 | | | | |

* significant at 0.05 level

Descriptive statistics showed that Y&AA group (median= 8.00; mean rank = 22.07) had higher scores than that N&AA group (median= 5.00; mean rank = 8.93). Mann-Whitney U value was found to be statistically significant U= 14.00 (z = -4.15), p <0.001 and the difference between Y&AA and N&AA groups was large (r = -1.07).

**Table 4. 129.B: Sight word Kan post intervention data Post-hoc analyses between Y&AA-AA**

| Groups | $n$ | Mean ranks | U | $z$ | $p$ | Effect size |
|--------|-----|-----------|------|--------|-------|-------------|
| Y&AA | 15 | 19.37 | 9.50 | -4.003 | .000* | -1.034 |
| AA | 12 | 7.29 | | | | |

* significant at 0.05 level

Descriptive statistics showed that Y&AA group (median= 8.00; mean rank = 19.37) had higher scores than that AA group (median= 5.00; mean rank = 7.29). Mann-Whitney U value was found to be statistically significant U= 9.50 (z = -4.00), p <0.001 and the difference between Y&AA and AA groups was large (r = -1.03).

**Table 4. 129.C: Sight word Kan post intervention data Post-hoc analyses between Y&AA-C**

| Groups | n | Mean ranks | U | z | p | Effect size |
|--------|----|------------|------|--------|-------|-------------|
| Y&AA | 15 | 22.60 | 6.00 | -4.466 | .000* | -1.154 |
| C | 15 | 8.40 | | | | |

* significant at 0.05 level

Descriptive statistics showed that Y&AA group (median= 8.00; mean rank = 22.60) had higher scores than that C group (median= 5.00; mean rank = 8.40). Mann-Whitney U value was found to be statistically significant U= 6.00 (z = -4.46), p <0.001 and the difference between Y&AA and C groups was large (r = -1.15).

**Table 4. 129.D: Sight word Kan post intervention data Post-hoc analyses between N&AA-AA**

| Groups | n | Mean ranks | U | z | p | Effect size |
|--------|----|------------|-------|-------|------|-------------|
| N&AA | 15 | 13.47 | 82.00 | -.412 | .680 | -0.106 |
| AA | 12 | 14.67 | | | | |

Descriptive statistics showed that N&AA group (median= 5.00; mean rank = 13.47) had equal scores as AA group (median= 5.00; mean rank = 14.67). Mann-Whitney U value was found to be statistically non significant U= 82.00 (z = -4.12), p =0.68.

**Table 4. 129.E: Sight word Kan post intervention data Post-hoc analyses between N&AA-C**

| Groups | n | Mean ranks | U | z | p | Effect size |
|--------|----|------------|-------|-------|------|-------------|
| N&AA | 15 | 16.93 | 91.00 | -.923 | .356 | -0.238 |
| C | 15 | 14.07 | | | | |

Descriptive statistics showed that N&AA group (median= 5.00; mean rank = 16.93) had equal scores as C group (median= 5.00; mean rank = 14.07). Mann-Whitney U value was found to be statistically non significant U= 91.00 (z = -.92), p =0.36.

**Table 4. 129.F: Sight word Kan post intervention data Post-hoc analyses between AA-C**

| Groups | $n$ | Mean ranks | U | $z$ | $p$ | Effect size |
|--------|-----|------------|------|--------|------|-------------|
| AA | 12 | 16.08 | 65.00 | -1.258 | .209 | -0.363 |
| C | 15 | 12.33 | | | | |

Descriptive statistics showed that AA group (median= 5.00; mean rank = 16.08) had equal scores as C group (median= 5.00; mean rank = 12.33). Mann-Whitney U value was found to be statistically non significant U= 65.00 (z = -1.26), p =0.21.

**4.7.3.5 Between group analyses for Sight word Kan follow up data**

**Table 4.130: Sight word Kan subtest data between groups analyses (Follow up data)**

| Groups | $n$ | Mean ranks | Chi sq | df | $p$ |
|--------|-----|------------|--------|-----|------|
| Y&AA | 15 | 49.93 | | | |
| N&AA | 15 | 24.40 | 38.129 | 2 | .000* |
| C | 15 | - | | | |
| AA | 12 | 26.67 | | | |

* significant at 0.05 level

There was a statistically significant difference between the groups on the levels of Kannada sight word reading skills in the follow up data ($x^2(2)$ = 38.13, $p$= .00) with a mean rank of 49.93 (Median= 11.00) for Y&AA group, 24.40 (Median= 6.00) for N&AA group, and 26.67 (Median= 6.00) for AA group.

**4.7.3.5. A. Post-hoc analyses for Sight word Kan follow up data**

**Table 4.130.A: Sight word Kan follow up data Post-hoc analyses between Y&AA-N&AA**

| Groups | $n$ | Mean ranks | U | $z$ | $p$ | Effect size |
|--------|-----|------------|------|--------|-------|-------------|
| Y&AA | 15 | 22.97 | 0.50 | -4.677 | .000* | -1.208 |
| N&AA | 15 | 8.03 | | | | |

* significant at 0.05 level

Descriptive statistics showed that Y&AA group (median= 11.00; mean rank = 22.97) had higher scores than that N&AA group (median= 6.00; mean rank = 8.03). Mann-Whitney U value was found to be statistically significant U= 0.50 (z = -4.47), p <0.001 and the difference between Y&AA and N&AA groups was large (r = -1.21).

**Table 4.130.B: Sight word Kan follow up data Post-hoc analyses between Y&AA-AA**

| Groups | n | Mean ranks | U | z | p | Effect size |
|--------|-----|------------|------|--------|-------|-------------|
| Y&AA | 15 | 19.97 | 0.50 | -4.420 | .000* | -1.142 |
| AA | 12 | 6.54 | | | | |

* significant at 0.05 level

Descriptive statistics showed that Y&AA group (median= 11.00; mean rank = 19.97) had higher scores than that AA group (median= 6.00; mean rank = 6.54). Mann-Whitney U value was found to be statistically significant U= 0.50 (z = -4.42), p <0.001 and the difference between Y&AA and AA groups was large (r = -1.14).

**Table 4.130.C: Sight word Kan follow up data Post-hoc analyses between N&AA-AA**

| Groups | n | Mean ranks | U | z | p | Effect size |
|--------|-----|------------|-------|-------|------|-------------|
| N&AA | 15 | 13.53 | 83.00 | -.362 | .717 | -0.093 |
| AA | 12 | 14.58 | | | | |

Descriptive statistics showed that N&AA group (median= 6.00; mean rank = 13.53) had equal scores as AA group (median= 6.00; mean rank = 14.58). Mann-Whitney U value was found to be statistically non significant U= 83.00 (z = -.36), p =0.36.

Graph 16

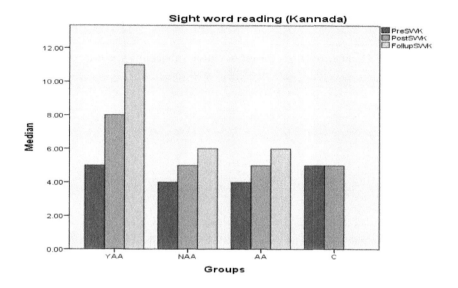

#### 4.7.4 Decoding Kannada

#### 4.7.4.1 Homogeneity test for intervention subgroups for Decoding Kan

Table 4.131: Homogeneity test for intervention subgroups pre-intervention data Decoding Kan

| Groups | n | Mean ranks | Chi sq | df | p |
|--------|---|------------|--------|-----|-----|
| Y&AA1 | 8 | 25.38 | | | |
| Y&AA2 | 7 | 17.21 | | | |
| N&AA1 | 7 | 26.57 | 5.04 | | |
| N&AA2 | 8 | 15.88 | | 5 | .41 |
| AA1 | 7 | 23.43 | | | |
| AA2 | 5 | 20.50 | | | |

There was no statistically significant difference ($p$=0.39) between the experimental groups carried out in two seasons in Sight word Kan subtest scores before the commencement of the intervention. Hence the groups Y&AA1 & Y&AA2, N&AA1 & N&AA2, AA1 & AA2 are combined respectively in further analysis

#### 4.7.4.2 Homogeneity test for Decoding Kan pre-intervention data

Table 4.132: Homogeneity test for Decoding Kan pre-intervention data

| Groups | n | Mean ranks | Chi sq | df | p |
|--------|-----|------------|--------|-----|------|
| Y&AA | 15 | 29.67 | | | |
| N&AA | 15 | 28.20 | .311 | 3 | .958 |
| C | 15 | 27.70 | | | |
| AA | 12 | 30.79 | | | |

There was no statistically significant difference ($p$=0.96) between the experimental and control groups in Kannada decoding skills before the start of the intervention.

187

### 4.7.4.3 Within group analysis for Decoding Kan

### 4.7.4.3.1 Within group analysis for Decoding Kan Y&AA group

**Table 4.133: Descriptive statistics for Decoding Kannada subtest data (Y&AA group)**

| Data | $n$ | Median | $M$ | $SD$ | Min | Max |
|------|-----|--------|-----|------|-----|-----|
| Pretest | 15 | 4.00 | 3.73 | 1.03 | 2.00 | 6.00 |
| Posttest | 15 | 5.00 | 4.80 | 1.01 | 3.00 | 7.00 |
| Follow up | 15 | 9.00 | 9.27 | 2.43 | 6.00 | 14.00 |

**Table 4.133.A: Pre, Post & Follow up intervention comparisons within (Y&AA) group**

| | $z$ | $p$ | Effect size |
|---|-----|-----|-------------|
| Pretest-Posttest | -3.066 | .002* | -0.792 |
| Pretest-Follow up | -3.431 | .001* | -0.886 |
| Posttest-Follow up | -3.431 | .001* | -0.886 |

* significant at 0.05 level

There was a significant increase from pretest (median= 4.00) to posttest (median= 5.00), z=-3.06, p<0.001, r= -0.79, pretest (median=4.00) to follow up (median=9.00)z=-3.43, p<0.001, r=-0.88 and posttest (median=5.00) to follow up (median=9.00) z=-3.43, p<0.001 r= -0.88 in the Kannada decoding scores, and the decrease was large. This indicates that the group has significantly improved from Y&AA intervention in their Kannada decoding skills and the improvement continued over a period of time till the follow up assessment was made.

### 4.7.4.3.2 Within group analysis for Decoding Kan N&AA group

**Table 4.134: Descriptive statistics for Decoding Kannada subtest data (N&AA group)**

| Data | $n$ | Median | $M$ | $SD$ | Min | Max |
|------|-----|--------|-----|------|-----|-----|
| Pretest | 15 | 4.00 | 3.53 | 1.87 | 1.00 | 6.00 |
| Posttest | 15 | 4.00 | 3.77 | .89 | 2.00 | 5.00 |
| Follow up | 15 | 6.00 | 5.97 | 1.13 | 4.00 | 8.00 |

**Table 4.134.A: Pre, Post & Follow up intervention comparisons within (N&AA) group**

|  | z | p | Effect size |
|---|---|---|---|
| Pretest-Posttest | -.443 | .658 | -0.114 |
| Pretest-Follow up | -3.204 | .001* | -0.827 |
| Posttest-Follow up | -3.441 | .001* | -0.889 |

* significant at 0.05 level

There was no significant difference from pretest (median= 4.00) to posttest (median= 4.00), z=-.44, p=.66, r= -0.11, but there was significant increase from pretest (median=4.00) to follow up (median=6.00)z=-3.20, p<0.001, r=-0.83 and posttest (median=4.00) to follow up (median=6.00) z=-3.44, p<0.001 r= -0.88 in the Kannada decoding scores, and the decrease was large. This indicates that the group has significantly improved from N&AA intervention in their Kannada decoding skills after the end of intervention.

### 4.7.4.3.3 Within group analysis for Decoding Kan AA group

**Table 4.135: Descriptive statistics for Decoding Kannada subtest data (AA group)**

| Data | n | Median | M | SD | Min | Max |
|---|---|---|---|---|---|---|
| Pretest | 12 | 4.00 | 3.75 | .62 | 3.00 | 5.00 |
| Posttest | 12 | 4.50 | 4.50 | .81 | 3.00 | 6.00 |
| Follow up | 12 | 7.00 | 6.77 | .88 | 5.00 | 8.00 |

**Table 4.135.A: Pre, Post & Follow up intervention comparisons within (AA) group**

|  | z | p | Effect size |
|---|---|---|---|
| Pretest-Posttest | -2.310 | .021* | -0.667 |
| Pretest-Follow up | -3.100 | .002* | -0.895 |
| Posttest-Follow up | -3.088 | .002* | -0.892 |

* significant at 0.05 level

There was a significant increase from pretest (median= 4.00) to posttest (median= 4.50), z=-2.31, p<0.001, r= -0.66, pretest (median=4.00) to follow up (median=7.00)z=-3.10, p<0.001, r=-0.89 and posttest (median=4.50) to follow up (median=7.00) z=-3.43, p<0.001 r= -0.89 in the Kannada decoding scores, and the increase was moderate to large. This indicates that the group has significantly improved from AA intervention in their Kannada decoding skills and the improvement continued over a period of time till the follow up assessment was made.

**4.7.4.3.4 Within group analysis for Decoding Kan C group**

**Table 4.136: Descriptive statistics for Decoding Kannada subtest data (C group)**

| Data | *n* | Median | *M* | *SD* | Min | Max |
|------|-----|--------|-----|------|-----|-----|
| Pretest | 15 | 3.00 | 3.60 | 1.12 | 2.00 | 6.00 |
| Posttest | 15 | 3.00 | 3.13 | .92 | 2.00 | 5.00 |
| Follow up | - | | | | | |

**Table 4.136.A: Pre, Post & Follow up intervention comparisons within (C) group**

| | *z* | *p* | Effect size |
|---|-----|-----|-------------|
| Pretest-Posttest | -1.355 | .176 | -0.350 |

There was no significant difference from pretest (median= 3.00) to posttest (median= 3.00), z=-1.35, p=.18, r= -0.35. This indicates that the group has not improved in the control group from pretest to posttest assessment.

**4.7.4.4 Between group analyses for Decoding Kan post intervention data**

**Table 4.137: Decoding Kan subtest data between groups analyses (Post-test data)**

| Groups | *n* | Mean ranks | *Chi sq* | *df* | *p* |
|--------|-----|-----------|----------|------|-----|
| Y&AA | 15 | 40.03 | | | |
| N&AA | 15 | 24.07 | 20.472 | 3 | .000* |
| C | 15 | 16.60 | | | |
| AA | 12 | 36.88 | | | |

* significant at 0.05 level

There was a statistically significant difference between the groups on the Kannada decoding scores in the posttest data ($x^2(2)$ = 20.47, $p$= .00) with a mean rank of 40.03 (Median= 5.00) for Y&AA group, 24.07 (Median= 4.00) for N&AA group, 16.60 (Median= 3.00) for C group and 36.88 (Median= 4.50) for AA group.

**4.7.4.4. A. Post-hoc analyses for Decoding Kan post intervention**

**Table 4. 137.A: Decoding Kan post intervention data Post-hoc analyses between Y&AA-N&AA**

| Groups | $n$ | Mean ranks | U | $z$ | $p$ | Effect size |
|--------|-----|-----------|------|--------|-------|-------------|
| Y&AA   | 15  | 19.83     | 47.50 | -2.805 | .005* | -0.724      |
| N&AA   | 15  | 11.17     |      |        |       |             |

* significant at 0.05 level

Descriptive statistics showed that Y&AA group (median= 5.00; mean rank = 19.83) had higher scores than that N&AA group (median= 4.00; mean rank = 11.17). Mann-Whitney U value was found to be statistically significant U= 47.50 ($z$ = -2.80), p <0.001 and the difference between Y&AA and N&AA groups was moderate (r = -0.72).

**Table 4. 137.B: Decoding Kan post intervention data Post-hoc analyses between Y&AA-AA**

| Groups | $n$ | Mean ranks | U | $z$ | $p$ | Effect size |
|--------|-----|-----------|-------|-------|------|-------------|
| Y&AA   | 15  | 14.93     | 76.00 | -.728 | .467 | -0.188      |
| AA     | 12  | 12.83     |       |       |      |             |

Descriptive statistics showed that Y&AA group (median= 5.00; mean rank = 14.93) had higher scores than that AA group (median= 4.50; mean rank = 12.83). Mann-Whitney U value was found to be statistically non significant U= 76.00 ($z$ = -.73), p =0.47.

**Table 4. 137.C: Decoding Kan post intervention data Post-hoc analyses between Y&AA-C**

| Groups | n | Mean ranks | U | z | p | Effect size |
|--------|---|-----------|-----|------|------|-------------|
| Y&AA | 15 | 21.27 | 26.00 | -3.689 | .000* | -0.953 |
| C | 15 | 9.73 | | | | |

* significant at 0.05 level

Descriptive statistics showed that Y&AA group (median= 5.00; mean rank = 21.27) had higher scores than that C group (median= 3.00; mean rank = 9.73). Mann-Whitney U value was found to be statistically significant U= 26.00 (z = -3.68), p <0.001 and the difference between Y&AA and C groups was large (r = -0.95).

**Table 4. 137.D: Decoding Kan post intervention data Post-hoc analyses between N&AA-AA**

| Groups | n | Mean ranks | U | z | p | Effect size |
|--------|---|-----------|-----|------|------|-------------|
| N&AA | 15 | 166.00 | 46.00 | -2.254 | .024* | -0.582 |
| AA | 12 | 212.00 | | | | |

* significant at 0.05 level

Descriptive statistics showed that N&AA group (median= 4.00; mean rank = 166.00) had lower scores than that AA group (median= 4.50; mean rank = 212.00). Mann-Whitney U value was found to be statistically significant U= 46.00 (z = -2.25), p <0.001 and the difference between N&AA and AA groups was moderate (r = -0.58).

**Table 4. 137.E: Decoding Kan post intervention data Post-hoc analyses between N&AA-C**

| Groups | n | Mean ranks | U | z | p | Effect size |
|--------|---|-----------|-----|------|------|-------------|
| N&AA | 15 | 17.83 | 77.50 | -1.528 | .127 | -0.394 |
| C | 15 | 13.17 | | | | |

Descriptive statistics showed that N&AA group (median= 4.00; mean rank = 17.83) had higher scores than that C group (median= 3.00; mean rank = 13.17). Mann-Whitney U value was found to be statistically non significant U= 77.50 (z = -1.58), p =.13.

**Table 4. 137.F: Decoding Kan post intervention data Post-hoc analyses between AA-C**

| Groups | $n$ | Mean ranks | U | $z$ | $p$ | Effect size |
|--------|-----|------------|-------|--------|-------|-------------|
| AA | 12 | 19.38 | 25.50 | -3.259 | .001* | -0.941 |
| C | 15 | 9.70 | | | | |

* significant at 0.05 level

Descriptive statistics showed that AA group (median= 4.50; mean rank = 19.38) had higher scores than that C group (median= 3.00; mean rank = 9.70). Mann-Whitney U value was found to be statistically significant U= 25.50 (z = -3.25), p <0.001 and the difference between AA and C groups was large (r = -0.94).

**4.7.4.5 Between group analyses for Decoding Kan follow up data**

**Table 4.138: Decoding Kan subtest data between groups analyses (Follow up data)**

| Groups | $n$ | Mean ranks | Chi sq | df | $p$ |
|--------|-----|------------|--------|----|-----|
| Y&AA | 15 | 46.77 | | | |
| N&AA | 15 | 24.00 | 35.098 | 2 | .000* |
| C | 15 | - | | | |
| AA | 12 | 33.42 | | | |

* significant at 0.05 level

There was a statistically significant difference between the groups on the Kannada decoding scores in the follow up data ($x^2(2) = 35.09$, $p= .00$) with a mean rank of 46.77 (Median= 9.00) for Y&AA group, 24.00 (Median= 6.00) for N&AA group and 33.42 (Median= 7.00) for AA group.

**4.7.4.5. A. Post-hoc analyses for Decoding Kan follow up data**

**Table 4.138.A: Decoding Kanfollow up data Post-hoc analyses between Y&AA-N&AA**

| Groups | $n$ | Mean ranks | U | $z$ | $p$ | Effect size |
|--------|-----|------------|-------|--------|-------|-------------|
| Y&AA | 15 | 21.80 | 18.00 | -3.975 | .000* | -1.027 |
| N&AA | 15 | 9.20 | | | | |

* significant at 0.05 level

Descriptive statistics showed that Y&AA group (median= 9.00; mean rank = 21.80) had higher scores than that N&AA group (median= 6.50; mean rank = 9.20). Mann-Whitney U value was found to be statistically significant U= 18.00 (z = -3.97), p <0.001 and the difference between Y&AA and N&AA groups was large (r = -1.03).

**Table 4.138.B: Decoding Kanfollow up data Post-hoc analyses between Y&AA-AA**

| Groups | n | Mean ranks | U | z | p | Effect size |
|--------|---|-----------|------|--------|-------|-------------|
| Y&AA | 15 | 18.07 | 29.00 | -3.049 | .002* | -0.787 |
| AA | 12 | 8.92 | | | | |

* significant at 0.05 level

Descriptive statistics showed that Y&AA group (median= 9.00; mean rank = 18.07) had higher scores than that AA group (median= 7.00; mean rank = 8.92). Mann-Whitney U value was found to be statistically significant U= 29.00 (z = -3.05), p <0.001 and the difference between Y&AA and AA groups was moderate (r = -0.78).

**Table 4.138.C: Decoding Kanfollow up data Post-hoc analyses between N&AA-AA**

| Groups | n | Mean ranks | U | z | p | Effect size |
|--------|---|-----------|------|--------|------|-------------|
| N&AA | 15 | 11.53 | 53.00 | -1.883 | .060 | -0.486 |
| AA | 12 | 17.08 | | | | |

Descriptive statistics showed that N&AA group (median= 6.00; mean rank = 11.53) had lower scores than that AA group (median= 7.00; mean rank = 17.08). Mann-Whitney U value was found to be statistically non significant U= 53.00 (z = -1.88), p =0.06.

Graph 17

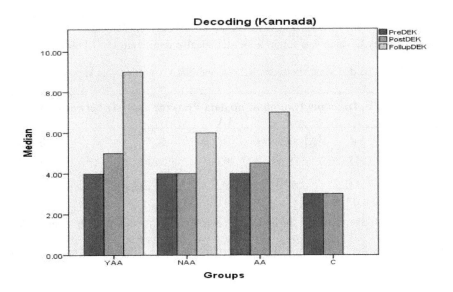

## 4.8 Testing Hypothesis 7: Practice of yoga will improve arithmetic efficiency in Children with LD

### 4.8.1 Arithmetic

#### 4.8.1.1 Homogeneity test for intervention subgroups for Arithmetic

**Table 4.139: Homogeneity test for intervention subgroups pre-intervention data Arithmetic**

| Groups | $n$ | Mean ranks | Chi sq | df | p |
|--------|-----|------------|--------|-----|-----|
| Y&AA1 | 8 | 20.63 | | | |
| Y&AA2 | 7 | 21.71 | | | |
| N&AA1 | 7 | 16.00 | 2.65 | | |
| N&AA2 | 8 | 23.50 | | 5 | .75 |
| AA1 | 7 | 25.93 | | | |
| AA2 | 5 | 20.90 | | | |

There was no statistically significant difference ($p$=0.75) between the experimental groups carried out in two seasons in Arithmetic subtest scores before the commencement of the intervention. Hence the groups Y&AA1 & Y&AA2, N&AA1 & N&AA2, AA1 & AA2 are combined respectively in further analysis

#### 4.8.1.2 Homogeneity test for Arithmetic pre-intervention data

**Table 4.140: Homogeneity test for Arithmetic pretest data**

| Groups | $n$ | Mean ranks | Chi sq | df | p |
|--------|-----|------------|--------|-----|-----|
| Y&AA | 15 | 29.50 | | | |
| N&AA | 15 | 27.97 | 1.254 | 3 | .740 |
| C | 15 | 26.23 | | | |
| AA | 12 | 33.13 | | | |

There was no statistically significant difference ($p$=0.74) between the experimental and control groups on levels of arithmetic performance before the start of the intervention.

196

### 4.8.1.3 Within group analysis for Arithmetic

### 4.8.1.3.1 Within group analysis for Arithmetic Y&AA group

#### Table 4.141: Descriptive statistics for Arithmetic subtest data (Y&AA group)

| Data | n | Median | M | SD | Min | Max |
|---|---|---|---|---|---|---|
| Pretest | 15 | 26.00 | 27.13 | 3.68 | 23.00 | 38.00 |
| Posttest | 15 | 49.00 | 49.93 | 3.22 | 46.00 | 58.00 |
| Follow up | 15 | 55.00 | 54.60 | 3.22 | 49.00 | 61.00 |

#### Table 4.141.A: Pre, Post & Follow up intervention comparisons within (Y&AA) group

| | z | p | Effect size |
|---|---|---|---|
| Pretest-Posttest | -3.41 | .001* | -0.881 |
| Pretest-Follow up | -3.41 | .001* | -0.881 |
| Posttest-Follow up | -3.42 | .001* | -0.883 |

* significant at 0.05 level

There was a significant increase from pretest (median= 26.00) to posttest (median= 49.00), z=-3.41, p<0.001, r= -0.88, pretest (median=26.00) to follow up (median=55.00)z=-3.41, p<0.001, r=-0.88 and posttest (median=49.00) to follow up (median=55.00) z=-3.42, p<0.001 r= -0.88 in the scores of arithmetic problem solving, and the increase was large. This indicates that the group has significantly improved from Y&AA intervention in their arithmetic problem solvingskill and the improvement continued over a period of time till the follow up assessment was made.

### 4.8.1.3.2 Within group analysis for Arithmetic N&AA group

#### Table 4.142: Descriptive statistics for Arithmetic subtest data (N&AA group)

| Data | n | Median | M | SD | Min | Max |
|---|---|---|---|---|---|---|
| Pretest | 15 | 26.00 | 26.53 | 3.68 | 19.00 | 33.00 |
| Posttest | 15 | 43.00 | 41.73 | 2.46 | 37.00 | 45.00 |
| Follow up | 15 | 50.00 | 50.37 | 2.02 | 47.00 | 54.00 |

**Table 4.142.A: Pre, Post & Follow up intervention comparisons within (N&AA) group**

|  | $z$ | $p$ | Effect size |
|---|---|---|---|
| Pretest-Posttest | -3.41 | .001* | -0.881 |
| Pretest-Follow up | -3.41 | .001* | -0.881 |
| Posttest-Follow up | -3.43 | .001* | -0.886 |

* significant at 0.05 level

There was a significant increase from pretest (median= 26.00) to posttest (median= 43.00), z=-3.41, p<0.001, r= -0.88, pretest (median=26.00) to follow up (median=50.00)z=-3.41, p<0.001, r=-0.88 and posttest (median=43.00) to follow up (median=50.00) z=-3.43, p<0.001 r= -0.88 in the scores of arithmetic problem solving, and the increase was large. This indicates that the group has significantly improved from N&AA intervention in their arithmetic problem solving skill and the improvement continued over a period of time till the follow up assessment was made.

### 4.8.1.3.3 Within group analysis for Arithmetic AA group

**Table 4.143: Descriptive statistics for Arithmetic subtest data (AA group)**

| Data | $n$ | Median | $M$ | $SD$ | Min | Max |
|---|---|---|---|---|---|---|
| Pretest | 12 | 27.00 | 27.27 | 3.26 | 21.00 | 32.00 |
| Posttest | 12 | 38.00 | 37.77 | 3.70 | 31.00 | 43.00 |
| Follow up | 12 | 44.50 | 43.00 | 3.67 | 35.00 | 46.00 |

**Table 4.143.A: Pre, Post & Follow up intervention comparisons within (AA) group**

|  | $z$ | $p$ | Effect size |
|---|---|---|---|
| Pretest-Posttest | -3.06 | .002* | -0.884 |
| Pretest-Follow up | -3.17 | .002* | -0.916 |
| Posttest-Follow up | -3.17 | .002* | -0.916 |

* significant at 0.05 level

There was a significant increase from pretest (median= 27.00) to posttest (median= 38.00), z=-3.06, p<0.001, r= -0.88, pretest (median=38.00) to follow up (median=44.50)z=-3.17, p<0.001, r=-0.91 and posttest (median=38.00) to follow up (median=44.50) z=-3.17, p<0.001 r= -0.91 in the scores of arithmetic problem solving, and the increase was large. This indicates that the group has significantly improved from AA intervention in their arithmetic problem solving skill and the improvement continued over a period of time till the follow up assessment was made.

#### 4.8.1.3.4 Within group analysis for Arithmetic C group

**Table 4.144: Descriptive statistics for Arithmetic subtest data (C group)**

| Data | $n$ | Median | $M$ | SD | Min | Max |
|---|---|---|---|---|---|---|
| Pretest | 15 | 27.00 | 25.66 | 3.39 | 19.00 | 31.00 |
| Posttest | 15 | 27.00 | 26.93 | 3.19 | 21.00 | 32.00 |
| Follow up | - | | | | | |

**Table 4.144.A: Pre, Post & Follow up intervention comparisons within (C) group**

| | $z$ | $p$ | Effect size |
|---|---|---|---|
| Pretest-Posttest | -1.78 | .075 | -0.459 |
| Pretest-Follow up | | | |
| Posttest-Follow up | | | |

There was no significant change from pretest (median= 27.00) to posttest (median= 27.00), z=-1.78, p= .075, r= -0.45 in the scores of arithmetic problem solving.

#### 4.8.1.4 Between group analyses for Arithmetic post intervention data

**Table 4.145: Arithmetic subtest data between groups analyses (Post-test data)**

| Groups | $n$ | Mean ranks | Chi sq | df | $p$ |
|---|---|---|---|---|---|
| Y&AA | 15 | 50.00 | | | |
| N&AA | 15 | 32.90 | 49.838 | 3 | .000* |
| C | 15 | 8.10 | | | |
| AA | 12 | 24.00 | | | |

* significant at 0.05 level

There was a statistically significant difference between the groups in arithmetic problem solving in the posttest data ($x^2(2)$ = 49.84, $p$= .00) with a mean rank of 50.00 (Median= 49.00) for Y&AA group, 32.90 (Median= 43.00) for N&AA group, 8.10 (Median= 27.00) for C group and 24.00 (Median= 38.00) for AA group.

**4.8.1.4.A. Post-hoc analyses for Arithmetic post intervention**

**Table 4.145.A: Arithmetic post intervention data Post-hoc analyses between Y&AA-N&AA**

| Groups | $n$ | Mean ranks | U | $z$ | $p$ | Effect size |
|--------|-----|-----------|-----|--------|-------|-------------|
| Y&AA | 15 | 23.00 | .00 | -4.684 | .000* | -1.210 |
| N&AA | 15 | 8.00 | | | | |

* significant at 0.05 level

Descriptive statistics showed that Y&AA group (median= 49.00; mean rank = 23.00) had higher scores than that N&AA group (median= 43.00; mean rank = 8.00). Mann-Whitney U value was found to be statistically significant U= .00 (z = -4.68), p <0.001 and the difference between Y&AA and N&AA groups was large (r = -1.21).

**Table 4. 145.B: Arithmetic post intervention data Post-hoc analyses between Y&AA-AA**

| Groups | $n$ | Mean ranks | U | $z$ | $p$ | Effect size |
|--------|-----|-----------|-----|--------|-------|-------------|
| Y&AA | 15 | 20.00 | .00 | -4.407 | .000* | -1.138 |
| AA | 12 | 6.50 | | | | |

* significant at 0.05 level

Descriptive statistics showed that Y&AA group (median= 49.00; mean rank = 20.00) had higher scores than that AA group (median= 38.00; mean rank = 6.50). Mann-Whitney U value was found to be statistically significant U= .00 (z = -4.40), p <0.001 and the difference between Y&AA and AA groups was large (r = -1.14).

**Table 4. 145.C: Arithmetic post intervention data Post-hoc analyses between Y&AA-C**

| Groups | n | Mean ranks | U | z | p | Effect size |
|--------|---|-----------|-----|--------|-------|-------------|
| Y&AA | 15 | 23.00 | .00 | -4.681 | .000* | -1.209 |
| C | 15 | 8.00 | | | | |

* significant at 0.05 level

Descriptive statistics showed that Y&AA group (median= 49.00; mean rank = 23.00) had higher scores than that C group (median= 27.00; mean rank = 8.00). Mann-Whitney U value was found to be statistically significant U= .00 (z = -4.68), p <0.001 and the difference between Y&AA and C groups was large (r = -1.21).

**Table 4. 145.D: Arithmetic post intervention data Post-hoc analyses between N&AA-AA**

| Groups | n | Mean ranks | U | z | p | Effect size |
|--------|---|-----------|-------|--------|-------|-------------|
| N&AA | 15 | 17.90 | 31.50 | -2.877 | .004* | -0.743 |
| AA | 12 | 9.13 | | | | |

* significant at 0.05 level

Descriptive statistics showed that N&AA group (median= 43.00; mean rank = 17.90) had higher scores than that AA group (median= 38.00; mean rank = 9.13). Mann-Whitney U value was found to be statistically significant U= 31.50 (z = -2.87), p <0.001 and the difference between N&AA and AA groups was large (r = -0.74).

**Table 4. 145.E: Arithmetic post intervention data Post-hoc analyses between N&AA-C**

| Groups | n | Mean ranks | U | z | p | Effect size |
|--------|---|-----------|-----|--------|-------|-------------|
| N&AA | 15 | 23.00 | .00 | -4.680 | .000* | -1.209 |
| C | 15 | 8.00 | | | | |

Descriptive statistics showed that N&AA group (median= 43.00; mean rank = 23.00) had higher scores than that C group (median= 27.00; mean rank = 8.00). Mann-Whitney U value was found to be statistically significant U= .00 (z = -4.68), p <0.001 and the difference between N&AA and C groups was large (r = -1.21).

**Table 4. 145.F: Arithmetic post intervention data Post-hoc analyses between AA-C**

| Groups | n | Mean ranks | U | z | p | Effect size |
|--------|---|-----------|-----|-------|-------|-------------|
| AA | 12 | 21.38 | 1.50 | -4.329 | .000* | -1.251 |
| C | 15 | 8.10 | | | | |

* significant at 0.05 level

Descriptive statistics showed that AA group (median= 38.00; mean rank = 21.38) had higher scores than that C group (median= 27.00; mean rank = 8.10). Mann-Whitney U value was found to be statistically significant U= 1.50 (z = -4.33), p <0.001 and the difference between AA and C groups was large (r = -1.25).

**4.8.1.5 Between group analyses for Arithmetic follow up data**

**Table 4.146: Arithmetic subtest data between groups analyses (Follow up data)**

| Groups | n | Mean ranks | Chi sq | df | p |
|--------|---|-----------|--------|-----|-----|
| Y&AA | 15 | 33.07 | | | |
| N&AA | 15 | 21.93 | 31.531 | 2 | .000* |
| C | 15 | | | | |
| AA | 12 | 6.50 | | | |

* significant at 0.05 level

There was a statistically significant difference between the groups in arithmetic problem solving in the follow up data ($x^2(2)$ = 31.53, $p$= .00) with a mean rank of 33.07 (Median= 55.00) for Y&AA group, 21.93 (Median= 50.00) for N&AA group, and 6.50 (Median= 44.50) for AA group.

**4.8.1.5. A. Post-hoc analyses for Arithmetic follow up data**

**Table 4.146.A: Arithmeticfollow up data Post-hoc analyses between Y&AA-N&AA**

| Groups | n | Mean ranks | z | p | Effect size |
|--------|---|-----------|--------|-------|-------------|
| Y&AA | 15 | 21.07 | -3.496 | .000* | -0.903 |
| N&AA | 15 | 9.93 | | | |

* significant at 0.05 level

**Table 4.146.B: Arithmeticfollow up data Post-hoc analyses between Y&AA-AA**

| Groups | *n* | Mean ranks | *z* | *p* | Effect size |
|--------|-----|-----------|-----|-----|-------------|
| Y&AA | 15 | 20.00 | -4.408 | .000* | -1.139 |
| AA | 12 | 6.50 | | | |

* significant at 0.05 level

**Table 4.146.C: Arithmeticfollow up data Post-hoc analyses between N&AA-AA**

| Groups | *n* | Mean ranks | *z* | *p* | Effect size |
|--------|-----|-----------|-----|-----|-------------|
| N&AA | 15 | 20.00 | -4.409 | .000* | -1.139 |
| AA | 12 | 6.50 | | | |

* significant at 0.05 level

Post hoc test shows that there is statistically significant difference between Y&AA and N&AA, Y&AA and AA, and N&AA and AA. Y&AA group performance was better than the other groups in follow up assessment

Graph 18

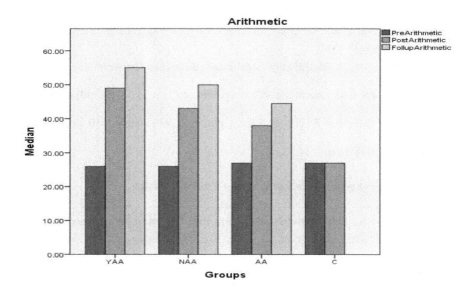

**4.9 Testing Hypothesis 8: Practice of yoga will improve behavioral adjustment in children with LD**

**4.9.1. Homogeneity test for intervention subgroups for Behv.Adjustment**

**Table 4.147:  Homogeneity test for Behavioral Adjustment pre intervention data**

| Groups | $n$ | Mean ranks | Chi sq | df | p |
|--------|-----|-----------|--------|-----|-----|
| Y&AA1 | 8 | 20.25 | | | |
| Y&AA2 | 7 | 14.64 | | | |
| N&AA1 | 7 | 24.00 | 14.25 | | |
| N&AA2 | 8 | 30.69 | | 5 | .014 |
| AA1 | 7 | 11.50 | | | |
| AA2 | 5 | 28.90 | | | |

* significant at 0.05 level

There was statistically significant difference ($p$=0.01) between experimental groups. Hence the groups are not combined in further analysis.

**4.9.2 Within group analysis for Behv.Adjustment**

**4.9.2.1 Within group analysis for Behv.Adjustment Y&AA1 group**

**Table 4.148: Descriptive statistics for subtest data (Y&AA1 group)**

| Data | $n$ | Median | $M$ | $SD$ | Min | Max |
|------|-----|--------|-----|------|-----|-----|
| Pretest | 8 | 5.00 | 4.87 | 1.24 | 3.00 | 7.00 |
| Posttest | 8 | 3.00 | 3.50 | .75 | 3.00 | 5.00 |
| Follow up | 8 | 2.00 | 2.00 | .75 | 1.00 | 3.00 |

**Table 4.148.A: Pre, Post & Follow up intervention comparisons within (Y&AA1) group**

| | $z$ | $p$ | Effect size |
|---|-----|-----|-------------|
| Pretest-Posttest | -2.33 | .020* | -0.82 |
| Pretest-Follow up | -2.53 | .011* | -0.89 |
| Posttest-Follow up | -2.58 | .010* | -0.91 |

* significant at 0.05 level

204

There was significant decrease from pretest (median= 5.00) to posttest (median= 3.00), z=-2.33, p<0.001, r= -0.82, pretest (median=5.00) to follow up (median=2.00) z=-2.53, p<0.001, r=-0.89 and posttest (median=3.00) to follow up (median=2.00) z=-2.58, p<0.001 r= -0.91 in the scores of behavioral adjustment, and the decrease was large.

### 4.9.2.2 Within group analysis for Behv.Adjustment Y&AA2 group

**Table 4.149: Descriptive statistics for subtest data (Y&AA2 group)**

| Data | n | Median | M | SD | Min | Max |
|---|---|---|---|---|---|---|
| Pretest | 7 | 4.00 | 4.14 | 1.34 | 2.00 | 6.00 |
| Posttest | 7 | 4.00 | 3.71 | 1.11 | 2.00 | 5.00 |
| Follow up | 7 | 2.00 | 2.14 | 0.69 | 1.00 | 3.00 |

**Table 4.149.A: Pre, Post & Follow up intervention comparisons within (Y&AA2) group**

| | z | p | Effect size |
|---|---|---|---|
| Pretest-Posttest | -1.00 | .317 | -0.378 |
| Pretest-Follow up | -2.13 | .033* | -0.806 |
| Posttest-Follow up | -2.05 | .040* | -0.776 |

* significant at 0.05 level

There was no significant decrease from pretest (median= 4.00) to posttest (median= 4.00), z=-1.00, p=0.32, r= -0.38, but there was sig decrease in pretest (median=4.00) to follow up (median=2.00) z=-2.3, p<0.001, r=-0.81 and posttest (median=4.00) to follow up (median=2.00) z=-2.05, p<0.001 r= -0.77 in the scores of behavioral adjustment, and the decrease was large.

### 4.9.2.3 Within group analysis for Behv.Adjustment N&AA1 group

#### Table 4.150: Descriptive statistics for subtest data (N&AA1 group)

| Data | $n$ | Median | $M$ | $SD$ | Min | Max |
|------|-----|--------|-----|------|-----|-----|
| Pretest | 7 | 5.00 | 5.28 | 1.11 | 4.00 | 7.00 |
| Posttest | 7 | 5.00 | 4.57 | 0.53 | 4.00 | 5.00 |
| Follow up | 7 | 2.00 | 2.28 | 0.75 | 1.00 | 3.00 |

#### Table 4.150.A: Pre, Post & Follow up intervention comparisons within (N&AA1) group

| | $z$ | $p$ | Effect size |
|---|---|---|---|
| Pretest-Posttest | -1.41 | .157 | -0.534 |
| Pretest-Follow up | -2.37 | .018* | -0.897 |
| Posttest-Follow up | -2.46 | .014* | -0.931 |

* significant at 0.05 level

There was no significant decrease from pretest (median= 5.00) to posttest (median= 5.00), z=-1.41, p=0.15, r= -0.53, but there was sig decrease in pretest (median=5.00) to follow up (median=2.00) z=-2.37, p<0.001, r=-0.89 and posttest (median=5.00) to follow up (median=2.00) z=-2.46, p<0.001 r= -0.93 in the scores of behavioral adjustment, and the decrease was large.

### 4.9.2.4 Within group analysis for Behv.Adjustment N&AA2 group

#### Table 4.151: Descriptive statistics for subtest data (N&AA2 group)

| Data | $n$ | Median | $M$ | $SD$ | Min | Max |
|------|-----|--------|-----|------|-----|-----|
| Pretest | 8 | 6.00 | 6.12 | 1.24 | 4.00 | 8.00 |
| Posttest | 8 | 4.50 | 4.37 | 1.06 | 3.00 | 6.00 |
| Follow up | 8 | 3.00 | 2.75 | 1.03 | 1.00 | 4.00 |

**Table 4.151.A: Pre, Post & Follow up intervention comparisons within (N&AA2) group**

| | $z$ | $p$ | Effect size |
|---|---|---|---|
| Pretest-Posttest | -2.56 | .010[*] | -0.907 |
| Pretest-Follow up | -2.53 | .011[*] | -0.897 |
| Posttest-Follow up | -2.26 | .024[*] | -0.801 |

[*]significant at 0.05 level

There was a significant decrease from pretest (median= 6.00) to posttest (median= 4.50), z=-2.56, p<0.001, r= -0.91, pretest (median=6.00) to follow up (median=3.00) z=-2.53, p<0.001, r=-0.89 and posttest (median=4.50) to follow up (median=3.00) z=-2.26, p<0.001 r= -0.80 in the scores of behavioral adjustment, and the decrease was large. This indicates that the group has significantly improved from N&AA2 intervention in their behavioral adjustment and the improvement continued over a period of time till the follow up assessment was made

### 4.9.2.5 Within group analysis for Behv.Adjustment AA1 group

**Table 4.152: Descriptive statistics for subtest data (AA1 group)**

| Data | $n$ | Median | $M$ | $SD$ | Min | Max |
|---|---|---|---|---|---|---|
| Pretest | 7 | 4.00 | 4.00 | 0.57 | 3.00 | 5.00 |
| Posttest | 7 | 3.00 | 3.00 | 1.00 | 1.00 | 4.00 |
| Follow up | 7 | 2.00 | 2.00 | 1.15 | 1.00 | 4.00 |

**Table 4.152.A: Pre, Post & Follow up intervention comparisons within (AA1) group**

| | $z$ | $p$ | Effect size |
|---|---|---|---|
| Pretest-Posttest | -1.84 | .066 | -0.696 |
| Pretest-Follow up | -2.21 | .027[*] | -0.837 |
| Posttest-Follow up | -1.82 | .068 | -0.689 |

[*]significant at 0.05 level

There was no significant decrease from pretest (median= 4.00) to posttest (median= 3.00), z=-1.84, p=0.66, r= -0.69, pretest (median=4.00) to follow up (median=2.00) z=-2.21, p<0.001, r=-0.84 and posttest (median=3.00) to follow up (median=2.00) z=-1.82, p=0.68 r= -0.68 in the scores of behavioral adjustment.

**4.9.2.6 Within group analysis for Behv.Adjustment AA2 group**

**Table 4.153: Descriptive statistics for subtest data (AA2group)**

| Data | $n$ | Median | $M$ | $SD$ | Min | Max |
|------|-----|--------|-----|------|-----|-----|
| Pretest | 5 | 6.00 | 6.00 | 1.58 | 4.00 | 8.00 |
| Posttest | 5 | 4.00 | 4.00 | 1.22 | 3.00 | 6.00 |
| Follow up | 5 | 3.00 | 2.40 | 0.89 | 1.00 | 3.00 |

**Table 4.153.A: Pre, Post & Follow up intervention comparisons within (AA2) group**

| | $z$ | $p$ | Effect size |
|------|-----|-----|-------------|
| Pretest-Posttest | -2.04 | .041[*] | -0.914 |
| Pretest-Follow up | -2.04 | .041[*] | -0.914 |
| Posttest-Follow up | -2.06 | .039[*] | -0.923 |

[*] significant at 0.05 level

There was a significant decrease from pretest (median= 6.00) to posttest (median= 4.00), z=-2.04, p<0.001, r= -0.91, pretest (median=6.00) to follow up (median=3.00) z=-2.04, p<0.001, r=-0.91 and posttest (median=4.00) to follow up (median=3.00) z=-2.06, p<0.001 r= -0.92 in the scores of behavioral adjustment, and the decrease was large. This indicates that the group has significantly improved from AA2 intervention in their behavioral adjustment and the improvement continued over a period of time till the follow up assessment was made

### 4.9.2.7 Within group analysis for Behv.Adjustment C group

**Table 4.154: Descriptive statistics for subtest data (C group)**

| Data | n | Median | M | SD | Min | Max |
|---|---|---|---|---|---|---|
| Pretest | 15 | 5.00 | 5.37 | 1.49 | 2.00 | 8.00 |
| Posttest | 15 | 5.00 | 5.57 | .83 | 4.00 | 7.00 |
| Follow up | | | | | | |

**Table 4.154.A: Pre, Post & Follow up intervention comparisons within (C) group**

| | z | p | Effect size |
|---|---|---|---|
| Pretest-Posttest | -.83 | .405 | -0.214 |

There was no decrease from pretest (median= 5.00) to posttest (median= 5.00), z=-.83, p<0.001, r= -0.21 in the scores of behavioral adjustment. Follow up data was not collected from C group. This indicates that the group has not changed from pretest to posttest in the control condition.

### 4.9.3.4 Between group analyses for Behv.Adjustment post intervention data

**Table 4.155: Between groups analyses Post-intervention data**

| Groups | n | Mean ranks | Chi sq | df | p |
|---|---|---|---|---|---|
| Y&AA1 | 8 | 17.44 | | | |
| Y&AA2 | 7 | 21.71 | | | |
| N&AA1 | 7 | 33.64 | | | |
| N&AA2 | 8 | 30.38 | 28.23 | 6 | .00 |
| AA1 | 7 | 12.86 | | | |
| AA2 | 5 | 24.30 | | | |
| C | 15 | 44.77 | | | |

* significant at 0.05 level

There was a statistically significant difference between the groups on the levels of behavioral adjustment in the posttest data ($x^2(2) = 28.23$, $p= .00$).

### 4.9.3.4.A. Post-hoc analyses for Behv.Adjustment post intervention

**Table 4.155.A: Behavioral Adjustment Post-intervention data Post-hoc analyses between YAA1-YAA2**

| Groups | $n$ | Mean ranks | U | $z$ | $p$ | Effect size |
|--------|-----|------------|-----|-------|------|-------------|
| YAA1 | 8 | 7.50 | 24 | -4.95 | .621 | -1.755 |
| YAA2 | 7 | 8.57 | | | | |

Mann-Whitney U value was found to be statistically non significant U= 24.00 (z = -4.95), p =.62

**Table 4.155.B: Behavioral Adjustment Post-intervention data Post-hoc analyses between YAA1-NAA1**

| Groups | $n$ | Mean ranks | U | $z$ | $p$ | Effect size |
|--------|-----|------------|------|-------|-------|-------------|
| YAA1 | 8 | 5.50 | 8.00 | -2.44 | .014* | -0.865 |
| NAA1 | 7 | 10.86 | | | | |

Mann-Whitney U value was found to be statistically significant U= 8.00 (z = - 2.44), p <0.001 and the difference between YAA1 and NAA1 groups was large (r = - .86).

**Table 4.155.C: Behavioral Adjustment Post-intervention data Post-hoc analyses between YAA1-NAA2**

| Groups | $n$ | Mean ranks | U | $z$ | $p$ | Effect size |
|--------|-----|------------|-------|-------|------|-------------|
| YAA1 | 8 | 6.56 | 16.50 | -1.72 | .084 | -0.609 |
| NAA2 | 8 | 10.44 | | | | |

Mann-Whitney U value was found to be statistically non significant U= 16.50 (z = -1.72), p =.08

**Table 4.155.D: Behavioral Adjustment Post-intervention data Post-hoc analyses between YAA1-AA1**

| Groups | $n$ | Mean ranks | U | $z$ | $p$ | Effect size |
|--------|-----|------------|-------|------|------|-------------|
| YAA1 | 8 | 8.75 | 22.00 | -.79 | .428 | -0.280 |
| AA1 | 7 | 7.14 | | | | |

Mann-Whitney U value was found to be statistically non significant U= 22.00

(z = -.79), p =.42

**Table 4.155.E: Behavioral Adjustment Post-intervention data Post-hoc analyses between YAA1-AA2**

| Groups | *n* | Mean ranks | U | *z* | *p* | Effect size |
|--------|-----|-----------|-------|-------|------|-------------|
| YAA1 | 8 | 6.38 | 15.00 | -.809 | .419 | -0.286 |
| AA2 | 5 | 8.00 | | | | |

Mann-Whitney U value was found to be statistically non significant U= 15.00

(z = -.80), p =.41

**Table 4.155.F: Behavioral Adjustment Post-intervention data Post-hoc analyses between YAA1-C**

| Groups | *n* | Mean ranks | U | *z* | *p* | Effect size |
|--------|-----|-----------|------|-------|--------|-------------|
| YAA1 | 8 | 5.25 | 6.00 | -3.62 | .00[*] | -1.283 |
| C | 15 | 15.60 | | | | |

[*]significant at 0.05 level

Mann-Whitney U value was found to be statistically significant U= 6.00 (z = -3.62), p <0.001 and the difference between YAA1 and C groups was large (r = -1.28).

**Table 4.155.G: Behavioral Adjustment Post-intervention data Post-hoc analyses between YAA2-NAA1**

| Groups | *n* | Mean ranks | U | *z* | *p* | Effect size |
|--------|-----|-----------|-------|-------|------|-------------|
| YAA2 | 7 | 5.86 | 13.00 | -1.56 | .11 | -.590 |
| NAA1 | 7 | 9.14 | | | | |

Mann-Whitney U value was found to be statistically non significant U= 19.00

(z = -1.08), p =.28

**Table 4.155.H: Behavioral Adjustment Post-intervention data Post-hoc analyses between YAA2-NAA2**

| Groups | *n* | Mean ranks | U | *z* | *p* | Effect size |
|--------|-----|-----------|-------|-------|------|-------------|
| YAA2 | 7 | 6.71 | 19.00 | -1.08 | .28 | -0.409 |
| NAA2 | 8 | 9.13 | | | | |

Mann-Whitney U value was found to be statistically non significant U= 19.00

(z = -1.08), p =.28

**Table 4.155.I: Behavioral Adjustment Post-intervention data Post-hoc analyses between YAA2-AA1**

| Groups | *n* | Mean ranks | U | *z* | *p* | Effect size |
|--------|-----|------------|------|------|------|-------------|
| YAA2 | 7 | 8.71 | 16.00 | -1.14 | .252 | -0.431 |
| AA1 | 7 | 6.29 | | | | |

Mann-Whitney U value was found to be statistically non significant U= 16.00

(z = -1.14), p =.80

**Table 4.155.J: Behavioral Adjustment Post-intervention data Post-hoc analyses between YAA2-AA2**

| Groups | *n* | Mean ranks | U | *z* | *p* | Effect size |
|--------|-----|------------|------|------|------|-------------|
| YAA2 | 7 | 6.29 | 16.00 | -.253 | .800 | -0.095 |
| AA2 | 5 | 6.80 | | | | |

Mann-Whitney U value was found to be statistically non significant U= 16.00

(z = -.25), p =.80

**Table 4.155.K: Behavioral Adjustment Post-intervention data Post-hoc analyses between YAA2-C**

| Groups | *n* | Mean ranks | U | *z* | *p* | Effect size |
|--------|-----|------------|------|------|------|-------------|
| YAA2 | 7 | 5.57 | 11.00 | -3.08 | .002* | -1.166 |
| C | 15 | 14.27 | | | | |

* significant at 0.05 level

Mann-Whitney U value was found to be statistically significant U= 11.00 (z =

-3.08), p <0.001 and the difference between YAA2 and C groups was large (r = -

1.16).

**Table 4.155.L: Behavioral Adjustment Post-intervention data Post-hoc analyses between NAA1-NAA2**

| Groups | n | Mean ranks | U | z | p | Effect size |
|---|---|---|---|---|---|---|
| NAA1 | 7 | 8.43 | 25.00 | -.374 | .709 | -0.141 |
| NAA2 | 8 | 7.63 | | | | |

Mann-Whitney U value was found to be statistically non significant U= 25.00

(z = -.37), p =.70

**Table 4.155.M: Behavioral Adjustment Post-intervention data Post-hoc analyses betweenNAA1-AA1**

| Groups | n | Mean ranks | U | z | p | Effect size |
|---|---|---|---|---|---|---|
| NAA1 | 7 | 10.57 | 3.00 | -2.877 | .004* | -1.089 |
| AA1 | 7 | 4.43 | | | | |

*significant at 0.05 level

Mann-Whitney U value was found to be statistically significant U= 3.00 (z = -

2.87), p <0.001 and the difference between NAA1 and AA1 groups was large (r = -

1.08).

**Table 4.155.N: Behavioral Adjustment Post-intervention data Post-hoc analyses between NAA1-AA2**

| Groups | n | Mean ranks | U | z | p | Effect size |
|---|---|---|---|---|---|---|
| NAA1 | 7 | 7.57 | 10.00 | -1.29 | .197 | -0.488 |
| AA2 | 5 | 5.00 | | | | |

Mann-Whitney U value was found to be statistically non significant U= 10.00

(z = -1.29), p =.19

**Table 4.155.O: Behavioral Adjustment Post-intervention data Post-hoc analyses between NAA1-C**

| Groups | n | Mean ranks | U | z | p | Effect size |
|---|---|---|---|---|---|---|
| NAA1 | 7 | 7.07 | 21.50 | -2.40 | .016* | -0.909 |
| C | 15 | 13.57 | | | | |

* significant at 0.05 level

Mann-Whitney U value was found to be statistically significant U= 21.50 (z =
-2.40), p <0.001 and the difference between NAA1 and C groups was large (r = -
0.91).

**Table 4.155.P: Behavioral Adjustment Post-intervention data Post-hoc analyses between NAA2-AA1**

| Groups | $n$ | Mean ranks | U | $z$ | $p$ | Effect size |
|--------|-----|-----------|-------|-------|--------|-------------|
| NAA2 | 8 | 10.25 | 10.00 | -2.18 | .029* | -0.773 |
| AA1 | 7 | 5.43 | | | | |

* significant at 0.05 level

Mann-Whitney U value was found to be statistically significant U= 10.00 (z =
-2.18), p <0.001 and the difference between NAA2 and AA1 groups was large (r = -
0.77).

**Table 4.155.Q: Behavioral Adjustment Post-intervention data Post-hoc analyses between NAA2-AA2**

| Groups | $n$ | Mean ranks | U | $z$ | $p$ | Effect size |
|--------|-----|-----------|-------|-------|--------|-------------|
| NAA2 | 8 | 7.56 | 15.50 | -.683 | .495 | -0.242 |
| AA2 | 5 | 6.10 | | | | |

Mann-Whitney U value was found to be statistically non significant U= 15.50
(z = -.68), p =.49

**Table 4.155.R: Behavioral Adjustment Post-intervention data Post-hoc analyses between NAA2-C**

| Groups | $n$ | Mean ranks | U | $z$ | $p$ | Effect size |
|--------|-----|-----------|-------|--------|--------|-------------|
| NAA2 | 8 | 7.88 | 27.00 | -2.273 | .032* | -0.806 |
| C | 15 | 14.20 | | | | |

* significant at 0.05 level

Mann-Whitney U value was found to be statistically significant U= 27.00 (z =
-2.27), p <0.001 and the difference between NAA2 and C groups was large (r = -
0.81).

**Table 4.155.S: Behavioral Adjustment Post-intervention data Post-hoc analyses between AA1-AA2**

| Groups | $n$ | Mean ranks | U | $z$ | $p$ | Effect size |
|--------|-----|-----------|-------|-------|------|-------------|
| AA1    | 7   | 5.43      | 10.00 | -1.32 | .185 | -0.5        |
| AA2    | 5   | 8.00      |       |       |      |             |

*significant at 0.05 level

Mann-Whitney U value was found to be statistically non significant U= 10.00 (z = -1.32), p =.18

**Table 4.155.T: Behavioral Adjustment Post-intervention data Post-hoc analyses between AA1-C**

| Groups | $n$ | Mean ranks | U | $z$ | $p$ | Effect size |
|--------|-----|-----------|------|--------|------|-------------|
| AA1    | 7   | 4.14      | 1.00 | -3.747 | .00* | -1.419      |
| C      | 15  | 14.93     |      |        |      |             |

* significant at 0.05 level

Mann-Whitney U value was found to be statistically significant U= 1.00 (z = -3.74), p <0.001 and the difference between AA1 and C groups was large (r = -1.41).

**Table 4.155.U: Behavioral Adjustment post-intervention data Post-hoc analyses between AA2-C**

| Groups | $n$ | Mean ranks | U | $z$ | $p$ | Effect size |
|--------|-----|-----------|-------|--------|-------|-------------|
| AA2    | 5   | 5.40      | 12.00 | -2.324 | .020* | -1.042      |
| C      | 15  | 12.20     |       |        |       |             |

*significant at 0.05 level

Mann-Whitney U value was found to be statistically significant U= 12.00 (z = -2.32), p <0.001 and the difference between AA2 and C groups was large (r = -1.11).

## 4.9.3.5 Between group analyses for Behv.Adjustment follow up data

### Table 4.156: Behavioral Adjustment between groups analyses (Follow up data)

| Groups | *n* | Mean ranks | *Chi sq* | *df* | *p* |
|--------|-----|-----------|----------|------|-----|
| Y&AA1  | 8   | 18.13     |          |      |     |
| Y&AA2  | 7   | 20.00     |          |      |     |
| N&AA1  | 7   | 22.14     |          |      |     |
| N&AA2  | 8   | 27.44     | 3.90     |      |     |
|        |     |           |          | 5    | .564 |
| AA1    | 7   | 17.64     |          |      |     |
| AA2    | 5   | 24.00     |          |      |     |

There was no statistically significant difference between the groups on the levels of behavioral adjustment in the follow up data ($x^2(2)$ = 3.90, $p$= .56) hence, no further analysis was done.

Graph 19

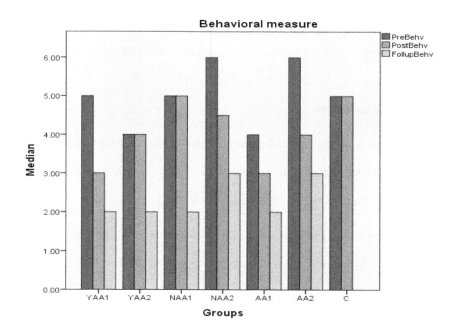

216

**4.10 Results**

**4.10.1 Results for Hypothesis 1: Practice of yoga will improve the planning process in children with LD**

- There was no difference between the four groups (YAA, NAA, AA, and C) before the start of intervention. The children showed average planning capacity before intervention ($M = 91.21$, $SD= 9.98$) as assessed by Cognitive Assessment System.

- The YAA group showed significant and large improvement at the end of intervention and sustained the effect over a period of time till the follow up assessment was made. (pretest median= 89.00; posttest median= 100.00; follow up median=100.00)

- The NAA group also improved significantly and largely at the end of intervention and the improvement continued significantly till the follow up assessment was made. (pretest median= 89.00; posttest median= 94.00; follow up median=98.00)

- The AA group did not show significant improvement at the end of intervention but had significant improvement when follow up assessment was made. (pretest median= 98.00; posttest median= 97.00; follow up median=102.00)

- There was a significant and moderate improvement in planning ability in control group at post test assessment. (pretest median= 89.00; posttest median= 92.00)

- There seem to be confounding effect of maturation in planning scores

- Since all the groups showed improvement, there was no significant difference between groups at post test assessment and follow up assessment

217

Though there were improvement in all the groups, at the end of post test and follow up all the children were still in average performance level as per the norm of the tool.

**4.10.2 Results for Hypothesis 2: Practice of yoga will improve the Attention process in children with LD**

- There was significant difference between the groups (YAA, NAA, AA, and C) before the start of intervention.

- Children in control group showed very poor performance in attention (Mean ranks= 19.17) where as children in NAA group had comparatively high performance (Mean ranks= 38.37). YAA group and AA groups had, Mean ranks= 30.40 and Mean ranks= 27.83 respectively.

- As a group children fell into low average performance level ($M = 82.77$, $SD= 9.87$) in attention before the start of intervention as assessed by CAS.

- The YAA group showed significant and large improvement at the end of intervention and sustained the effect over a period of time till the follow up assessment was made. (pretest median= 84.00; posttest median= 108.00; follow up median=102.00)

- The NAA group also showed significant and large improvement at the end of intervention and the improvement continued significantly till the follow up assessment was made. (pretest median= 88.00; posttest median= 94.00; follow up median=100.00)

- The AA group showed significant and moderate improvement at the end of intervention and had significant and large improvement when follow up assessment was made. (pretest median= 82.00; posttest median= 84.00; follow up median=95.00)

- There was a no difference in pre and post test assessment scores in C group. (pretest median= 75.00; posttest median= 77.00)

- There was significant difference between the groups at post test assessment. YAA group had maximum scores (mean rank= 45.97) compared to NAA (mean rank= 34.03), AA (mean rank= 20.92) and C (mean rank= 13.47) groups. There was significant difference between YAA-NAA, YAA-AA and YAA-C, NAA-AA, NAA-C groups. AA-C did not show significant difference.

- There was also significant difference between the groups at follow up assessment. YAA group had maximum scores (mean rank= 26.77) followed by NAA (mean rank= 23.03), and AA (mean rank= 13.00) groups. There was significant difference between YAA-AA and NAA-AA groups. And there was no difference between YAA and NAA groups at follow up assessment.

- At the end of intervention and follow up assessment children's performance improved from low average to average performance in all the three intervention groups.

In both post test and follow up assessments YAA group showed maximum improvement compared to all the other groups

### 4.10.3 Results for Hypothesis 3: Practice of yoga will improve simultaneous process in children with LD

- There was no difference between the four groups (YAA, NAA, AA, and C) before the start of intervention. The children showed average performance in simultaneous processing before intervention ($M$ = 90.44, $SD$= 12.97) as assessed by CAS

- All the three groups YAA (pretest median= 92.00; posttest median= 98.00; follow up median=102.00), NAA (pretest median= 98.00; posttest median= 102.00; follow up median=102.00) and AA (pretest median= 95.00; posttest median= 98.00; follow up median=100.00) showed significant and large improvement at the end of intervention and sustained the effect over a period of time till the follow up assessment was made.

- There was a no difference in pre and post test assessment scores in C group (pretest median= 87.00; posttest median= 89.00).

- There was significant difference between groups at posttest assessment. NAA group had maximum score (mean rank= 35.30) followed by YAA (mean rank= 34.87), AA (mean rank= 29.38) and C (mean rank= 16.53) groups. There was no difference between YAA-NAA, YAA-AA, and NAA-AA. But there was significant difference between YAA-C , NAA-C, and AA-C indicating all the groups were better than the control group

- There was no significant difference between groups at follow up assessment

Though there were improvements in all the groups, at the end of post test and follow up all the children were still in average performance level as per the norm of the tool.

**4.10.4 Results for Hypothesis 4: Practice of yoga will improve successive process in children with LD**

- There was significant difference between the groups (YAA, NAA, AA, and C) before the start of intervention.

- Children in AA group showed better performance in successive processing (mean rank= 39.17) followed by NAA group (mean rank= 29.93), C group (mean rank= 27.17) and YAA group (mean rank= 21.77). As a group children fell into low average performance level ($M$ = 84.58, $SD$= 11.09) in successive processing before the start of intervention.

- The YAA group showed significant and large improvement (pretest median= 77.00; posttest median= 94.00; follow up median=100.00) at the end of intervention and sustained the effect over a period of time till the follow up assessment was made.

- The NAA group also showed significant and large improvement (pretest median= 86.00; posttest median= 90.00; follow up median=98.00) at the end of intervention and the improvement continued significantly till the follow up assessment was made.

- The AA group did not show significant improvement in the post test assessment (pretest median= 90.00; posttest median= 92.00; follow up median=100.00) but showed significant and large improvement in follow up assessment.

- There was no difference in pre and post test assessment score in C group (pretest median= 79.00; posttest median= 81.00).

- There was significant difference between groups in posttest assessment. YAA group had maximum score (mean rank= 37.07) followed by AA (mean rank= 30.63), NAA (mean rank= 28.23) group and C (mean rank= 20.40) group. There was no difference between YAA-NAA, YAA-AA, NAA-AA, NAA-C and AA-C. But there was significant difference between YAA-C, indicating all the groups were better than the control group

- There was no significant difference between groups at follow up assessment

**4.10.5 Results for Hypothesis 5: Practice of yoga will improve phonological process in children with LD**

<u>Elision</u>

- There was no significant difference between the four groups (YAA, NAA, AA, and C) before the start of intervention.

- The YAA group showed significant and large improvement (pretest median= 4.00; posttest median= 12.00; follow up median=13.00) at the end of intervention and continued significant improvement over a period of time till the follow up assessment was made.

- The NAA group showed significant improvement (pretest median= 4.00; posttest median=12 .00; follow up median=13.00) at the end of intervention and continued significant improvement over a period of time till the follow up assessment was made.

- The AA group showed significant improvement in the post test assessment (pretest median= 5.00; posttest median= 11.50; follow up median=13.50) at the end of intervention and continued significant improvement over a period of time till the follow up assessment was made.

- There was no difference in pre and post test assessment score in C group (pretest median=4.00; posttest median= 4.00).

- There was significant difference between groups at posttest assessment. YAA group had maximum score (mean rank= 38.57) followed by NAA (mean rank= 35.50), AA (mean rank= 35.17) and C (mean rank= 8.00) groups. There was significant difference between YAA-C, NAA-C, and AA-C. And there were no significant difference between YAA-NAA, YAA-AA, and NAA-AA indicating that YAA group was significantly better than all the other groups

- There was no significant difference between groups at follow up assessment.

## Blending words

- There was no significant difference between the four groups (YAA, NAA, AA, and C) before the start of intervention.

- The YAA group showed significant and large improvement (pretest median= 5.00; posttest median= 13.00; follow up median=13.00) at the end of intervention and retained improvement over a period of time till the follow up assessment was made.

- The NAA group showed significant improvement (pretest median= 5.00; posttest median= 12.00; follow up median=13.00) at the end of intervention and retained improvement over a period of time till the follow up assessment was made.

- The AA group showed significant improvement in the post test assessment (pretest median= 5.00; posttest median= 13.00; follow up median=13.50) at the end of intervention and retained improvement over a period of time till the follow up assessment was made.

223

- There was no difference in pre and post test assessment score in C group (pretest median= 6.00; posttest median= 5.00).

- There was significant difference between groups at posttest assessment. AA group had maximum score (mean rank= 39.21) followed by YAA (mean rank= 26.30), NAA (mean rank= 34.47) and C (mean rank= 8.07) groups. There was significant difference between YAA-C, NAA-C, and AA-C. And there were no significant difference between YAA-NAA, YAA-AA and NAA-AA.

- There was no significant difference between groups at follow up assessment.

## Blending non words

- There was no significant difference between the four groups (YAA, NAA, AA, and C) before the start of intervention.

- The YAA group showed significant and large improvement (pretest median= 6.00; posttest median= 13.00; follow up median=13.00) at the end of intervention and retained effect over a period of time till the follow up assessment was made.

- The NAA group showed significant improvement (pretest median= 7.00; posttest median= 11.00; follow up median=12.00).

- The AA group showed significant improvement in the post test assessment (pretest median= 6.50; posttest median= 10.00; follow up median=12.50) and showed significant and large improvement in follow up assessment.

- There was no difference in pre and post test assessment score in C group (pretest median= 6.00; posttest median= 6.00).

- There was significant difference between groups at posttest assessment. YAA group had maximum score (mean rank= 40.47) followed by NAA (mean rank= 37.70), AA (mean rank= 29.79) and C (mean rank= 8.20) groups. There was significant difference between YAA-AA, YAA-C, NAA-C, and AA-C. And there were no significant difference between YAA-NAA, and NAA-AA.

- There was no significant difference between groups at follow up assessment.

## Segmenting non words

- There was no significant difference between the four groups (YAA, NAA, AA, and C) before the start of intervention.

- The YAA group showed significant and large improvement (pretest median= 5.00; posttest median= 8.00; follow up median=11.00) at the end of intervention and continued significant improvement over a period of time till the follow up assessment was made.

- The NAA group showed significant improvement (pretest median= 4.00; posttest median= 8.00; follow up median=10.00) at the end of intervention and continued significant improvement over a period of time till the follow up assessment was made.

- The AA group did not show significant improvement in the post test assessment (pretest median= 8.00; posttest median= 8.00; follow up median=13.00) but showed significant and large improvement in follow up assessment.

- There was significant decrease from pre to post test assessment score in C group (pretest median= 5.00; posttest median= 4.00).

- There was significant difference between groups at posttest assessment. NAA group had maximum score (mean rank= 37.93) followed by YAA (mean rank= 35.57), AA (mean rank= 34.54) and C (mean rank= 9.07) groups. There was significant difference between YAA-C, NAA-C, and AA-C. And there were no significant difference between YAA-NAA, YAA-AA and NAA-AA.

- There was significant difference between groups at follow up assessment. AA group had maximum score (mean rank= 29.00) followed by YAA (mean rank= 20.87), and NAA (mean rank= 16.13). There was significant difference between NAA-AA and no significant difference between YAA-NAA, and YAA-AA.

**Phoneme reversal English**

- There was no significant difference between the four groups (YAA, NAA, AA, and C) before the start of intervention.

- All the three groups YAA (pretest median= 2.00; posttest median= 9.00; follow up median=12.00), NAA (pretest median= 2.00; posttest median= 9.00; follow up median=12.00) and AA (pretest median= 2.00; posttest median= 5.30; follow up median=7.30) showed significant and large improvement at the end of intervention and continued to improve over a period of time till the follow up assessment was made.

- There was no difference in pre and post test assessment score in C group (pretest median= 2.00; posttest median= 2.00).

- There was significant difference between groups at posttest assessment. YAA group had maximum score (mean rank= 40.20) followed by NAA (mean rank= 39.33), NAA (mean rank= 28.17) and C (mean rank= 8.13) groups.

226

There was significant difference between YAA-AA, YAA-C, NAA-AA, NAA-C and AA-C. And there was no significant difference between YAA-NAA.

- There was significant difference between groups at follow up assessment. YAA and NAA had equal scores (mean rank= 27.50) and AA (mean rank= 6.50). There was significant difference between YAA-AA, and NAA-AA and no significant difference between YAA-NAA.

**Phoneme Oddity**

- There was no significant difference between the four groups (YAA, NAA, AA, and C) before the start of intervention.

- The YAA group showed significant and large improvement (pretest median= .00; posttest median= 3.00; follow up median=4.00) at the end of intervention and sustained improvement over a period of time till the follow up assessment was made.

- The NAA group did not show significant improvement (pretest median= .00; posttest median= 1.00; follow up median=2.00) at the end of intervention and at follow up assessment.

- The AA group did show significant improvement in the post test assessment (pretest median= .00; posttest median= 1.00; follow up median=1.00) and sustained improvement in follow up assessment.

- There was no difference in pre and post test assessment score in C group (pretest median= .00; posttest median= .00).

- There was significant difference between groups at posttest assessment. YAA group had maximum score (mean rank= 44.37) followed by NAA (mean rank= 34.04), AA (mean rank= 20.53) and C (mean rank= 18.07) groups. There was significant difference between YAA-NAA, YAA-AA, YAA-C and NAA-C. But there were no significant difference between NAA-AA, and AA-C indicating that YAA group was significantly better than all the other groups

- There was significant difference between groups at follow up assessment. YAA group had maximum score (mean rank= 32.27) followed by NAA (mean rank= 18.73), and AA (mean rank= 11.50). There was significant difference between YAA-NAA, and YAA-AA and no significant difference between NAA-AA.

- Both at post test and follow up assessments YAA group was significantly better than the other groups.

**Phoneme deletion**

- There was no significant difference between the four groups (YAA, NAA, AA, and C) before the start of intervention.

- The YAA group showed significant and large improvement (pretest median= .00; posttest median= 5.00; follow up median=6.00) at the end of intervention and continued significant improvement over a period of time till the follow up assessment was made.

- The NAA group did not show significant improvement (pretest median= .00; posttest median= 1.00; follow up median=1.00) at the end of intervention and follow up assessment.

- The AA group showed significant improvement in the post test assessment (pretest median= .00; posttest median= 1.50; follow up median=1.50) and sustained the effect in follow up assessment.

228

- There was no difference in pre and post test assessment score in C group (pretest median= .00; posttest median= 1.00).

- There was significant difference between groups at posttest assessment. YAA group had maximum score (mean rank= 49.83) followed by AA (mean rank= 25.88), NAA (mean rank= 20.33) and C (mean rank= 19.33) groups. There was significant difference between YAA-NAA, YAA-C, and YAA-AA. But there were no significant difference between NAA-AA, NAA-C and NAA-C.

- There was significant difference between groups at follow up assessment. YAA group had maximum score (mean rank= 35.00) followed by AA (mean rank= 16.21), and NAA (mean rank= 12.23). There was significant difference between YAA-NAA, and no significant difference between YAA-AA and NAA-AA.

- Both at post test and follow up assessments YAA group was significantly better than the other groups.

**Spoonerism**

- There was significant difference between the four groups (YAA, NAA, AA, and C) before the start of intervention.

- The YAA group showed significant and large improvement (pretest median= .00; posttest median= 5.00; follow up median=6.00) at the end of intervention and continued significant improvement over a period of time till the follow up assessment was made.

- The NAA group did not show significant improvement in post test but showed moderate improvement in follow up assessment. (pretest median= 00.00; posttest median= 00.00; follow up median=1.00).

229

- The AA group showed significant improvement in the post test assessment (pretest median= .00; posttest median= 1.00; follow up median=1.00) and sustained effect in follow up assessment.

- There was no difference in pre and post test assessment score in C group (pretest median= .00; posttest median= .00).

- There was significant difference between groups at posttest assessment. YAA group had maximum score (mean rank= 49.80) followed by AA (mean rank= 24.54), NAA (mean rank= 21.27) and C (mean rank= 19.50) groups. There was significant difference between YAA-NAA, YAA-AA, and YAA-C. But there were no significant difference between NAA-AA, NAA-C and AA-C indicating that YAA group was significantly better than all the other groups

- There was significant difference between groups at follow up assessment. YAA group had maximum score (mean rank= 35.00) followed by AA (mean rank= 15.33), and NAA (mean rank= 12.93). There was significant difference between YAA-NAA, and YAA-AA and no significant difference between NAA-AA.

- Both at post test and follow up assessments YAA group was significantly better than the other groups.

### Phoneme reversal Kannada

- There was no significant difference between the four groups (YAA, NAA, AA, and C) before the start of intervention.

- The YAA group showed significant and large improvement (pretest median= 1.00; posttest median= 2.00; follow up median=3.00) at the end of intervention and continued significant improvement over a period of time till the follow up assessment was made.

- The NAA group did not show significant improvement (pretest median= .00; posttest median= .00; follow up median=.00).

- The AA group showed significant improvement in the post test assessment (pretest median= .00; posttest median= 1.00; follow up median=1.00) but showed significant and large improvement in follow up assessment.

- There was no difference in pre and post test assessment score in C group (pretest median= .00; posttest median= .00).

- There was significant difference between groups at posttest assessment. YAA group had maximum score (mean rank= 48.00) followed by AA (mean rank= 27.60), NAA (mean rank= 22.60) and C (mean rank= 17.50) groups. There was significant difference between YAA-NAA, YAA-C, YAA-AA, and AA-C. But there were no significant difference between NAA-AA, and NAA-C indicating that YAA group was significantly better than all the other groups

- There was significant difference between groups at follow up assessment. YAA group had maximum score (mean rank= 33.77) followed by AA (mean rank= 16.42), and NAA (mean rank= 13.30). There was significant difference between YAA-NAA, and YAA-AA and no significant difference between NAA-AA.

- Both at post test and follow up assessments YAA group was significantly better than the other groups.

### 4.10.6 Results for Hypothesis 6: Practice of yoga will improve word reading efficiency in Children with LD

<u>Sight word reading English</u>

- There was significant difference between the four groups (YAA, NAA, AA, and C) before the start of intervention. AA group had better performance (mean rank= 38.38) followed by YAA (mean rank= 31.50), C (mean rank= 27.67) and NAA (mean rank= 20.33)

- The YAA group showed significant and large improvement (pretest median= 19.00; posttest median= 29.00; follow up median=31.00) at the end of intervention and continued significant improvement over a period of time till the follow up assessment was made.

- The NAA group did not show significant improvement (pretest median= 16.00; posttest median= 16.00; follow up median=20.00) at the end of intervention but showed significant improvement at follow up assessment.

- The AA group did not showed significant improvement in the post test assessment (pretest median= 23.00; posttest median= 25.00; follow up median=27.00) but showed significant and large improvement in follow up assessment.

- There was no difference in pre and post test assessment score in C group (pretest median= 20.00; posttest median= 17.00).

- There was significant difference between groups at posttest assessment. YAA group had maximum score (mean rank= 44.37) followed by AA (mean rank= 34.04), C (mean rank= 20.53) and NAA (mean rank= 18.07) groups. There was significant difference between YAA-NAA, YAA-C, NAA-AA, and AA-

C. But there were no significant difference between YAA-AA, and NAA-C indicating that YAA group was significantly better than all the other groups

- There was significant difference between groups at follow up assessment. YAA group had maximum score (mean rank= 29.33) followed by AA (mean rank= 23.88), and NAA (mean rank= 11.77). There was significant difference between YAA-NAA, and YAA-AA and no significant difference between NAA-AA.

- Both at post test and follow up assessments YAA group was significantly better than the other groups.

## Decoding English

- There was no difference between the four groups (YAA, NAA, AA, and C) before the start of intervention

- The YAA group showed significant and large improvement (pretest median= 11.00; posttest median= 30.00; follow up median=30.00) at the end of intervention and continued significant improvement over a period of time till the follow up assessment was made.

- The NAA group did show significant improvement (pretest median= 10.00; posttest median= 11.00; follow up median=20.00) at the end of intervention and also showed significant improvement at follow up assessment.

- The AA group showed significant and moderate improvement in the post test assessment (pretest median= 12.00; posttest median= 30.00; follow up median=30.00) but not in the follow up assessment.

- There was no difference in pre and post test assessment score in C group (pretest median= 11.00; posttest median= 10.00).

233

- There was significant difference between groups at posttest assessment. YAA group had maximum score (mean rank= 42.87) followed by AA (mean rank= 41.21), NAA (mean rank= 19.60) and C (mean rank= 14.77) groups. There was significant difference between YAA-NAA, YAA-C, NAA-AA, and AA-C. But there were no significant difference between YAA-AA, and NAA-C indicating that YAA group was significantly better than all the other groups

- There was significant difference between groups at follow up assessment. YAA group had maximum score (mean rank= 28.53) followed by AA (mean rank= 24.42), and NAA (mean rank= 12.13). There was significant difference between YAA-NAA, and NAA-AA and no significant difference between YAA-AA.

- Both at post test and follow up assessments YAA group was significantly better than the other groups.

## Sight word reading Kannada

- There was no difference between the four groups (YAA, NAA, AA, and C) before the start of intervention

- All the three groups YAA (pretest median= 5.00; posttest median= 8.00; follow up median=11.00), NAA (pretest median= 4.00; posttest median= 5.00; follow up median=6.00) and AA (pretest median= 4.00; posttest median= 5.00; follow up median=6.00) showed significant and large improvement at the end of intervention and continued to improve over a period of time till the follow up assessment was made.

- There was no difference in pre and post test assessment score in C group (pretest median= 5.00; posttest median= 5.00).

234

- There was significant difference between groups at posttest assessment. YAA group had maximum score (mean rank= 48.03) followed by AA (mean rank= 25.04), NAA (mean rank= 23.33) and C (mean rank= 18.80) groups. There was significant difference between YAA-NAA, YAA-AA, and YAA-C. But there were no significant difference between NAA-AA, NAA-C and AA-C indicating that YAA group was significantly better than all the other groups

- There was significant difference between groups at follow up assessment. YAA group had maximum score (mean rank= 49.93) followed by AA (mean rank= 26.67), and NAA (mean rank= 24.40). There was significant difference between YAA-NAA, YAA-AA and no significant difference between NAA-AA.

- Both at post test and follow up assessments YAA group was significantly better than the other groups.

## Decoding Kannada

- There was no difference between the four groups (YAA, NAA, AA, and C) before the start of intervention

- The YAA group showed significant and large improvement (pretest median= 4.00; posttest median= 5.00; follow up median=9.00) at the end of intervention and continued significant improvement over a period of time till the follow up assessment was made.

- The NAA group did not show significant improvement (pretest median= 4.00; posttest median= 4.00; follow up median=6.00) at the end of intervention but showed significant improvement at follow up assessment.

235

- The AA group showed significant and moderate improvement in the post test assessment (pretest median= 4.00; posttest median= 4.50; follow up median=7.00) and showed significant and large improvement in follow up assessment.

- There was no difference in pre and post test assessment score in C group (pretest median= 3.00; posttest median= 3.00).

- There was significant difference between groups at posttest assessment. YAA group had maximum score (mean rank= 40.03) followed by AA (mean rank= 36.88), NAA (mean rank= 24.07) and C (mean rank= 16.60) groups. There was significant difference between YAA-NAA, YAA-C, NAA-AA, and AA-C. But there were no significant difference between YAA-AA, and NAA-C indicating that YAA group was significantly better than all the other groups

- There was significant difference between groups at follow up assessment. YAA group had maximum score (mean rank= 46.77) followed by AA (mean rank= 33.42), and NAA (mean rank= 24.00). There was significant difference between YAA-NAA, and YAA-AA and no significant difference between NAA-AA.

- Both at post test and follow up assessments YAA group was significantly better than the other groups.

**4.10.7 Results for Hypothesis 7: Practice of yoga will improve arithmetic efficiency in Children with LD**

- There was no difference between the four groups (YAA, NAA, AA, and C) before the start of intervention. The children showed below average performance in arithmetic before intervention ($M = 26.59$, $SD = 3.46$)

- All the three groups YAA (pretest median= 26.00; posttest median= 49.00; follow up median=55.00), NAA (pretest median= 26.00; posttest median= 43.00; follow up median=50.00) and AA (pretest median= 27.00; posttest median= 38.00; follow up median=44.50) showed significant and large improvement at the end of intervention and continued to improve over a period of time till the follow up assessment was made.

- There was a no difference in pre and post test assessment scores in C group (pretest median= 27.00; posttest median= 27.00).

- There was significant difference between groups at posttest assessment. YAA group had maximum score (mean rank= 50.00) followed by NAA (mean rank= 32.90), AA (mean rank= 24.00) and C (mean rank= 8.10) groups. There was significant difference between YAA-NAA, YAA-AA, YAA-C, NAA-AA, NAA-C and AA-C. indicating that YAA group was significantly better than all the other groups

- There was significant difference between groups at follow up assessment. YAA group had maximum score (mean rank= 33.07) followed by NAA (mean rank= 21.93), and AA (mean rank= 6.50). There was significant difference between YAA-NAA, YAA-AA and NAA-AA.

- Both at post test and follow up assessments YAA group was significantly better than the other groups.

**4.10.8 Results for Hypothesis 8: Practice of yoga will improve behavioral adjustment in Children with LD**

- There was no statistically significant difference between the groups before the commencement of intervention. The mean performance of the group was $M$=5.11, $SD$= 1.38.

- All the groups YAA (pretest median= 5.00; posttest median= 3.00; follow up median=2.00), NAA (pretest median=6.00; posttest median= 5.00; follow up median=3.00) and AA (pretest median= 4.00; posttest median= 3.00; follow up median=2.00) except control group (pretest median= 5.00; posttest median= 5.00) improved in behavioral adjustment and continued to improve even after the end of intervention

- There was significant difference between the groups in the posttest assessment. AA group showed maximum improvement (mean rank= 17.63) followed by YAA (mean rank= 19.43), NAA (mean rank= 31.90) and C (mean rank= 44.77) groups. There was significant difference between YAA-NAA, YAA-C, NAA-AA, NAA-C, and AA-C. There was no significant difference between YAA-AA.

- There was no significant difference between groups in the follow up assessment.

- YAA and AA groups showed equal improvements with each other and more improvement compared to NAA group.

- Control group showed same scores in pre and post tests and did not improve. Hence it can be said that there was no maturation effect on behavioral adjustment.

- Effect of only Yoga is difficult to say because both YAA and AA groups improved equally

*Chapter - V*

**DISCUSSION**

## 5.1 Planning

Planning is a higher cognitive process which involves formulation, evaluation and selection of a sequence of thoughts and actions to achieve a desired goal. The capacity to generate and organize the necessary step sequence to carry out a goal-directed behavior develops through out childhood and even during the first years of adolescence (Ricle, et al 2014). Studies have shown positive correlation between planning and mathematical ability in children (Nagleri, & Gottling, 1997). Children with LD show poor planning ability that reflects in their academic performances especially in arithmetic problem solving ability.

Previous studies have shown improvement in tower of London test following yoga intervention for a period of 30 days in children (Manjunath, & Telles, 2001). Schmalzl 2015, hypothesizes that movements involved in yoga involve executive functioning, procedural learning and planning which is mediated by basal ganglia via loops with cortico-striatal proections from the dorsolateral prefrontal cortex, the orbitofrontal cortex and anterior cingulated cortex.

In the present study, children have shown large (effect size= -0.88) improvement in planning subtest from pre to post intervention assessment but the control group has also showed significant (effect size= -0.76) improvement from pretest to posttest scores in the planning. Hence it is difficult to conclude whether yoga intervention improved children's planning ability in the preset study.

## 5.2 Attention

Attention involves selectively focusing on a discrete aspect of subjective or objective information, while ignoring other perceivable information. All of the yoga practices involve attention to bodily and mental states. Attentions to interoceptive, proprioceptive, kinesthetic, tactile, spatial information, breath, thoughts are intrinsic in all yoga practices. Structural changes in the brain areas like insular cortex, primary and secondary cortices, and anterior precuneous, reported in the yoga practitioners have been associated with introceptive, tactile and proprioceptive sensations. (Fox et al, 2014; Villemure et al, 2014; Tomasino et al, 2013; Frolinger et al, 2012). Kerr et al, 2013 showed that body focused attention elicit 7-14 Hz alpha rhythm which is associated with inhibition control. Long term changes in the prefrontal cortex activation due to body focused mindfulness practices have been reported by Davidson etal, 2003; Farb et al, 2013. The alpha rhythm in occipital regions is associated with state of relaxed wakefulness. The defocus and relaxation of ocular convergence in eye exercises and gaze training seem to produce these activation (Schmalzl, 2015). Inhibiting saccades and redirecting gaze to a target involves inhibition and performance monitoring which enhances attentional control in practitioners. Behavioral studies have also show improvement in attention in children with attentional disorders (Jensen, & Kenny, 2004; Harrison et al, 2004)

In the present study, children have shown large (effect size= -0.88) improvement in attention subtest from pre to post intervention assessment and have shown greater improvement compared to other groups. Even in the follow up studies Y&AA group had highest scores compared to the other groups. Hence the result seems to be consistent with the previous studies. It can be concluded that yoga practice improved attention in children with LD in the present study.

### 5.3 Simultaneous processing

Simultaneous processing is the process of combining unconnected and discrete information into a coherent whole to assist in comprehension and interpretation. The secondary and tertiary zones of occipital, parietal and temporal lobes posterior to the

241

central sulcus of the brain are the units responsible for simultaneous processing and they involve receiving, processing, and retaining information. It is hypothesized that yoga practice enhances neural circuits involved in the integration of top down and bottom up information. Yoga practice involves processing of bottom-up sensation and metabolic related information and top down attention and metacognition related processes. As a result of this, the bidirectional neurocircuitry in the hippocampus and the amygdala with the prefrontal areas involved in attentional control seem to enhance (schmalzl et al, 2015). Structural changes in the white matter pathways in rostro-caudal fiber pathways that connect dorsal temporo-parietal regions with prefrontal region have been observed following yoga practice (Fox et al, 2014). These pathways play important role in connecting parietal body awareness regions and prefrontal executive regions. Functional brain changes associated with meditation practices have shown changes in the areas like superior parietal lobule, inferior parietal lobule and supramarginal gyrus which have been involved in integrating multimodal spatial information in body centered coordinates, computation of size and shape of body parts and disembodiment and altered integration of multisensory information respectively. Studies have shown that age related decline in fluid intelligence were smaller in yoga practitioners and meditators compared to controls (Prakash et al., 2012; van Leeuwen et al., 2009)

In the present study, There was significant and large (effect size= -0.88) improvement in Y&AA and N&AA group (effect size= -0.88) in the posttest assessment, while AA group improved moderately (effect size= -0.71). Hence the large improvements in Y&AA ad N&AA groups as compared to AA and C groups can be attributed to the cognitive specific intervention these groups received. Hence it can be said that yoga has shown positive influence in improving simultaneous processing in children with LD.

## 5.4 Successive processing

Successive processing is involved with the use of stimuli arranged in a specific serial order. It involves serial organization of information like sounds or movements in order. It is integral to working with sounds or phononological processing in early reading. It also involves attentioanl and working memory components. The procedural learning of motor sequence and working memory to hold instructions in mind and select specific sequential motor activation may have potentiality to facilitate successive processing ability.

In the present study, both Y&AA and &NAA groups have shown large improvement in post assessment (effect size=-.088, -0.89 respectively). Where as AA group has not shown significant improvement in posttest assessment. Hence the improvement can be attributed to cognitive specific interventions and it can be said that yoga practice has resulted in improved successive processing in children with LD.

## 5.5 Phonological processing

Phonological processing consists of short-term maintenance of sound sequences in auditory memory during analysis of their auditory, somatosensory, and motor properties to support phonemic categorization.Categorization of ambiguous syllables engages a dorsal pathway, from primary auditory cortex to posterior temporal gyrus and ventral parietal regions, associated with auditory short-term memory and interaction with somatosensory and motor areas. (Liebenthal et al, 2013)

Phonological processing also involves rapid temporal processing characterizing phonological inputs which is same as sequential/successive processing ability.

In the present study, Phonological processing in English has improved largely in all the groups Y&AA, N&AA and AA. Reading and phonological processing have reciprocal influence on each other. The reading training given in AA intervention may have an effect on the phonological processing in English. Since children have shown improvement in successive processing in Y&AA and N&AA groups, this may have also influenced their phonological processing in English.

Phonological processing in Kannada has shown interesting results though. Y&AA group predominantly showed large improvement in post intervention assessment. The phonological processing tasks involved high attentional control, working memory and visual representation. A study conducted by the researcher showed that children when given phonological tasks in Kannada prefer visually processing the phoneme markers within the Kannada letters and mentally manipulate them, then to auditorily process them. (Poonacha, S & Salagamme, K.K,2014). Studies related to visual sequential processing have reported that children with LD take longer to process spatial-temporal order judgment tasks (Liebenthal et al, 2013).

Yoga techniques like eye exercise and visualization techniques alpha rhythm and state of wakeful relaxation. The Basal ganglia loops with cortico-striatal projections from frontal andsupplemental eye fields via the superior culliculus are known to be involved in voluntary eye movements. They seem to control saccadic eye movements, prevent from distracting visualinputs and improve spatial orientation. Behavioral researches have shown improvement in visual selective attention (Telles et al., 1995), and decreased visual reaction time (Narayana, 2009) found and have attributed the results to increased alertness and visuospatial attention promoted by the yoga practice.

## 5.6 Reading efficiency

Word Reading skills involve capability to convert graphemes to phonemes and to quickly recognize the word's structural and phonological features. In reading tasks speed does matter because speed determines ones mastery over the acquired skill. Reading is influenced by phonological processing skills, successive temporal processing, and automaticity. One of the theories for deficits in reading, the magnocellular hypothesis attributes impaired reading to impaired monitoring of ocularmovements, leading to visual confusion, superposition and distortion during reading.

In the present study, both in English and Kannada sight word reading subtests, which require visual processing of words Y&AA group has shown greater improvement (effect size=-.79, -.088 respectively) in post intervention assessment compared to other groups. In phonological decoding subtests, Y&AA group has showed moderate improvement in English (effect size=-.56) and Kannada (effect size=-.79)

## 5.7 Arithmetic ability

Arithmetic problem solving skills develop in stages with the development of pre operational, concrete operational and abstract operational skills in children. The development relies on cognitive maturity and development of planning ability in children. Children typically go through developmental stages as explained by piaget before they reach the stage where they can operate with abstract number concepts in arithmetic problem solving. In the present study all the three intervention groups have shown large improvement in post intervention assessment. Hence it is difficult to say the effect of yoga on arithmetic improvement in Y&AA group

## 5.8 Behavioral adjustment

Children with LD, generally show adjustment problems in school environment. Commonly observed behaviors include truancy, being destructive with other's objects, bullying, frequently engaging in fist fights, disobedience, lying, stealing. Some children show internalized problem behaviors like anxiety, fidgety, worried, tearful, irritability, thumb sucking, nail biting, frequent complaints of aches and pains etc. If unaddressed, these problems can persists through their school life and hamper development of health personality.

The yoga methods provide sensitivity to one's bodily and emotional states may help one better understand and cope with the problem. While some studies have shown that increased bodyly awareness can increase anxiety in children, majority of yoga studies have reported decreased anxiety, depression and better social adjustment.

In the present study, it is difficult to make conclusive judgment about the effect of yoga on behavioral adjustment because children in all the intervention groups have shown increased behavioral adjustment in school environment. It can be said that attention given to children in any form of intervention can help them improve in behavioral adjustments.

## 5.9 Conclusion

Previous studies have shown enhanced cognitive abilities like planning, attention, spatial and verbal memory, reaction time, cognitive flexibility etc following yoga intervention. Imaging studies have shown increased connectivity and grey matter volume in yoga practitioners. Yoga has consistently shown positive effects on

246

the body and mind in majority of studies reported. In the preset study also, children who received yoga intervention improved as equally as children in neuropsychological intervention which was developed exclusively for the improvement of PASS and phonological processes. This implies that yoga may have worked as effectively as neuropsychological intervention. But it should also be noted that yoga practiced merely as a physical exercise without internal focus, may not produce the desired effect. The maximum effects of yoga can be reaped only if yoga is practiced with all its components; movement, breath awareness, coordination, internal focus, body awareness, gaze, relaxation, and visualization incorporated coherently. It should also be noted that, yoga teaching methods should be designed keeping children's age in mind and methods be made comprehensible to them. Since the yoga techniques are very subjective in nature how each individual understands and experiences it is difficult to assess, hence the teaching methods must be made as objective and clear and concrete for children to understand and experience it. From the present study one can conclude that yoga has beneficial effects on cognitive processes and can be used as cognitive focused intervention for children with LD.

## 5.10 Implications of the study

The aim of the study was to evaluate the effectiveness of yoga as intervention for LD. Because LD intervention is time consuming and individualized program, an effective and alternative remediation method is the need of the hour. A cognition focused intervention which can be given to considerably large number of children would be beneficial in order to deliver service and attention to larger number of children with LD. The present study has shown that yoga can be used as an alterative intervention for neuropsychologically based intervention. Hence yoga based

247

intervention can be used in schools and special schools as a complementary intervention along with specific academic skill training.

## 5.11 Limitations of the study

Participant selection and distribution of participants to intervention groups were not randomized. This could have led to biased and homogeneous groups. The participants were mostly those who could commute easily to the place of intervention. Hence the participants were not very good representative samples.

The follow up assessment for control group was not done due to the inability to trace the participants after a period of about two and a half years. Hence the maturation effect post assessment period could not be controlled to make conclusive judgment about the maintenance effect of the intervention.

## 5.12 Recommendations for further research

Future research can be done with proper randomized control group to evaluate the effect of yoga on cognitive functions of children with LD. Research can be done to exploring individual yoga techniques on specific cognitive skills and yoga based cognitive therapy can be developed to help children with LD.

Printed by BoD™in Norderstedt, Germany